2ND EDITION

P9-DTA-167

MELODY • LYRICS • CHORD BOXES • TABLATURE

THE BEST CHRISTMAS GUITAR FAKE BOOK EVER

150 Songs!

ISBN 0-7935-1663-3

HAL•LEONARD®
CORPORATION

7777 W. BLUEMOUND RD. P.O. BOX 13819 MILWAUKEE, WI 53213

Visit Hal Leonard Online at
www.halleonard.com

CONTENTS

A Caroling We Go

Music and Lyrics by Johnny Marks

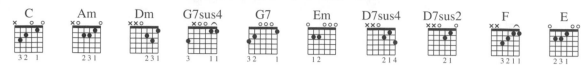

Strum Pattern: 8
Pick Pattern: 8

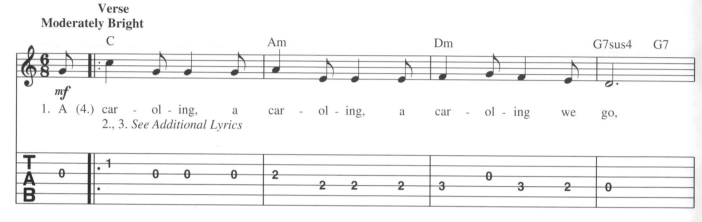

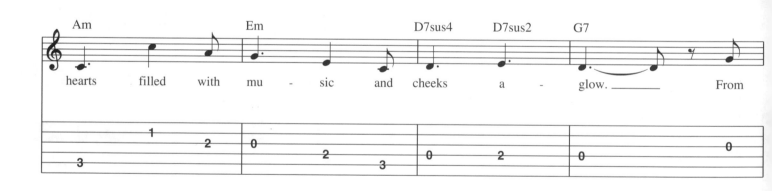

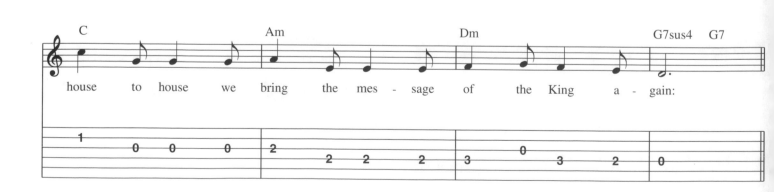

Chorus

Peace on _____ earth, good will to

men, peace on _____ earth, good will to

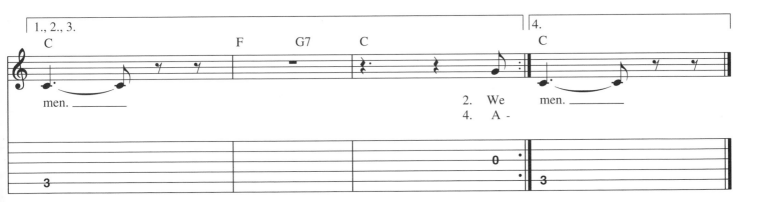

men. _____

2. We men. _____
4. A -

Additional Lyrics

2. We bring you season's greetings as we wish the best to you,
   And may our wish last the whole year through.
   Come join us if you will as we are singing once again:

3. Now you may have your holly and perhaps some mistletoe,
   Maybe in a fir tree and maybe snow.
   But wouldn't it be wonderful if we could have again:

All Through the Night

Welsh Folksong

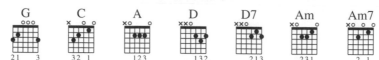

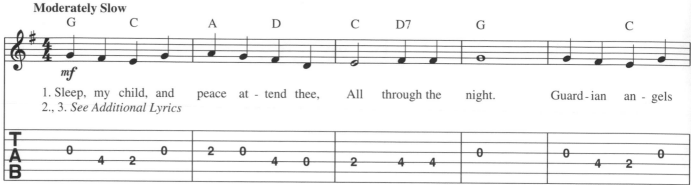

Strum Pattern: 4
Pick Pattern: 3

Verse
Moderately Slow

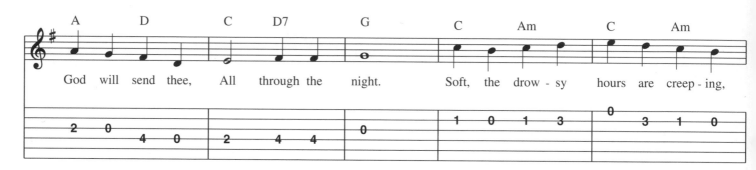

1. Sleep, my child, and peace at - tend thee, All through the night. Guard - ian an - gels
2., 3. *See Additional Lyrics*

God will send thee, All through the night. Soft, the drow - sy hours are creep - ing,

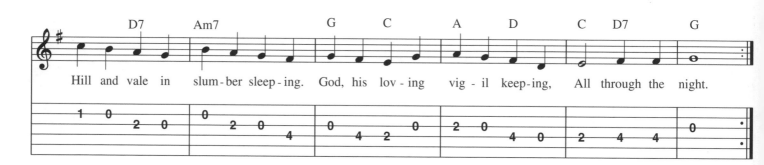

Hill and vale in slum - ber sleep - ing. God, his lov - ing vig - il keep - ing, All through the night.

Additional Lyrics

2. While the moon, her watch is keeping,
   All through the night.
   While the weary world is sleeping,
   All through the night.
   Through your dreams you're swiftly stealing,
   Visions of delight revealing,
   Christmas time is so appealing,
   All through the night.

3. You, my God, a babe of wonder,
   All through the night.
   Dreams you can't break from thunder,
   All through the night.
   Children's dreams cannot be broken.
   Life is but a lovely token.
   Christmas should be softly spoken,
   All through the night.

Almost Day
(It's Almost Day)

Words and Music by Huddie Ledbetter

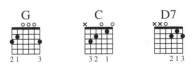

Strum Pattern: 10
Pick Pattern: 10

Verse

Moderate Square Dance

1. Chick-ens a-crowin' for mid-night, __ it's al - most day. Chick-ens a-crowin' for
2. *See Additional Lyrics*

mid-night, __ it's al - most day. Can-dy canes __ and sug-ar - plums, __ on Christ - mas

Day. Can-dy canes __ and sug-ar - plums, __ on Christ - mas Day. Day.

Additional Lyrics

2. Mama'll stuff a turkey on Christmas Day.
   Mama'll stuff a turkey on Christmas Day.
   Santa Claus is coming on Christmas Day.
   Santa Claus is coming on Christmas Day.

Angels From the Realms of Glory

Words by James Montgomery
Music by Henry T. Smart

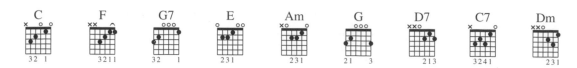

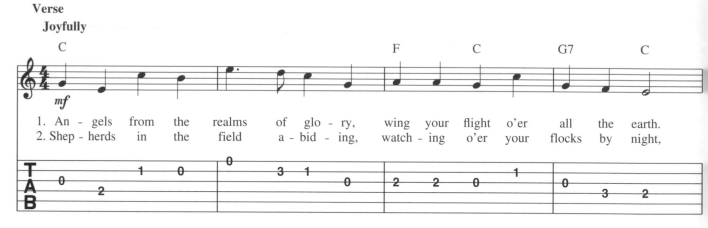

Strum Pattern: 3
Pick Pattern: 5

Verse
Joyfully

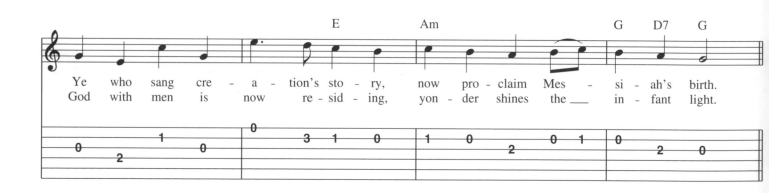

1. An - gels from the realms of glo - ry, wing your flight o'er all the earth.
2. Shep - herds in the field a - bid - ing, watch - ing o'er your flocks by night,

Ye who sang cre - a - tion's sto - ry, now pro - claim Mes - si - ah's birth.
God with men is now re - sid - ing, yon - der shines the ___ in - fant light.

Chorus

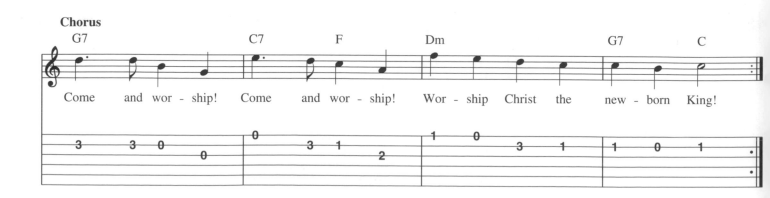

Come and wor - ship! Come and wor - ship! Wor - ship Christ the new - born King!

Angels We Have Heard on High

Traditional French Carol
Translated by James Chadwick

Strum Pattern: 6
Pick Pattern: 6

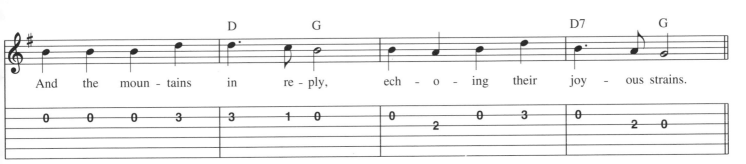

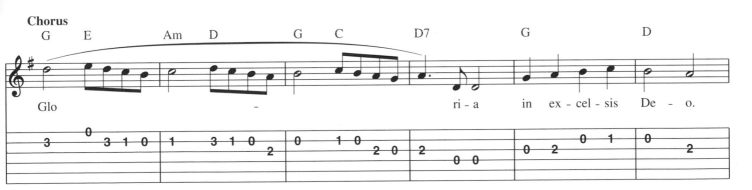

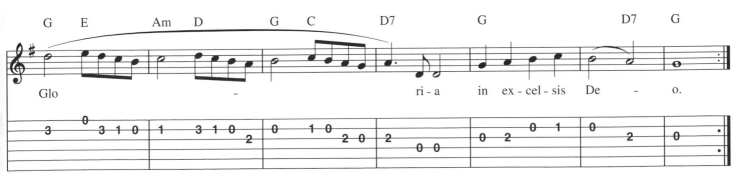

Additional Lyrics

2. Shepherds why this jubilee,
   Why your joyous strains prolong?
   What the gladsome tidings be
   Which inspire your heavenly song?

As Each Happy Christmas

Traditional

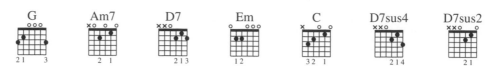

Strum Pattern: 4
Pick Pattern: 3

Moderately slow

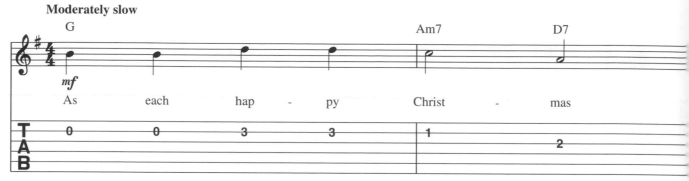

As each hap - py Christ - mas

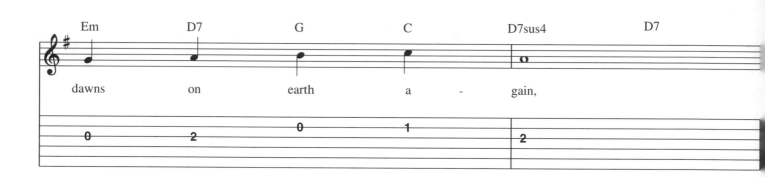

dawns on earth a - gain,

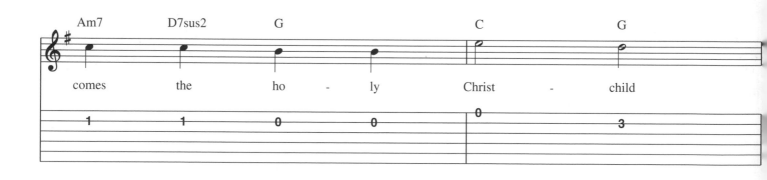

comes the ho - ly Christ - child

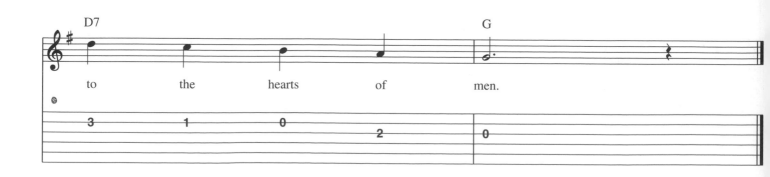

to the hearts of men.

As Lately We Watched

19th Century Austrian Carol

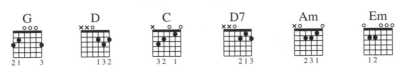

Strum Pattern: 7
Pick Pattern: 7

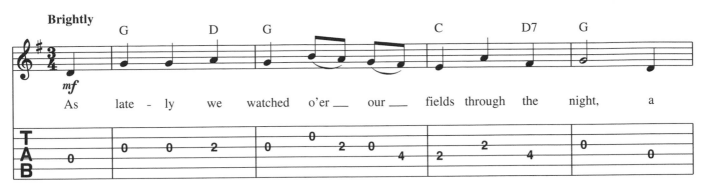

As late - ly we watched o'er ___ our ___ fields through the night, a

star there was seen of ___ such ___ glo - ri - ous light.

All through ___ the ___ night, an - gels ___ did ___ sing, in

car - ols so sweet of ___ the ___ birth of the King.

As With Gladness Men of Old

Words by William Chatterton Dix
Music by Conrad Kocher

Strum Pattern: 4
Pick Pattern: 5

Verse
Brightly

1. As with __ glad - ness men of old did the guid - ing star be - hold;
2., 3., 4. *See Additional Lyrics*

As with __ joy they hailed its light, lead - ing on - ward, beam - ing bright;

So, most gra - cious Lord, may we ev - er - more be led to Thee.

Additional Lyrics

2. As with joyful steps they sped,
   To that lowly manger bed,
   There to bend the knee before
   Him who Heaven and Earth adore,
   So may we with willing feet
   Ever seek thy mercy seat.

3. As they offered gifts most rare
   At that manger rude and bare,
   So may we with holy joy,
   Pure and free from sin's alloy,
   All our costliest treasures bring,
   Christ, to Thee, our heavenly King.

4. Holy Jesus, every day
   Keep us in the narrow way;
   And, when earthly things are past,
   Bring our ransomed souls at last
   Where they need no star to guide,
   Where no clouds Thy glory hide.

Auld Lang Syne

Words by Robert Burns
Traditional Scottish Melody

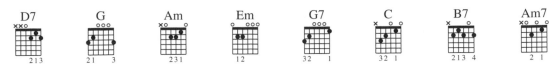

Strum Pattern: 3
Pick Pattern: 3

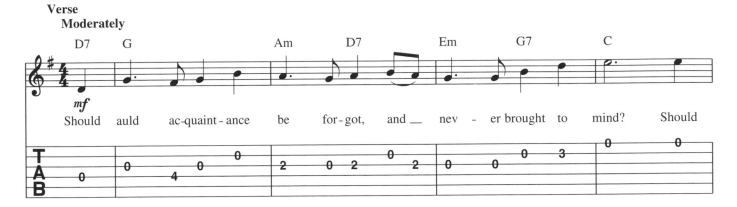

Verse
Moderately

Should auld ac-quaint-ance be for-got, and __ nev - er brought to mind? Should

auld ac-quaint - ance be for - got and __ days of Auld Lang Syne. For

Chorus

Auld __ Lang __ Syne, my dear, for Auld __ Lang __ Syne. We'll

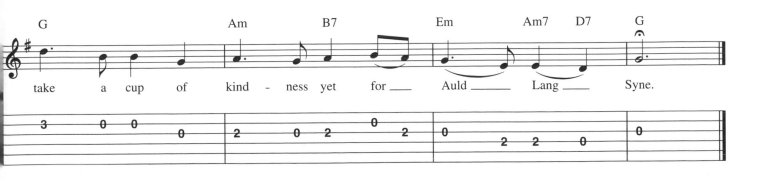

take a cup of kind - ness yet for __ Auld __ Lang __ Syne.

At the Hour of Midnight

Traditional

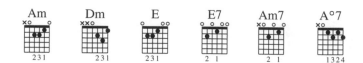

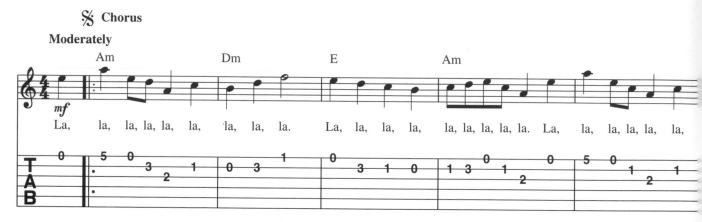

Strum Pattern: 4
Pick Pattern: 5

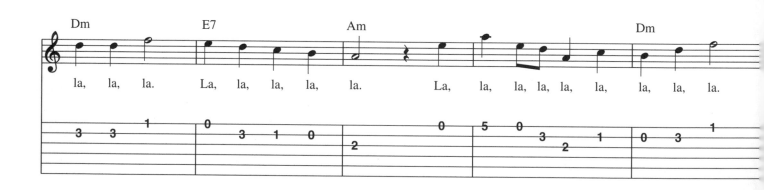

Verse

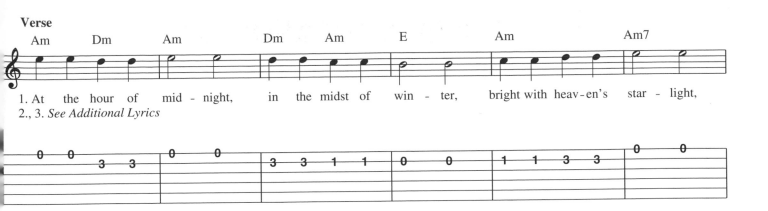

1. At the hour of mid - night, in the midst of win - ter, bright with heav-en's star - light,
2., 3. *See Additional Lyrics*

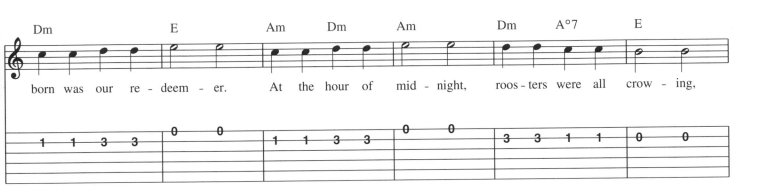

born was our re - deem - er. At the hour of mid - night, roos - ters were all crow - ing,

⊕ Coda

D.S. al Coda

"Christ, our heav'n-ly sun - light comes, his peace be - stow - ing. La, cov - ers. La,   la.

Additional Lyrics

2. Heaven's King eternal on the straw is lying.
   Mule and ox stand near Him; from the cold He's crying.
   Spreading hay to warm Him, ox o'er Jesus hovers;
   But the mule is wicked—he the Babe uncovers.

3. Mary weeps in pity for her suff'ring darling,
   Wishing for protection from the cold winds howling.
   "Tend'rest little Savior, O my Jesus,
   All my love forever, sweetest Son so precious."

Away in a Manger

Words by Martin Luther
Music by Jonathan E. Spillman

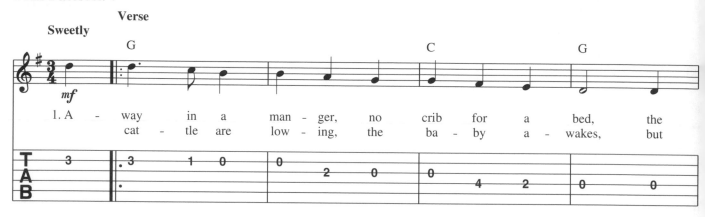

Strum Pattern: 9
Pick Pattern: 7

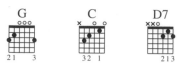

Sweetly

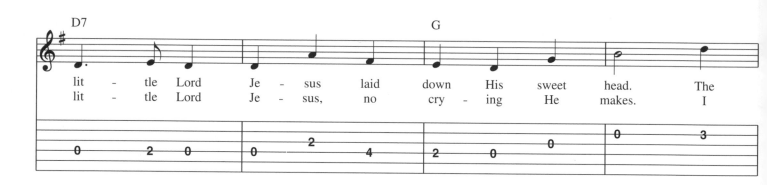

1. A - way in a man - ger, no crib for a bed, the
   cat - tle are low - ing, the ba - by a - wakes, but

lit - tle Lord Je - sus laid down His sweet head. The
lit - tle Lord Je - sus, no cry - ing He makes. I

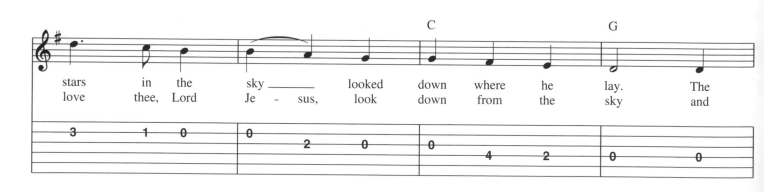

stars in the sky _____ looked down where he lay. The
love thee, Lord Je - sus, look down from the sky and

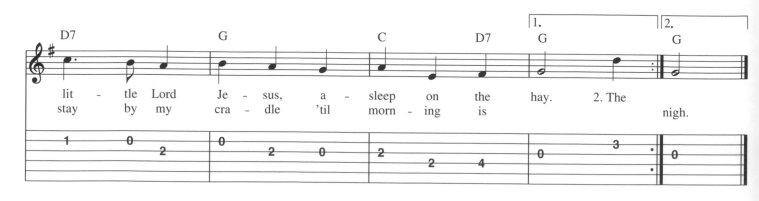

lit - tle Lord Je - sus, a - sleep on the hay. 2. The
stay by my cra - dle 'til morn - ing is nigh.

Copyright © 2002 by HAL LEONARD CORPORATION

A Baby in the Cradle

By D.G. Corner

Strum Pattern: 8
Pick Pattern: 8

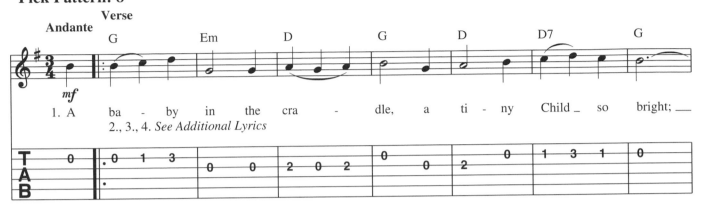

1. A ba - by in the cra - dle, a ti - ny Child so bright; ___
2., 3., 4. *See Additional Lyrics*

___ He shin - eth as a mir - ror re - flects a no - ble

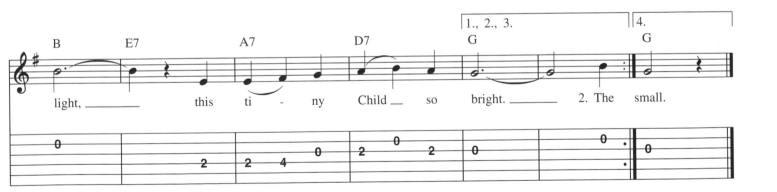

light, _____ this ti - ny Child so bright. _____ 2. The small.

Additional Lyrics

2. The Child of whom we're speaking
   Is Jesus Christ, the Lord;
   He brings us peace and brotherhood
   If we but heed His word,
   Doth Jesus Christ, the Lord.

3. And he who rocks the cradle
   Of the sweet Child so fine
   Must serve with joy and heartiness,
   Be humble and be kind,
   For Mary's Child so fine.

4. O Jesus, dearest Savior,
   Although Thou art so small,
   With Thy great love o'erflowing
   Come flooding through my soul,
   Thou lovely Babe so small.

Because It's Christmas
(For All the Children)

Music by Barry Manilow
Lyric by Bruce Sussman and Jack Feldman

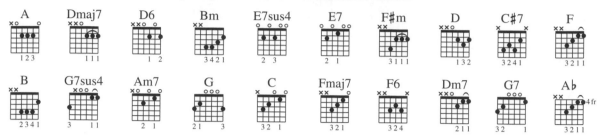

Strum Pattern: 4
Pick Pattern: 3

Verse
Moderately Slow

1. To-night the stars shine for the chil - dren and light the way for dreams to
2. *See Additional Lyrics*

fly.   To-night our love comes wrapped in _____ rib - bons.

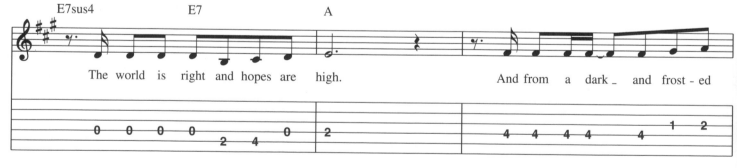

The world is right and hopes are high.   And from a dark and frost-ed

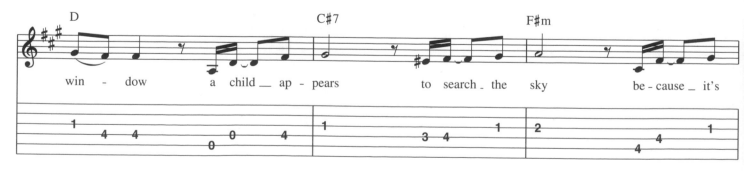

win - dow   a child ap - pears   to search the sky   be-cause it's

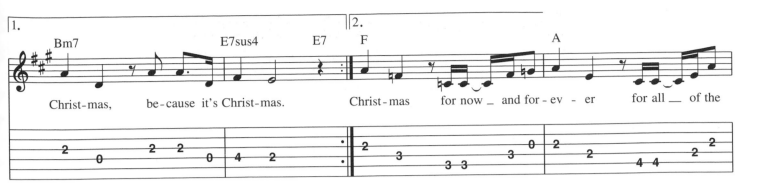

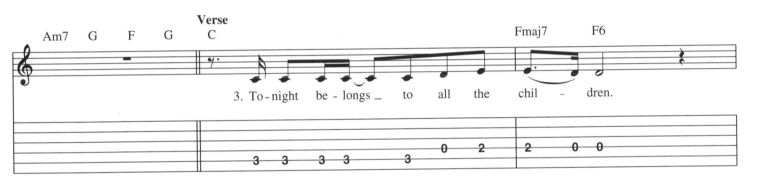

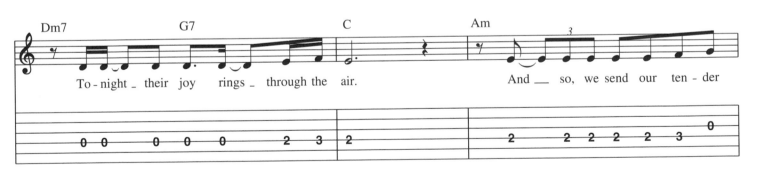

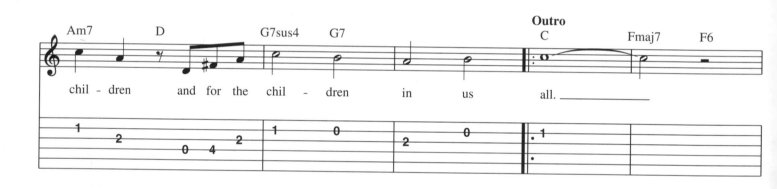

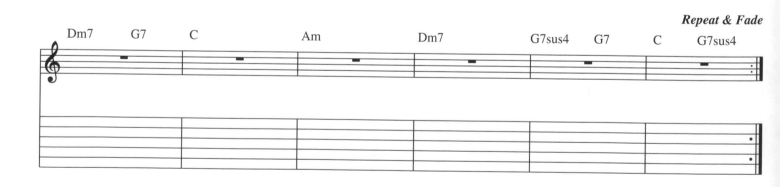

Additional Lyrics

2. Tonight belongs to all the children.
   Tonight their joy rings through the air.
   And so, we send our tender blessings
   To all the children ev'rywhere
   To see the smiles and hear the laughter,
   A time to give, a time to share
   Because it's Christmas for now and forever
   For all of the children in us all.

A Boy Is Born in Bethlehem

Traditional

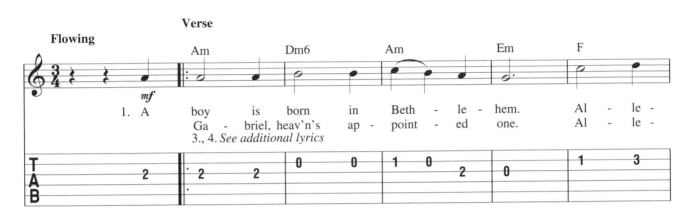

Strum Pattern: 8
Pick Pattern: 9

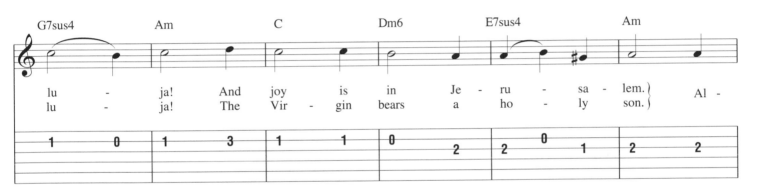

1. A boy is born in Beth - le - hem. Al - le -
   Ga - briel, heav'n's ap - point - ed one. Al - le -
   3., 4. *See additional lyrics*

lu - ja! And joy is in Je - ru - sa - lem. Al -
lu - ja! The Vir - gin bears a ho - ly son.

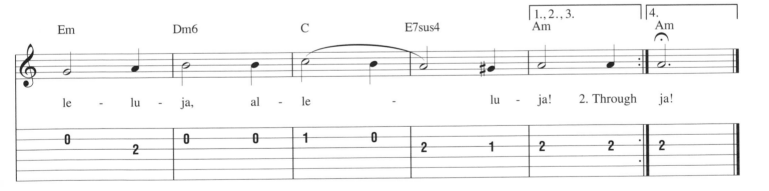

le - lu - ja, al - le - lu - ja! 2. Through ja!

Additional Lyrics

3. The wisest kings of Orient.
   Alleluja!
   Gold, frankincense, and myrrh present.
   Alleluja, alleluja!

4. Laud to the Holy Trinity.
   Alleluja!
   All thanks and praise to God most high.
   Alleluja, alleluja!

Bring a Torch, Jeannette, Isabella

17th Century French Provençal Carol

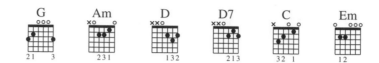

Strum Pattern: 8, 9
Pick Pattern: 8, 7

Verse
Brightly

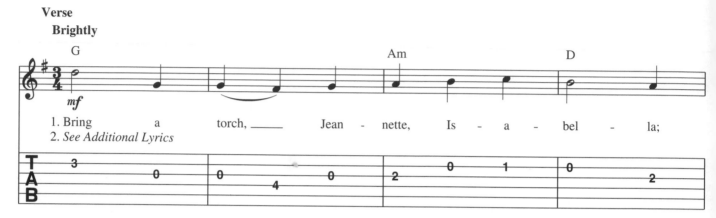

1. Bring a torch, _____ Jean - nette, Is - a - bel - la;
2. *See Additional Lyrics*

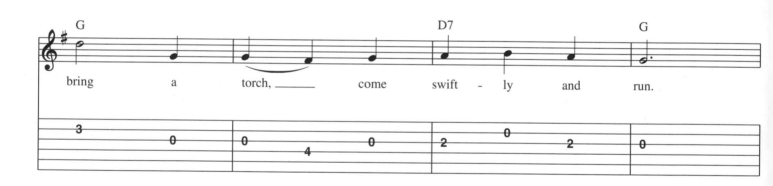

bring a torch, _____ come swift - ly and run.

Christ is born, tell the folk of the vil - lage,

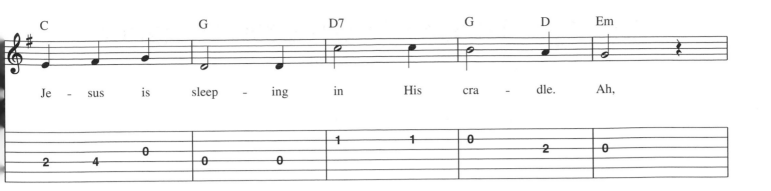

Je - sus   is   sleep - ing   in   His   cra - dle.   Ah,

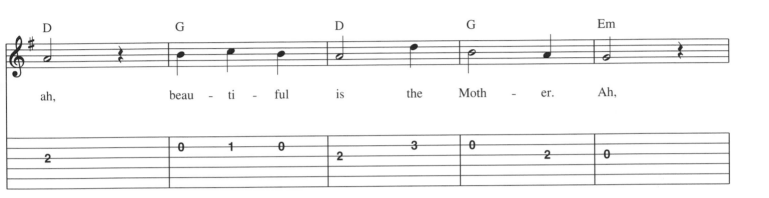

ah,   beau - ti - ful   is   the   Moth - er.   Ah,

ah,   beau - ti - ful   is   her   Son. _____

Additional Lyrics

2. Hasten now, good folk of the village,
   Hasten now, the Christ Child to see.
   You will find him asleep in a manger,
   Quitely come and whisper softly.
   Hush, hush, peacefully now he slumbers,
   Hush, hush, peacefully now He sleeps.

Burgundian Carol

Words and Music by Oscar Brand

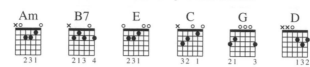

Strum Pattern: 8

Pick Pattern: 8

Verse

Moderately

1. The win - ter sea - son of the year, when
2. *See Additional Lyrics*

to this world our Lord was born, the

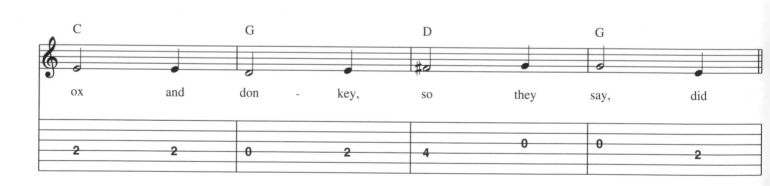

ox and don - key, so they say, did

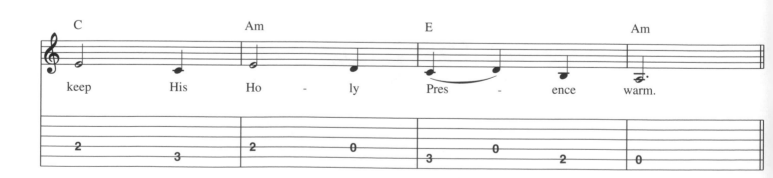

keep His Ho - ly Pres - ence warm.

Chorus

How man - y ox - en and don - keys now, if

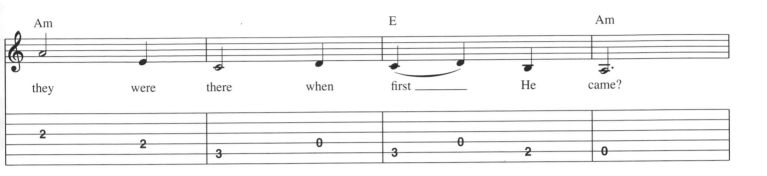

they were there when first _____ He came?

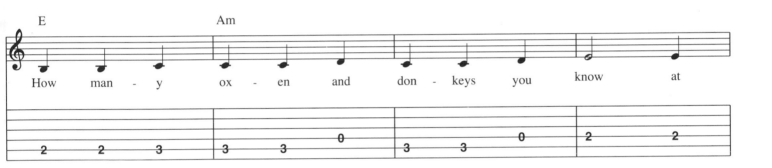

How man - y ox - en and don - keys you know at

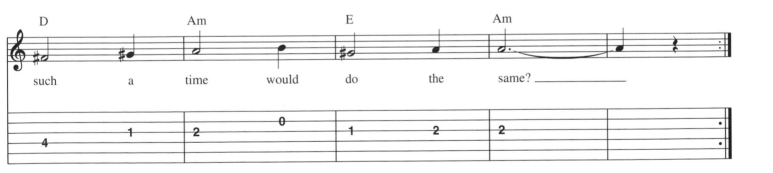

such a time would do the same? _____

Additional Lyrics

2. As soon as to these humble beasts
   Appeared our Lord, so mild and sweet,
   With joy they knelt before His grace
   And gently kissed His tiny feet.

Chorus If we, like oxen and donkeys then,
   In spite of all the things we've heard,
   Would like to be oxen and donkeys then,
   We'd hear the truth, believe His word.

Carol of the Bells

Ukrainian Christmas Carol

Strum Pattern: 8, 9
Pick Pattern: 8, 9

Exuberantly

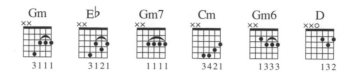

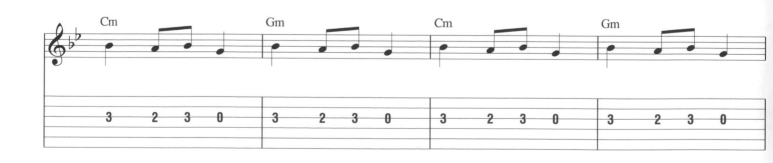

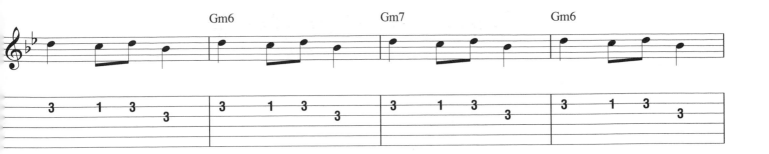

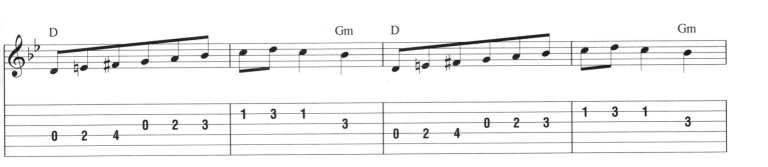

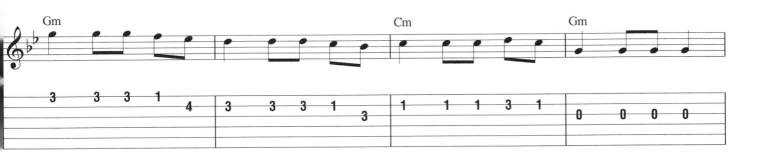

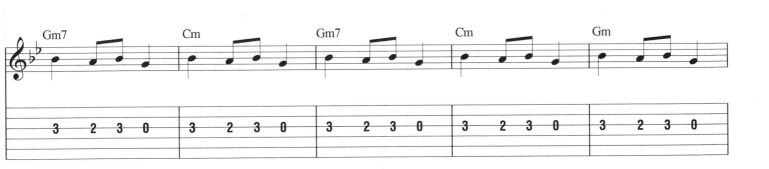

Caroling, Caroling

Words by Wihla Hutson
Music by Alfred Burt

Strum Pattern: 8

Pick Pattern: 8

Verse
With A Lilt

1. Car - ol - ing, car - ol - ing, now we go; Christ - mas bells are ring - ing! Car - ol - ing, car - ol - ing,
2., 3. *See Additional Lyrics*

through the snow; Christ - mas bells are ring - ing! Joy - ous voic - es sweet and clear,

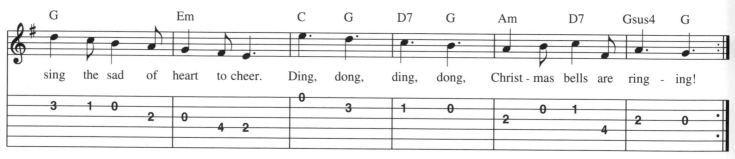

sing the sad of heart to cheer. Ding, dong, ding, dong, Christ - mas bells are ring - ing!

Additional Lyrics

2. Caroling, caroling, through the town;
Christmas bells are ringing!
Caroling, caroling, up and down;
Christmas bells are ringing!
Mark ye well the song we sing,
Gladsome tidings now we bring.
Ding, dong, ding, dong,
Christmas Bells are ringing!

3. Caroling, caroling, near and far;
Christmas bells are ringing!
Following, following yonder star;
Christmas bells are ringing!
Sing we all this happy morn,
"Lo, the King of heav'n is born!"
Ding, dong, ding, dong,
Christmas bells are ringing!

A Child Is Born in Bethlehem

14th-Century Latin Text adapted by Nicolai F.S. Grundtvig

Traditional Danish Melody

Strum Pattern: 4
Pick Pattern: 3

Verse
Moderately

1. A Child is born in Beth - le - hem, in Beth - le -
2., 3., 4. *See Additional Lyrics*

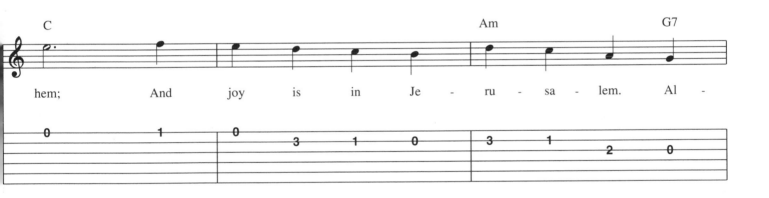

hem; And joy is in Je - ru - sa - lem. Al -

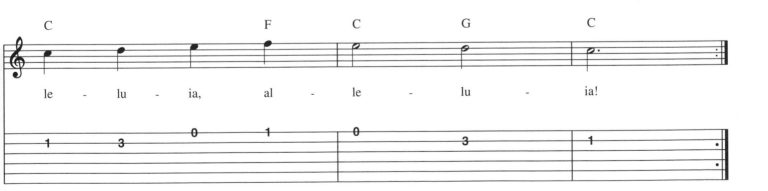

le - lu - ia, al - le - lu - ia!

Additional Lyrics

2. A lowly maiden all alone,
So all alone,
Gave birth to God's own Holy Son.
Alleluia, alleluia!

3. She chose a manger for His bed,
For Jesus' bed.
God's angels sang for joy o'erhead,
Alleluia, alleluia!

4. Give thanks and praise eternally,
Eternally,
To God, the Holy Trinity.
Alleluia, alleluia!

The Chipmunk Song

Words and Music by Ross Bagdasarian

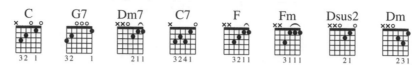

Strum Pattern: 8
Pick Pattern: 8

Verse
Happily

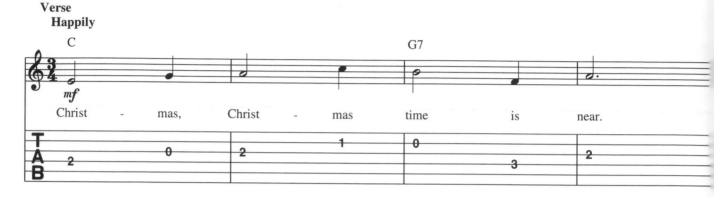

Christ - mas, Christ - mas time is near.

Time for toys and time for cheer.

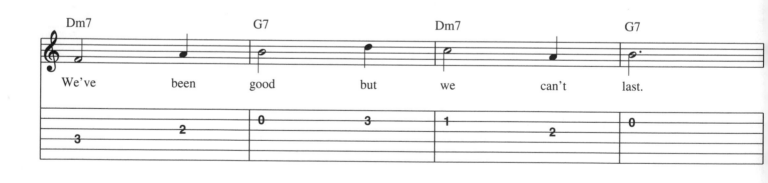

We've been good but we can't last.

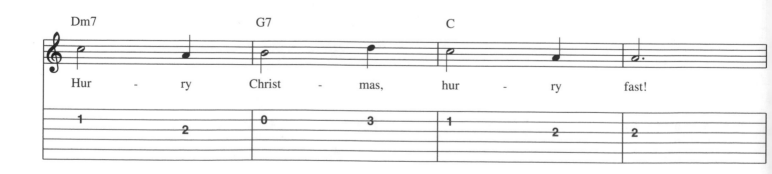

Hur - ry Christ - mas, hur - ry fast!

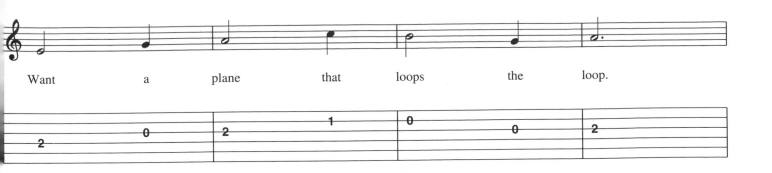

Want   a   plane   that   loops   the   loop.

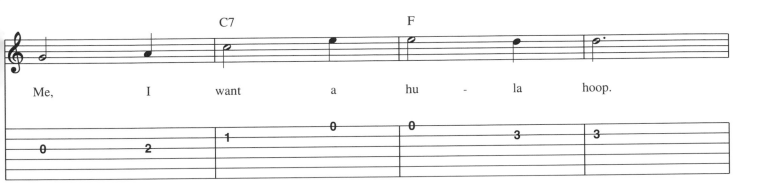

Me,   I   want   a   hu -   la   hoop.

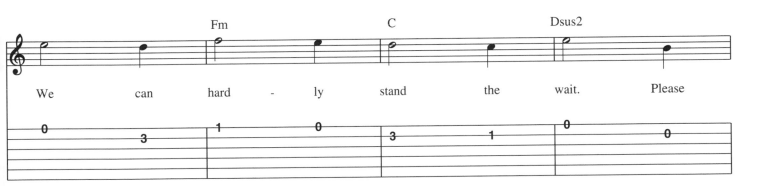

We   can   hard -   ly   stand   the   wait.   Please

Christ -   mas,   don't   be   late. _____

Christ Was Born on Christmas Day

Traditional

Strum Pattern: 8
Pick Pattern: 8

Lilting

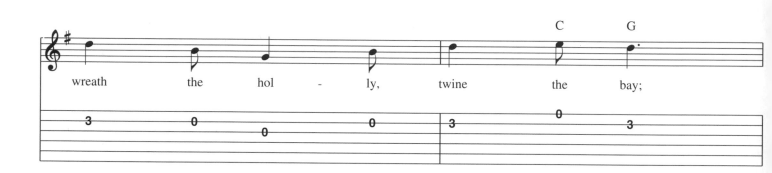

Christ was born on Christ - mas Day,

wreath the hol - ly, twine the bay;

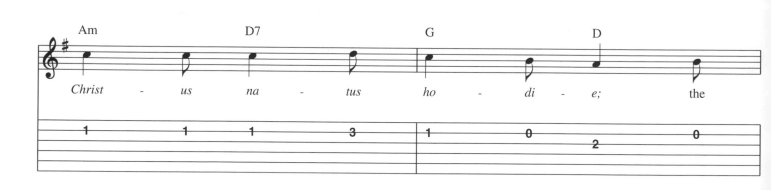

Christ - us na - tus ho - di - e; the

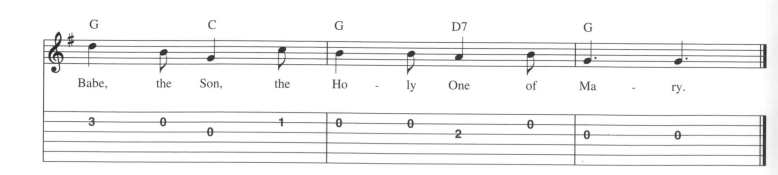

Babe, the Son, the Ho - ly One of Ma - ry.

Come, All Ye Shepherds

Traditional Czech Text
Traditional Moravian Melody

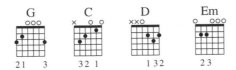

Strum Pattern: 8, 9
Pick Pattern: 8, 9

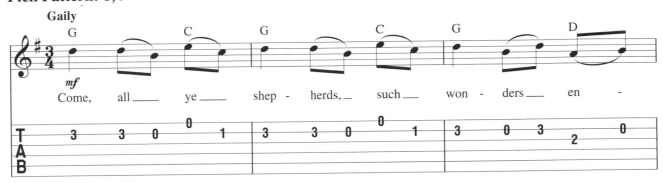

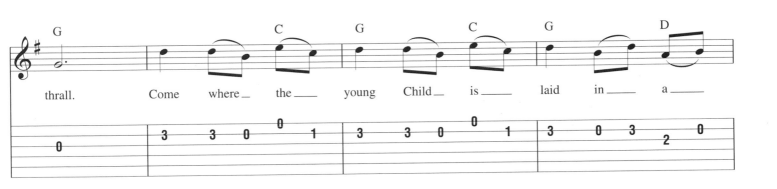

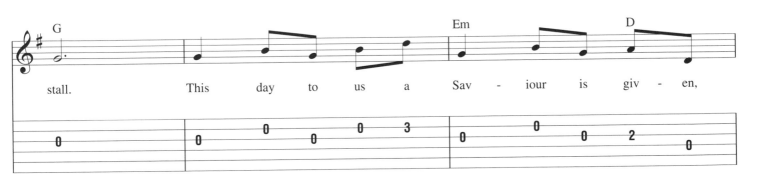

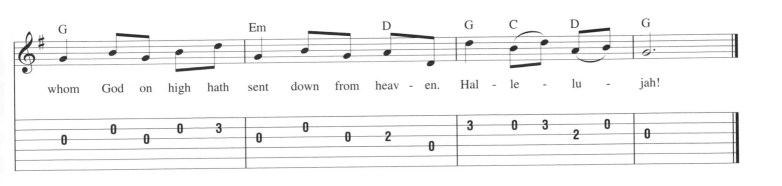

Christians, Awake!
Salute the Happy Morn

Traditional

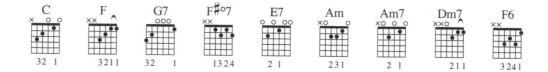

Strum Pattern: 2, 3
Pick Pattern: 1, 6

Verse

Moderately

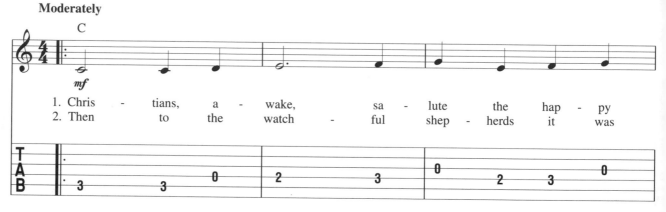

1. Chris - tians, a - wake, sa - lute the hap - py
2. Then to the watch - ful shep - herds it was

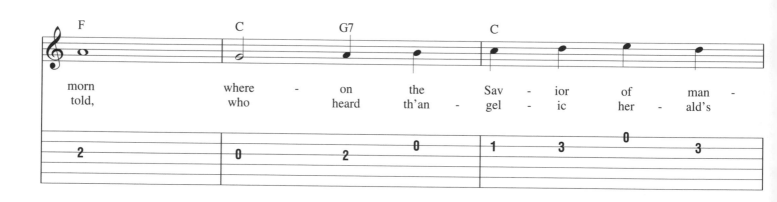

morn
told, where - on the Sav - ior of man -
who heard the th'an - gel - ic her - ald's

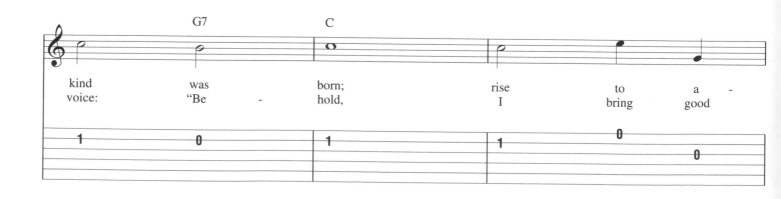

kind was born;
voice: "Be - hold, I bring good

dore the mys - ter - y of love which hosts of
ti - dings of a Sav - ior's birth to you and

an - gels chant - ed from a - bove; with them the
all the na - tions up - on earth; this day hath

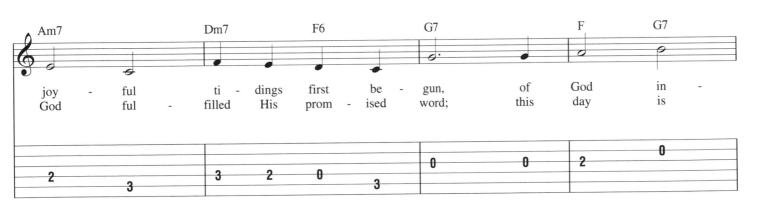

joy - ful ti - dings first be - gun, of God in -
God ful - filled His prom - ised word; this day is

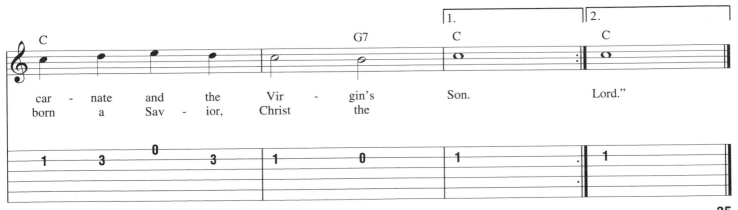

car - nate and the Vir - gin's Son.
born a Sav - ior, Christ the Lord."

C-H-R-I-S-T-M-A-S

Words by Jenny Lou Carson
Music by Eddy Arnold

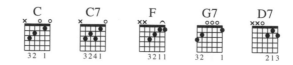

Strum Pattern: 3
Pick Pattern: 3

Verse
Brightly

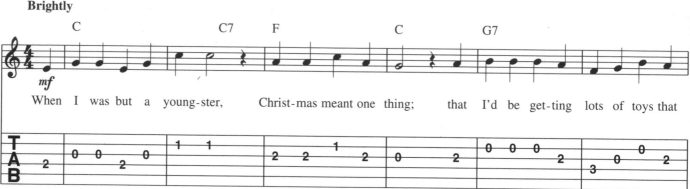

When I was but a young-ster, Christ-mas meant one thing; that I'd be get-ting lots of toys that

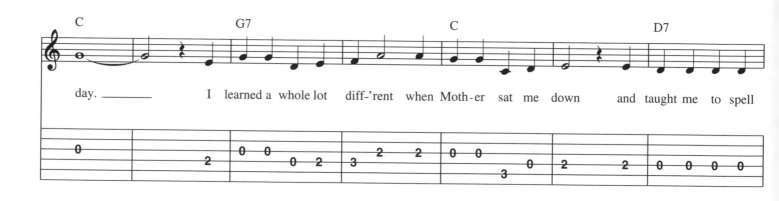

day. _____ I learned a whole lot diff'rent when Moth-er sat me down and taught me to spell

Chorus

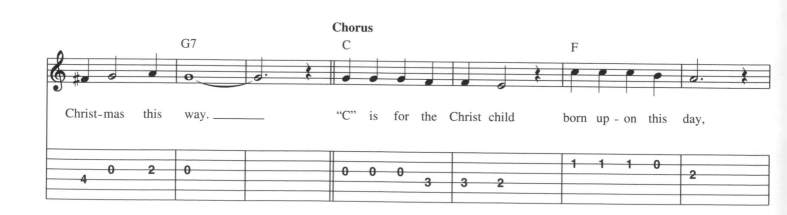

Christ-mas this way. _____ "C" is for the Christ child born up-on this day,

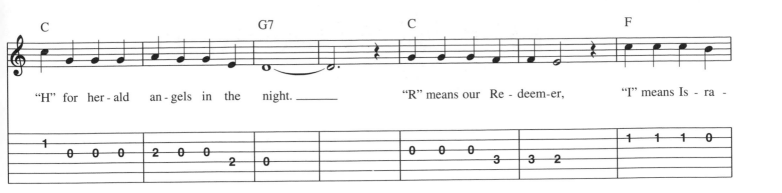

"H" for her-ald an-gels in the night. _____ "R" means our Re-deem-er, "I" means Is - ra -

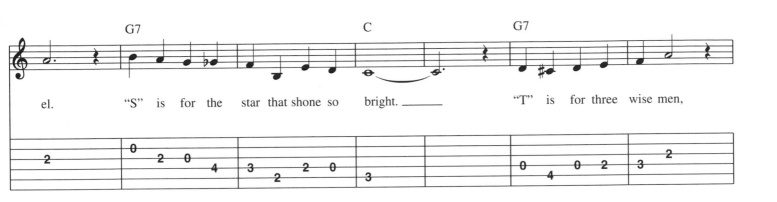

el. "S" is for the star that shone so bright. _____ "T" is for three wise men,

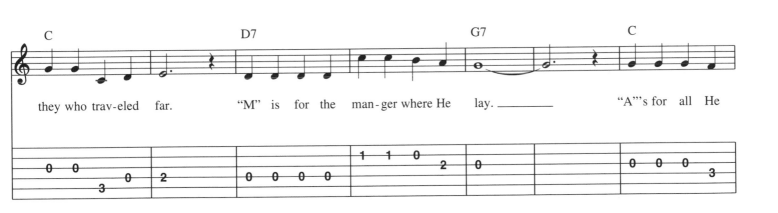

they who trav-eled far. "M" is for the man-ger where He lay. _____ "A"'s for all He

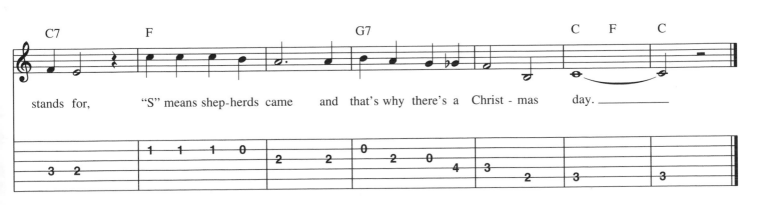

stands for, "S" means shep-herds came and that's why there's a Christ - mas day. _____

Christmas Is A-Comin'
(May God Bless You)

Words and Music by Frank Luther

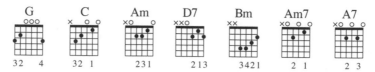

Strum Pattern: 2, 3
Pick Pattern: 2, 3

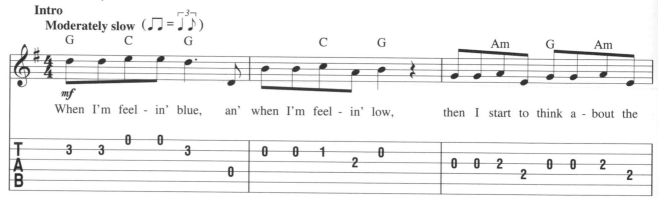

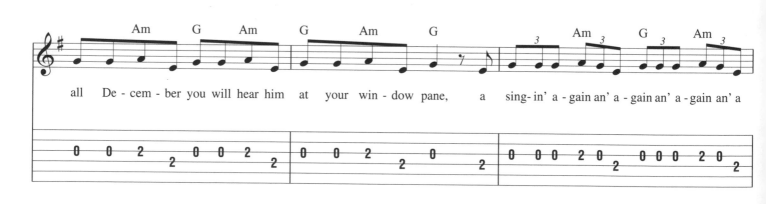

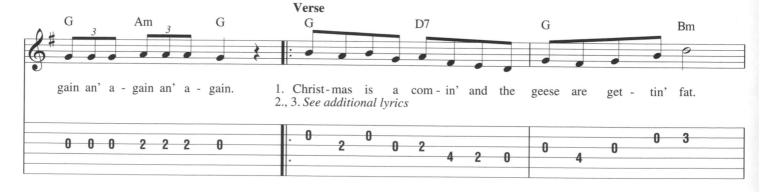

Additional Lyrics

2. Christmas is a comin' and the lights are on the tree.
   How about a turkey leg for poor old me?
   If you haven't got a turkey leg a turkey wing-'ll do.
   If you haven't got a turkey wing, may God bless you.
   God bless you, gentlemen, God bless you.
   If you haven't got a turkey wing, may God bless you.

3. Christmas is a comin' and the egg is in the nog,
   Please to let me sit around your old yule log.
   If you'd rather I didn't sit around, to stand around-'ll do,
   If you'd rather I didn't stand around, may God bless you.
   God bless you, gentlemen, God bless you.
   If you'd rather I didn't stand around may God bless you.
   If you haven't got a thing for me, may God bless you.

The Christmas Song
(Chestnuts Roasting on an Open Fire)

Music and Lyric by Mel Torme and Robert Wells

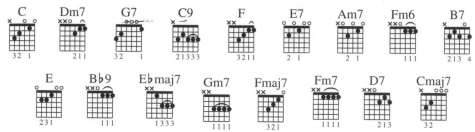

Strum Pattern: 2
Pick Pattern: 3

Verse
Sentimentally

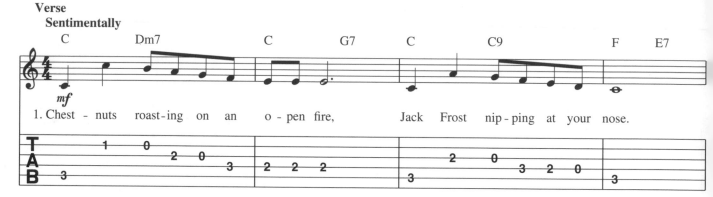

1. Chest - nuts roast - ing on an o - pen fire, Jack Frost nip - ping at your nose.

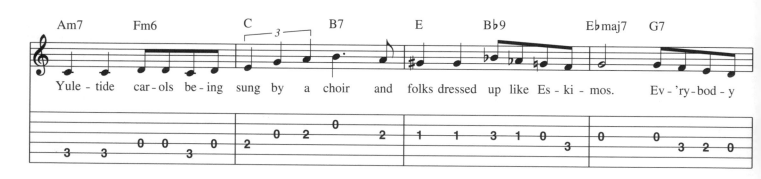

Yule - tide car - ols be - ing sung by a choir and folks dressed up like Es - ki - mos. Ev - 'ry - bod - y

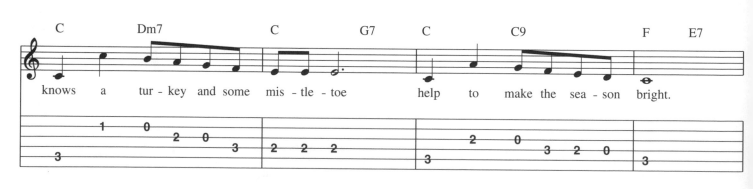

knows a tur - key and some mis - tle - toe help to make the sea - son bright.

Ti - ny tots with their eyes all a - glow will find it hard to sleep to - night. They know that

Bridge

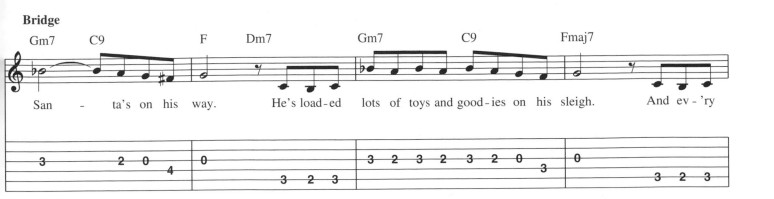

San - ta's on his way. He's load-ed lots of toys and good-ies on his sleigh. And ev-'ry

moth-er's child __ is gon-na spy _____ to see if rein-deer _ real-ly know how to fly. 2. And

Verse

so I'm of-fer-ing this sim-ple phrase to kids from one to nine-ty - two. Al -

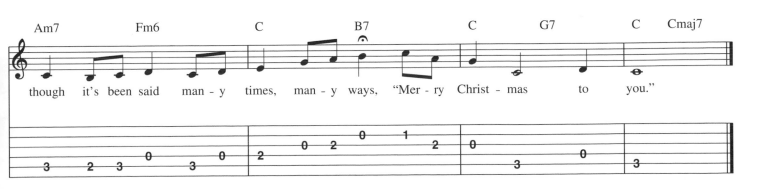

though it's been said man - y times, man - y ways, "Mer - ry Christ - mas to you."

Christmas Time Is Here

from A CHARLIE BROWN CHRISTMAS

Words by Lee Mendelson
Music by Vince Guaraldi

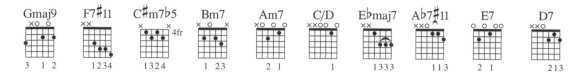

Gmaj9 F7#11 C#m7♭5 Bm7 Am7 C/D E♭maj7 A♭7#11 E7 D7

Strum Pattern: 8, 9
Pick Pattern: 8, 9

Verse
Slowly

1. Christ - mas time ___ is here, hap - pi - ness ___ and
2. Snow - flakes in ___ the air, car - ols ev - 'ry -

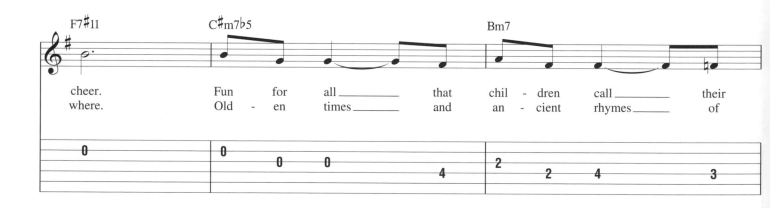

cheer. Fun for all ___ that chil - dren call ___ their
where. Old - en times ___ and an - cient rhymes ___ of

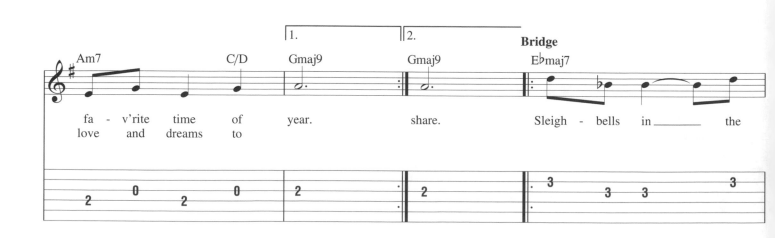

fa - v'rite time of year. share.
love and dreams to

Bridge

Sleigh - bells in ___ the

air, beau - ty ev - 'ry - where. Yule - tide by _____ the

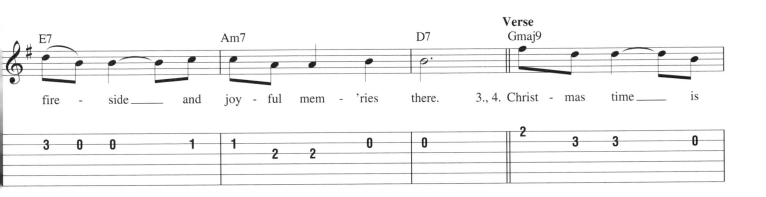

fire - side _____ and joy - ful mem - 'ries there. 3., 4. Christ - mas time _____ is

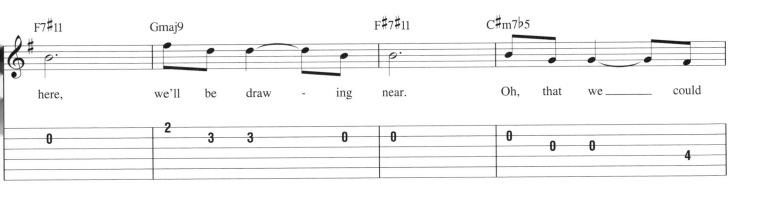

here, we'll be draw - ing near. Oh, that we _____ could

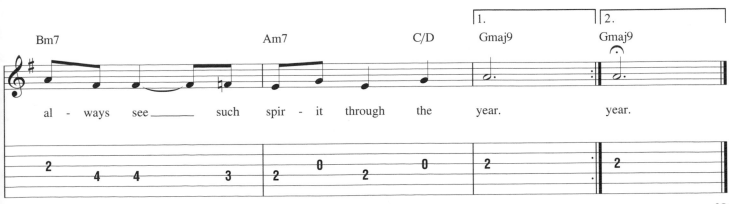

al - ways see _____ such spir - it through the year. year.

The Christmas Waltz

Words by Sammy Cahn
Music by Jule Styne

Strum Pattern: 9
Pick Pattern: 7

Verse
Moderately

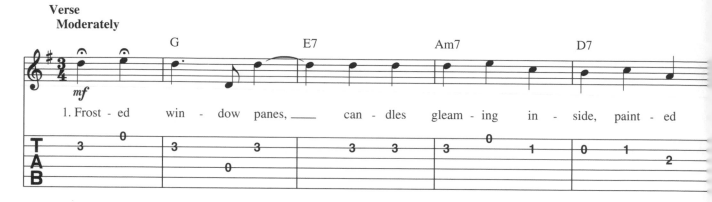

1. Frost-ed win-dow panes, ___ can-dles gleam-ing in - side, paint-ed

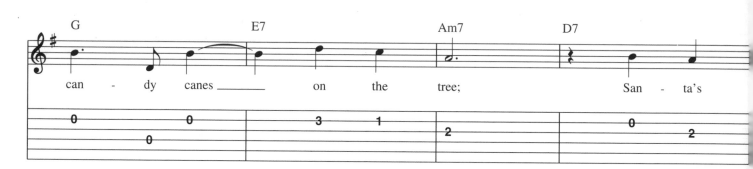

can - dy canes ___ on the tree; San - ta's

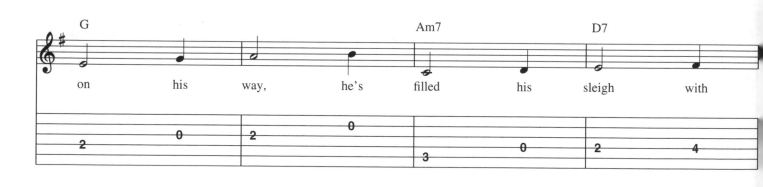

on his way, he's filled his sleigh with

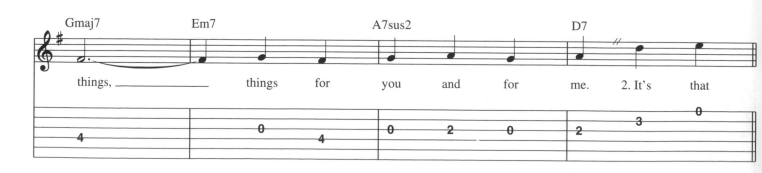

things, ___ things for you and for me. 2. It's that

Verse

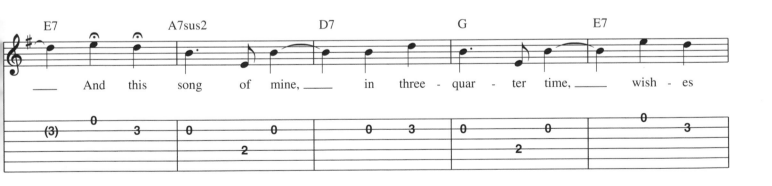

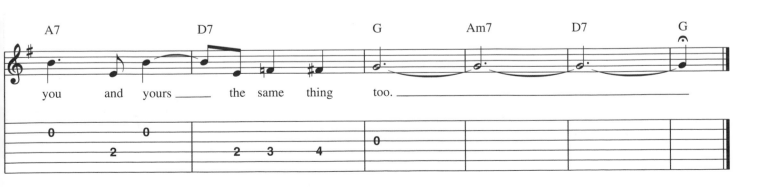

Come, Thou Long-Expected Jesus

Words by Charles Wesley
Music by Rowland Hugh Prichard

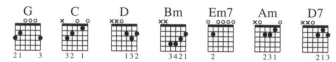

Strum Pattern: 8, 7
Pick Pattern: 8, 7

Verse
Moderately

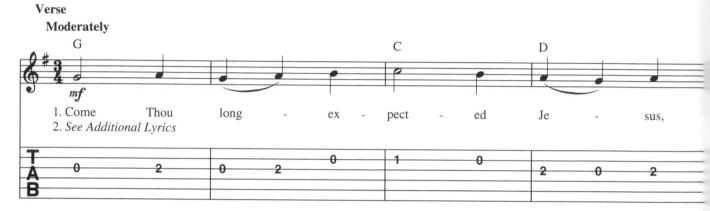

1. Come Thou long - ex - pect - ed Je - sus,
2. *See Additional Lyrics*

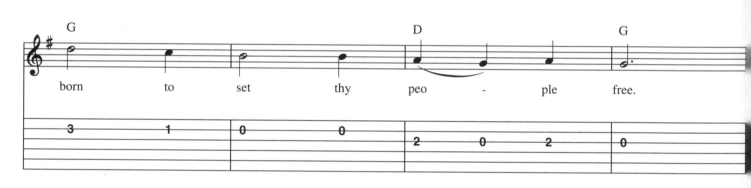

born to set thy peo - ple free.

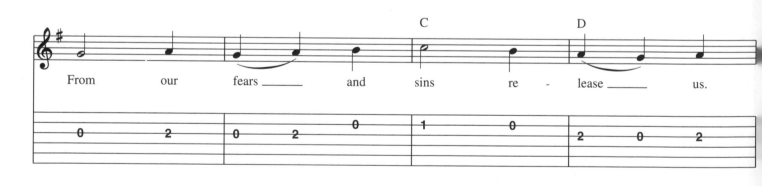

From our fears _____ and sins re - lease _____ us.

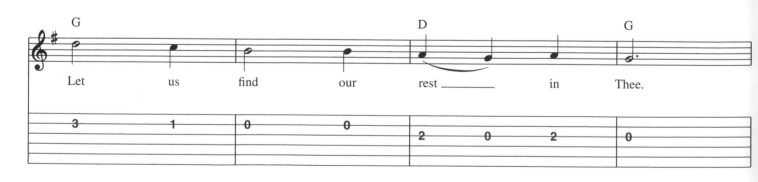

Let us find our rest _____ in Thee.

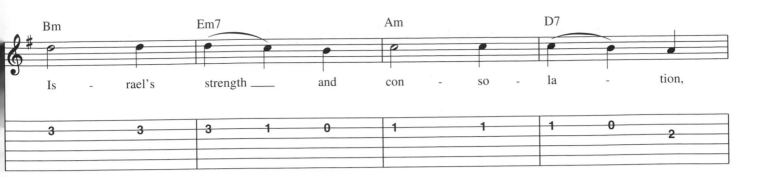

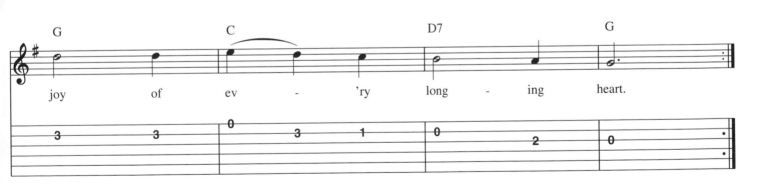

Additional Lyrics

2. Born thy people to deliver,
Born a child and yet a king.
Born to reign in us forever,
Now thy gracious kingdom bring.
By thine own eternal Spirit,
Rule in all our hearts alone.
By thine all-sufficient merit,
Raise us to thy glorious throne.

Coventry Carol

Words by Robert Croo
Traditional English Melody

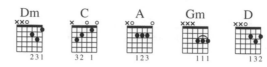

Strum Pattern: 7, 9
Pick Pattern: 7, 9

Verse
Tenderly

1. Lul - lay, thou lit - tle ti - ny child. By, by, lul -
2., 3., 4. *See Additional Lyrics*

ly, lul - lay. _____ Lul - lay, thou lit - tle

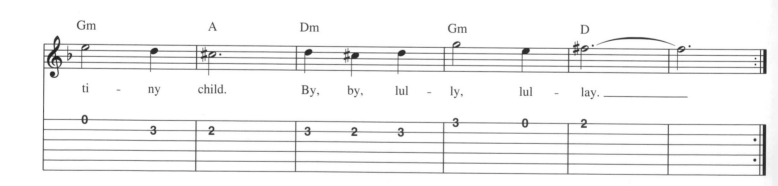

ti - ny child. By, by, lul - ly, lul - lay. _____

Additional Lyrics

2. Oh, sisters too,
   How may we do,
   For to preserve this day?
   This poor youngling,
   For whom we sing
   By, by, lully lullay.

3. Herod the king,
   In his raging,
   Charged he hath this day.
   His men of might,
   In his own sight,
   All young children to slay.

4. That woe is me,
   Poor child for thee!
   And ever morn and day,
   For thy parting
   Neither say nor sing
   By, by, lully lullay!

A Day, Bright Day of Glory

Traditional

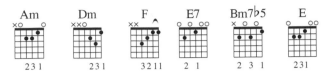

Strum Pattern: 8, 9
Pick Pattern: 7, 8

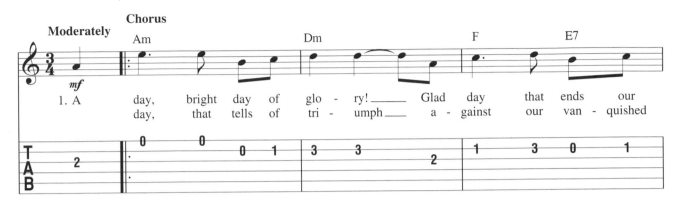

1. A day, bright day of glo - ry!____ Glad day that ends our
   day, that tells of tri - umph____ a - gainst our van - quished

woe! A foe: For us this Christ - mas sun - rise_____ this

bright De - cem - ber morn, so sing let us be joy - ous_____ for

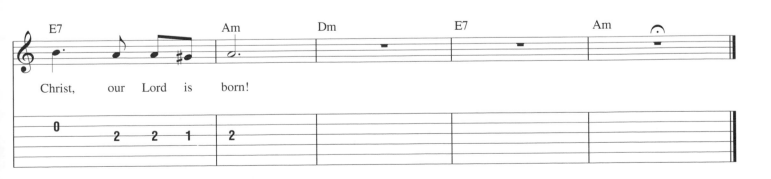

Christ, our Lord is born!

Deck the Hall

Traditional Welsh Carol

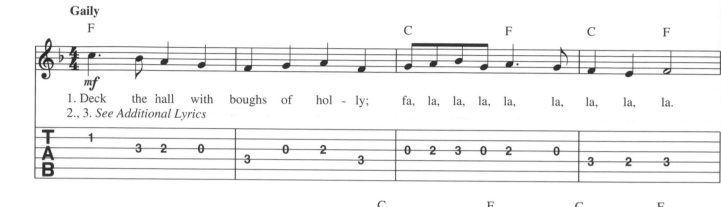

Strum Pattern: 4, 6
Pick Pattern: 5, 6

Verse
Gaily

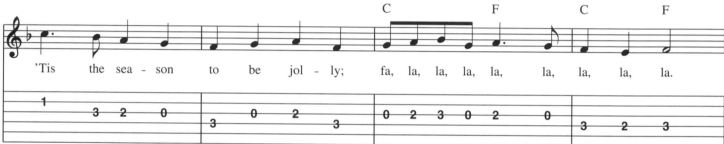

1. Deck the hall with boughs of hol - ly; fa, la, la, la, la, la, la, la, la.
2., 3. *See Additional Lyrics*

'Tis the sea - son to be jol - ly; fa, la, la, la, la, la, la, la, la.

Don we now our gay ap - par - el; fa, la, la, la, la, la, la, la, la.

Troll the an - cient yule - tide car - ol; fa, la, la, la, la, la, la, la, la.

Additional Lyrics

2. See the blazing yule before us;
   Fa, la, la, la, la, la, la, la, la.
   Strike the harp and join the chorus;
   Fa, la, la, la, la, la, la, la, la.
   Follow me in merry measure;
   Fa, la, la, la, la, la, la, la, la, la.
   While I tell of Yuletide treasure;
   Fa, la, la, la, la, la, la, la, la.

3. Fast away the old year passes;
   Fa, la, la, la, la, la, la, la, la.
   Hail the new ye lads and lasses;
   Fa, la, la, la, la, la, la, la, la.
   Sing we joyous, all together;
   Fa, la, la, la, la, la, la, la, la.
   Heedless of the wind and weather;
   Fa, la, la, la, la, la, la, la, la.

Everywhere, Everywhere, Christmas Tonight

By Lewis H. Redner and Phillip Brooks

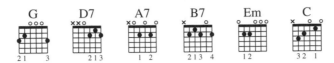

Strum Pattern: 7
Pick Pattern: 7

Verse
Moderately

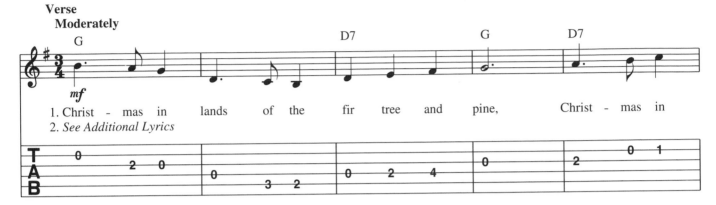

1. Christ - mas in lands of the fir tree and pine, Christ - mas in
2. *See Additional Lyrics*

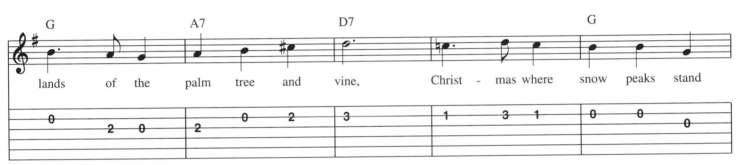

lands of the palm tree and vine, Christ - mas where snow peaks stand

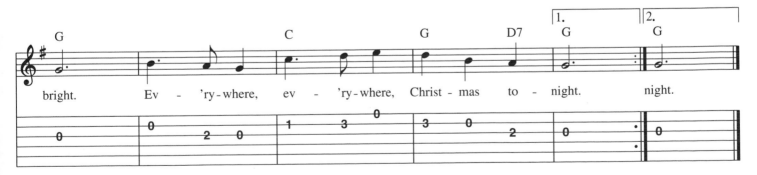

sol - emn and white Christ - mas where corn - fields lie sun - ny and

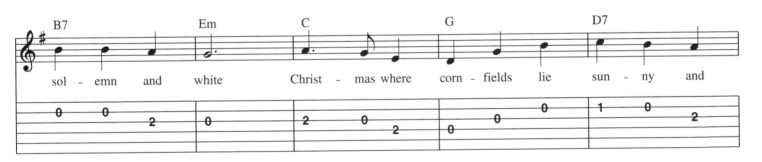

bright. Ev - 'ry - where, ev - 'ry - where, Christ - mas to - night. night.

Additional Lyrics

2. Christmas where children are hopeful and gay,
   Christmas where old men are patient and gray,
   Christmas where peace like a dove in its flight
   Broods o'er brave men in the thick of the fight.
   Ev'rywhere, ev'rywhere, Christmas tonight.

Ding Dong!
Merrily on High!

French Carol

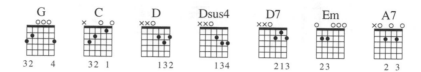

Strum Pattern: 2, 5
Pick Pattern: 2, 4

Intro
Moderately

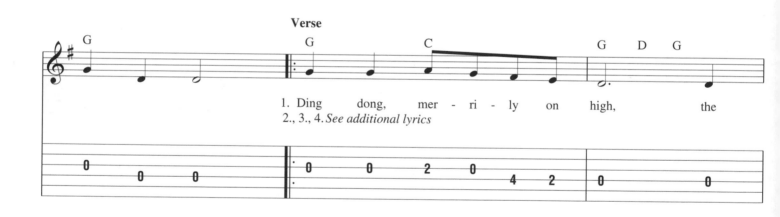

Verse

1. Ding   dong,   mer - ri - ly   on   high,   the
2., 3., 4. *See additional lyrics*

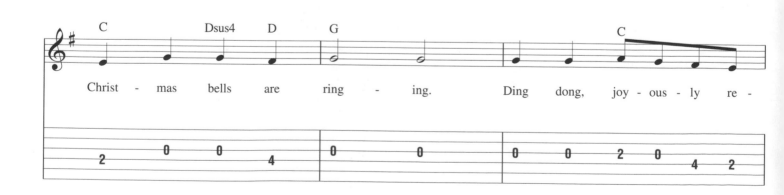

Christ - mas   bells   are   ring - ing.   Ding   dong,   joy - ous - ly   re -

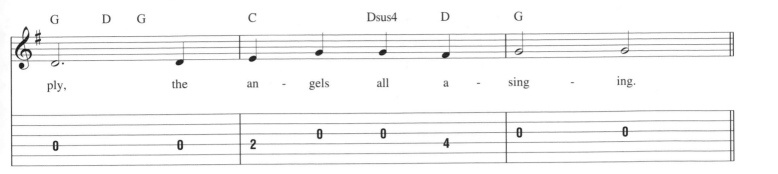

ply,   the   an - gels   all   a - sing - ing.

Chorus

Glo

ri - a,   Ho -

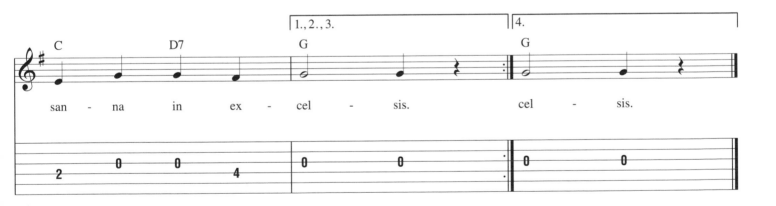

| 1., 2., 3. | 4. |

san - na   in   ex - cel - sis.   cel - sis.

Additional Lyrics

2. Ding dong, carol all the bells,
   Ring out the Christmas story.
   Ding dong, sound the good noels;
   God's Son has come in glory.

3. Praise Him! People far and near,
   And join the angels singing.
   Ding dong, everywhere we hear
   The Christmas bells a ringing.

4. Hear them ring this happy morn!
   Our God a gift has given:
   Ding dong, Jesus Christ is born!
   A precious Child from heaven.

Do They Know It's Christmas?

Words and Music by M. Ure and B. Geldof

Strum Pattern: 3, 4
Pick Pattern: 3, 4

Verse

Moderate Rock

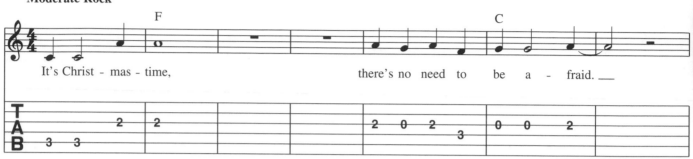

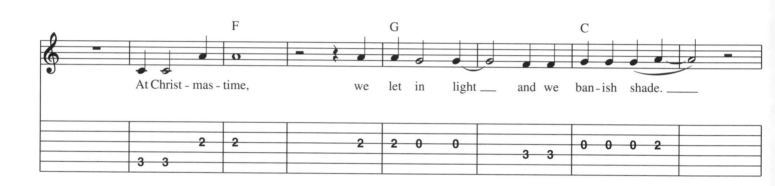

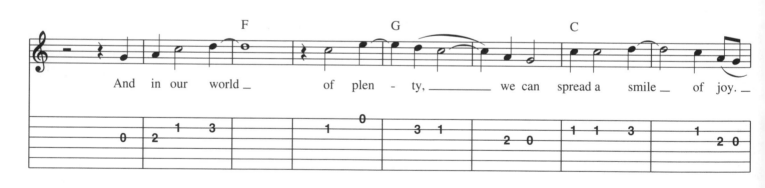

But say a prayer, to pray for the oth - er ones

at Christ - mas - time. It's hard, but __ when you're hav - ing fun

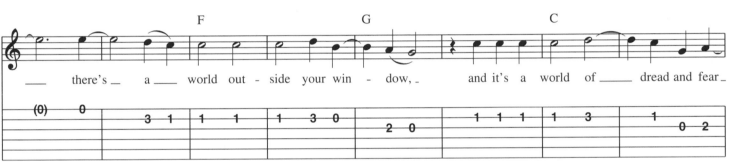

__ there's __ a __ world out - side your win - dow, __ and it's a world of _____ dread and fear

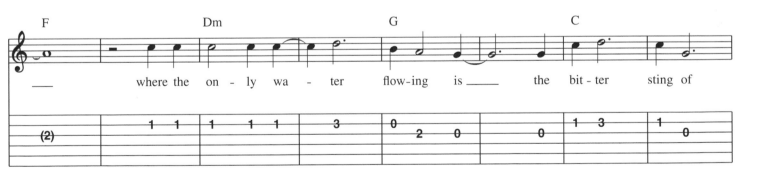

__ where the on - ly wa - ter flow-ing is _____ the bit - ter sting of

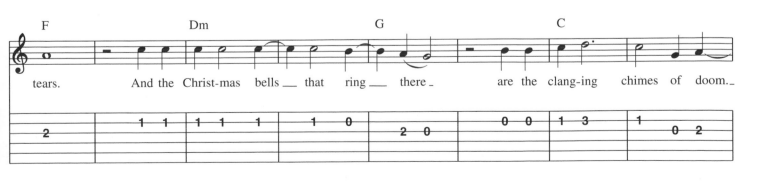

tears. And the Christ-mas bells __ that ring __ there _ are the clang-ing chimes of doom.

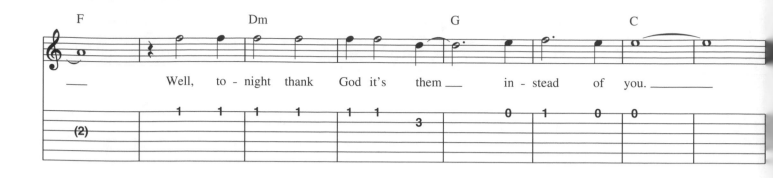

Well, to - night thank God it's them ___ in - stead of you. _____

And there won't be snow ___ in Af - ri - ca ___ this Christ - mas - time, ___

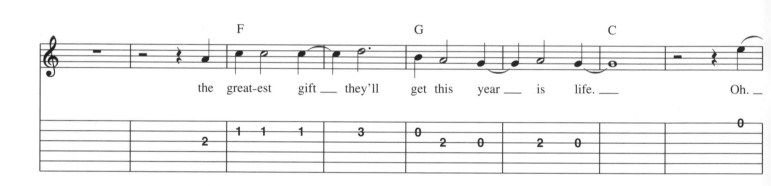

the great-est gift ___ they'll get this year ___ is life. ___ Oh. ___

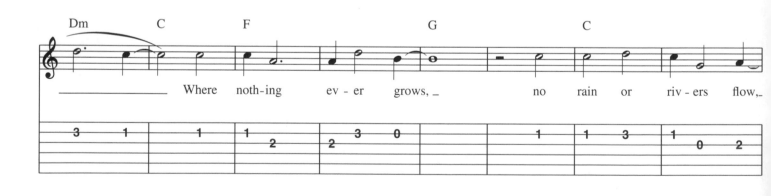

_____ Where noth-ing ev - er grows, _ no rain or riv - ers flow, _

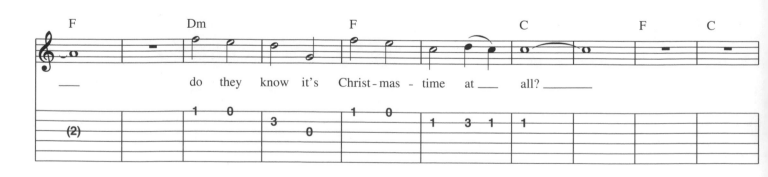

___ do they know it's Christ - mas - time at ___ all? _____

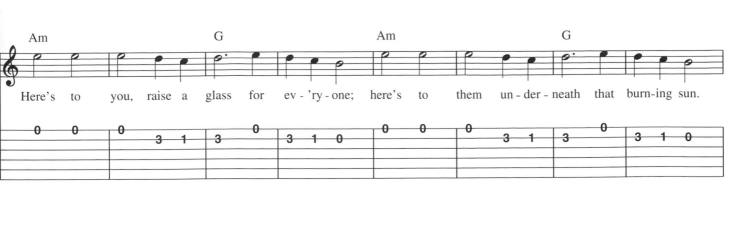

Here's to you, raise a glass for ev-'ry-one; here's to them un-der-neath that burn-ing sun.

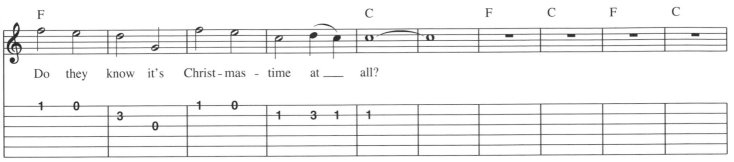

Do they know it's Christ - mas - time at ___ all?

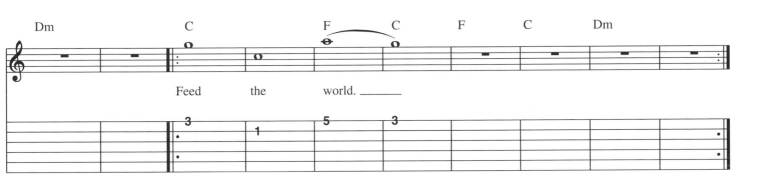

Feed the world. _____

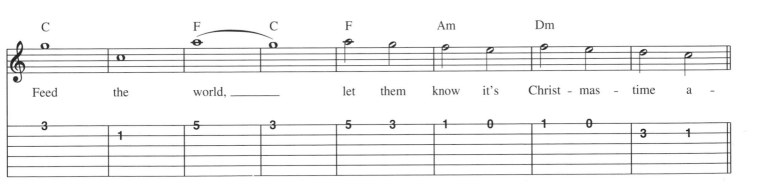

Feed the world, _____ let them know it's Christ - mas - time a -

Repeat & Fade

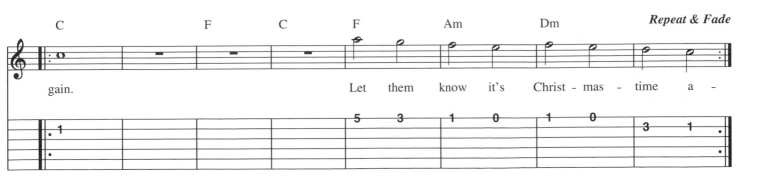

gain. Let them know it's Christ - mas - time a -

Feliz Navidad

Music and Lyrics by Jose Feliciano

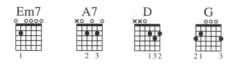

Strum Pattern: 2, 1
Pick Pattern: 4, 2

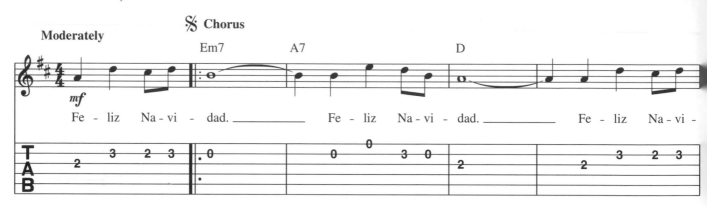

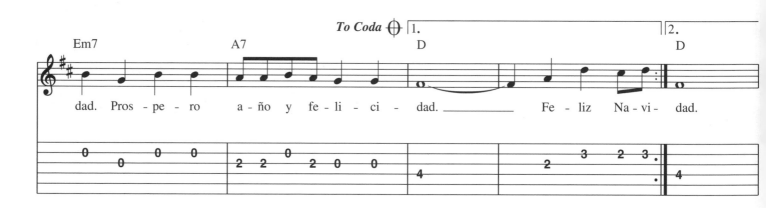

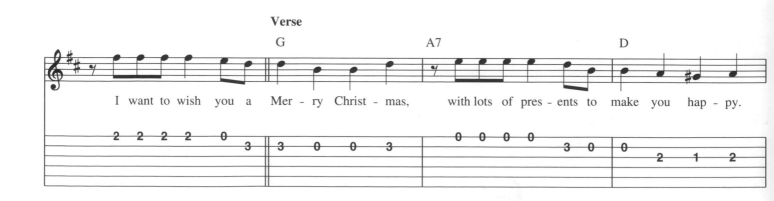

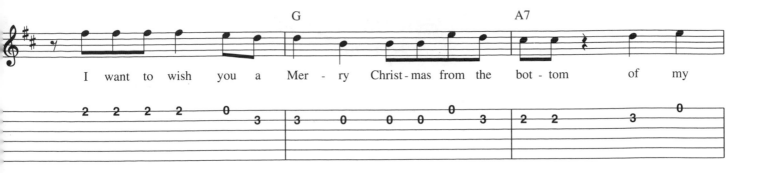

I want to wish you a Mer - ry Christ - mas from the bot - tom of my

heart. _____ I want to wish you a Mer - ry Christ - mas,

with mis - tle - toe and _ lots of cheer. _ With lots of laugh - ter through - out the years from the

D.S. al Coda
(with repeat)

⊕ *Coda*

bot - tom of my heart. _____ Fe - liz Na - vi -

dad. _____

The First Noël

17th Century English Carol
Music from W. Sandys' Christmas Carols

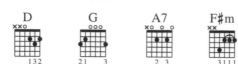

Strum Pattern: 7, 8
Pick Pattern: 9, 8

Verse
Moderately Slow

1. The first No - ël, the an - gel did say, was to cer - tain poor
2.-5. *See Additional Lyrics*

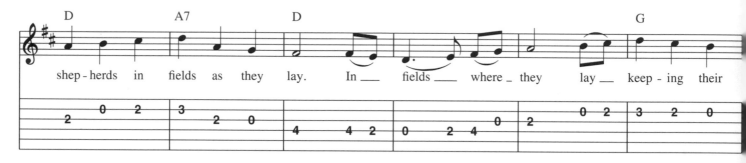

shep - herds in fields as they lay. In fields where they lay keep - ing their

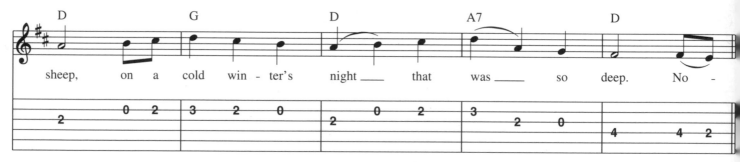

sheep, on a cold win - ter's night that was so deep. No -

Chorus

ël, No - ël, No - ël, No - ël, born is the King of Is - ra - el.

Additional Lyrics

2. They looked up and saw a star
   Shining in the East, beyond them far.
   And to the earth it gave great light
   And so it continued both day and night.

3. And by the light of that same star,
   Three wise man came from country far;
   To seek for a King was their intent,
   And to follow the star wherever it went.

4. This star drew nigh to the northwest,
   O'er Bethlehem it took its rest;
   And there it did both stop and stay,
   Right over the place where Jesus lay.

5. Then entered in those wise men three,
   Full reverently upon their knee;
   And offered there in His presence,
   Their gold, and myrrh, and frankincense.

The Friendly Beasts

Traditional English Carol

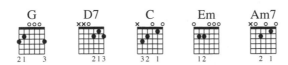

Strum Pattern: 8
Pick Pattern: 9

Verse
Moderately

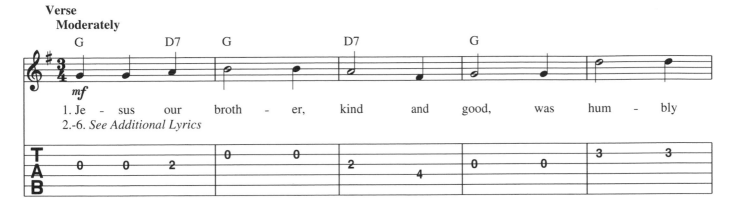

1. Je - sus our broth - er, kind and good, was hum - bly
2.-6. *See Additional Lyrics*

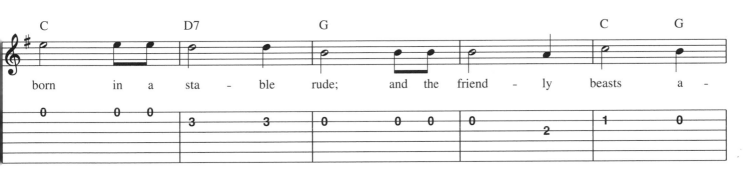

born in a sta - ble rude; and the friend - ly beasts a -

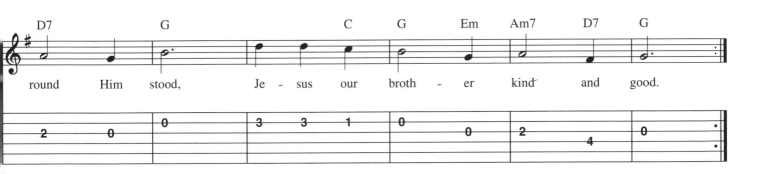

round Him stood, Je - sus our broth - er kind and good.

Additional Lyrics

2. "I," said the donkey, shaggy and brown,
   "I carried his mother up hill and down.
   I carried his mother to Bethlehem town."
   "I," said the donkey, shaggy and brown.

3. "I," said the cow, all white and red,
   "I gave Him my manger for His bed;
   I gave Him my hay to pillow His head."
   "I," said the cow, all white and red.

4. "I," said the sheep with the curly horn,
   "I gave Him my wool for His blanket warm;
   He wore my coat on Christmas morn."
   "I," said the sheep with the curly horn.

5. "I," said the dove from the rafters high,
   "I cooed Him to sleep that He would not cry;
   We cooed Him to sleep, my mate and I."
   "I," said the dove from the rafters high.

6. Thus every beast by some good spell,
   In the stable dark was glad to tell
   Of the gift he gave Emmanuel,
   The gift he gave Emmanuel.

From Heaven Above to the Earth I Come

Words and Music by Martin Luther

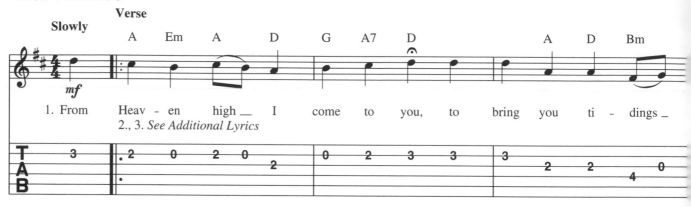

Strum Pattern: 4
Pick Pattern: 3

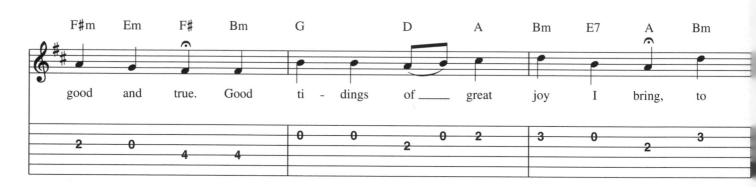

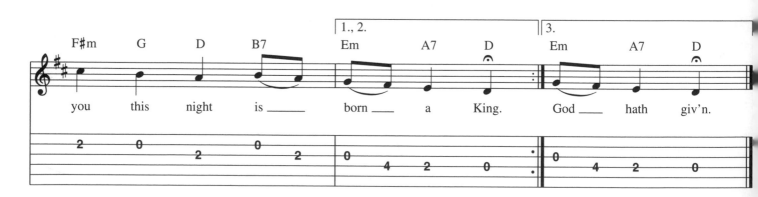

Additional Lyrics

2. This King is but a little child,
His mother blessed Mary mild.
His cradle is but now a stall,
Yet He brings joy and peace to all.

3. Now let us all with songs of cheer,
Follow the shepherds and draw near,
To find the wondrous gift of Heav'n,
The Blessed Christ whom God hath giv'n.

Frosty the Snow Man

Words and Music by Steve Nelson and Jack Rollins

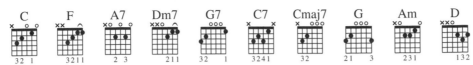

Strum Pattern: 3, 2
Pick Pattern: 3, 4

Verse
Moderately Fast

1. Frost - y, the snow man was a jol - ly hap - py
3. Frost - y, the snow man knew the sun was hot that

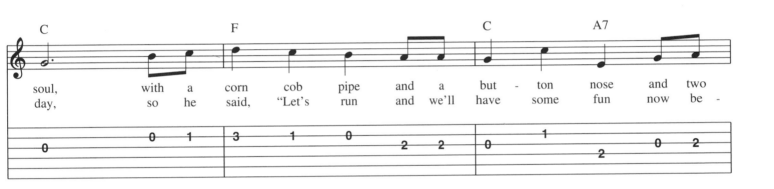

soul, with a corn cob pipe and a but - ton nose and two
day, so he said, "Let's run and we'll have some fun now be -

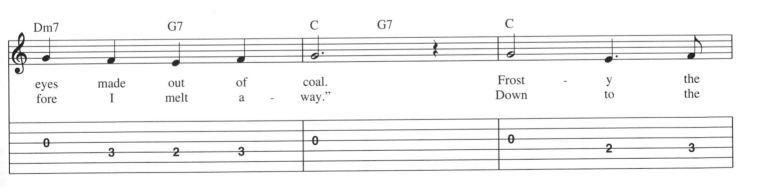

eyes made out of coal. Frost - y the
fore I melt a - way." Down to the

snow man is a fair - y tale they say. He was
vil - lage with a broom - stick in his hand, run - ning

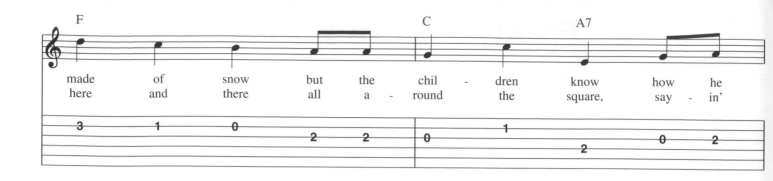

made   of   snow   but   the   chil - dren   know   how   he
here   and   there   all   a - round   the   know   square,   say - in'

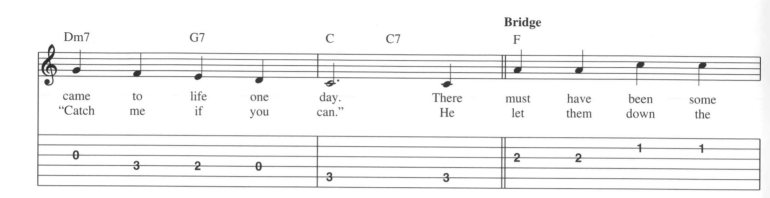

Bridge

came   to   life   one   day.   There   must   have   been   some
"Catch   me   if   you   can."   He   let   must   have   them   been   down   some   the

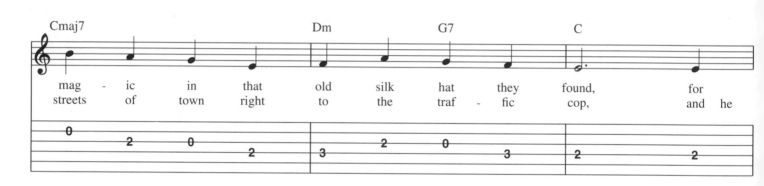

mag - ic   in   that   old   silk   hat   they   found,   for
streets   of   in   town   right   old   to   the   hat   traf - fic   cop,   and   he

when   they   placed   it   on   his   head   he   be - gan   to   dance   a -
on - ly   paused   a   mo - ment   when _____   he   heard   him   hol - ler,

Verse

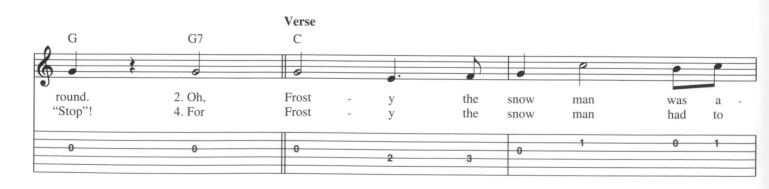

round.   2. Oh,   Frost - y   the   snow   man   was   a -
"Stop"!   4. For   Frost - y   the   snow   man   had   to

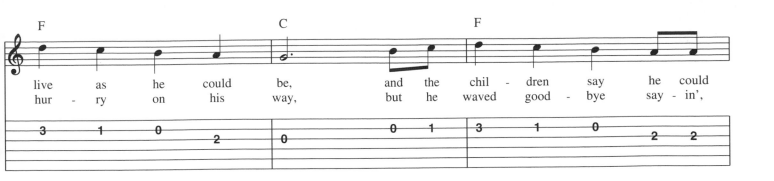

live   as   he   could   be,   and the chil - dren say   he could
hur - ry   on   his   way,   but he waved good - bye say - in',

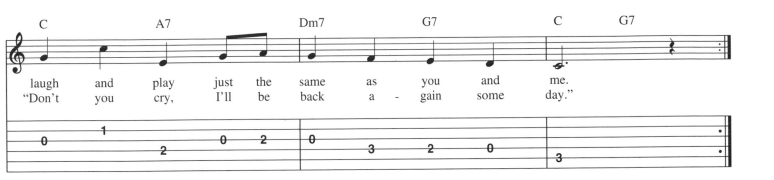

laugh   and   play   just the same as you and me.
"Don't you   cry, I'll be back a - gain some day."

Outro

Thup - et - y   thump thump, thump - et - y   thump thump,

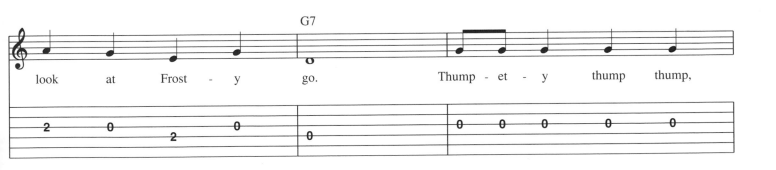

look   at   Frost - y   go.   Thump - et - y   thump thump,

thump - et - y   thump thump, o - ver the hills of snow.

From the Eastern Mountains

Traditional

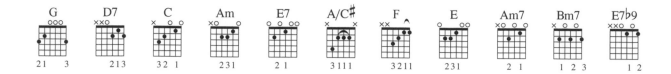

Strum Pattern: 2, 3
Pick Pattern: 2, 3

Verse
Moderately slow

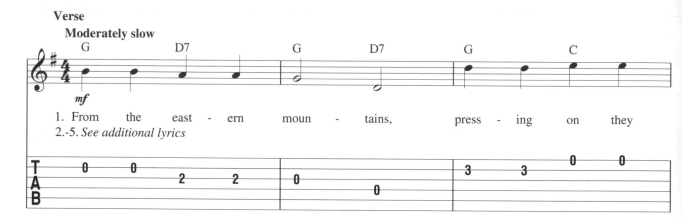

1. From the east - ern moun - tains, press - ing on they
2.-5. *See additional lyrics*

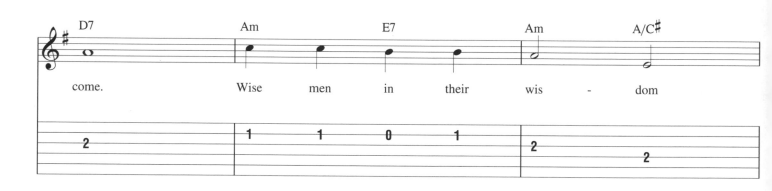

come. Wise men in their wis - dom

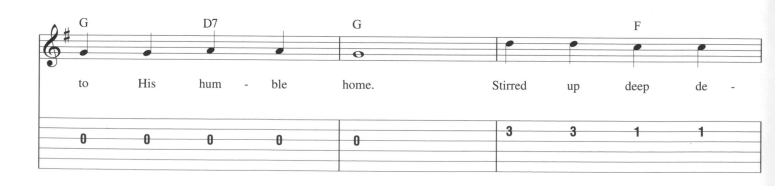

to His hum - ble home. Stirred up deep de -

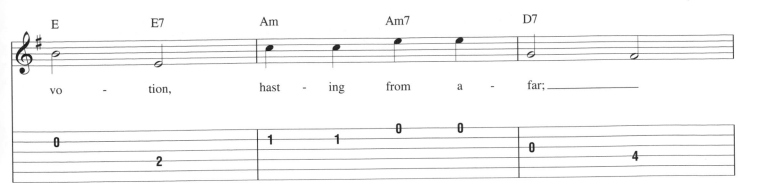

vo - tion, hast - ing from a - far; _____

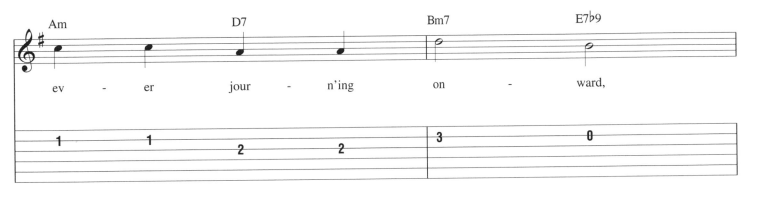

ev - er jour - n'ing on - ward,

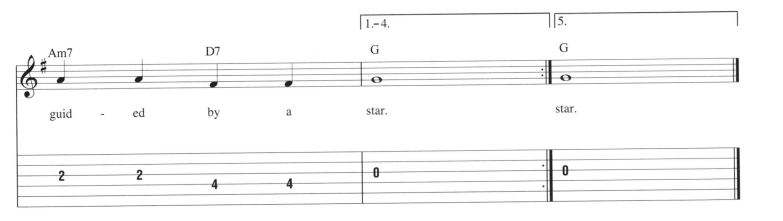

guid - ed by a star.   star.

Additional Lyrics

2. There their Lord and Savior
   Meek and lowly lay,
   Wondrous light that led them
   Onward on their way.
   Ever now to lighten
   Nations from afar,
   As they journey homeward
   By that guiding star.

3. Thou who in a manger,
   Once hast lowly lain.
   Who dost now in glory,
   O'er all kingdoms reign.
   Gather in the heathen
   Who in lands afar,
   Ne'er have seen the brightness
   Of Thy guiding star.

4. Gather in the outcasts,
   All who have astray.
   Throw Thy radiance o'er them,
   Guide them on their way.
   Those who never knew Thee,
   Those who have wandered far,
   Guide them by the brightness
   Of Thy guiding star.

5. Onward through the darkness
   Of the lonely night,
   Shining still before them
   With Thy kindly light.
   Guide them, Jew and Gentile,
   Homeward from afar.
   Young and old together,
   By Thy guiding star.

Fum, Fum, Fum

Traditional Catalonian Carol

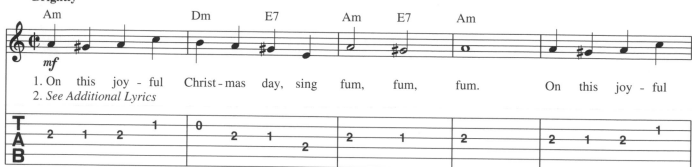

Strum Pattern: 4
Pick Pattern: 3

Verse
Brightly

1. On this joy - ful Christ - mas day, sing fum, fum, fum. On this joy - ful
2. *See Additional Lyrics*

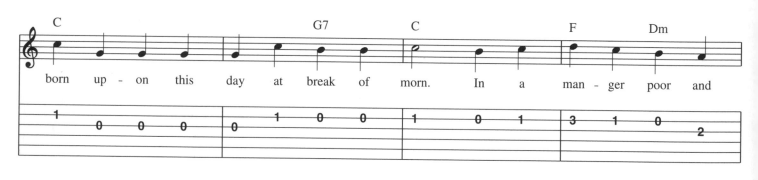

Christ - mas day, sing fum, fum, fum. For a bless - ed babe was

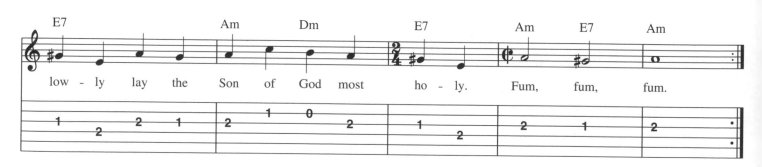

born up - on this day at break of morn. In a man - ger poor and

low - ly lay the Son of God most ho - ly. Fum, fum, fum.

Additional Lyrics

2. Thanks to God for holidays, sing fum, fum, fum.
   Thanks to God for holidays, sing fum, fum, fum.
   Now we all our voices raise.
   And sing a song of grateful praise.
   Celebrate in song and story, all the wonders of his glory.
   Fum, fum, fum.

Gather Around the Christmas Tree

By John H. Hopkins

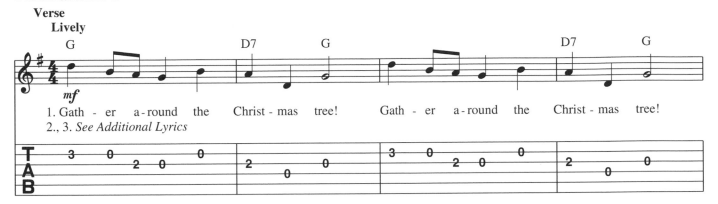

Strum Pattern: 4
Pick Pattern: 5

Verse
Lively

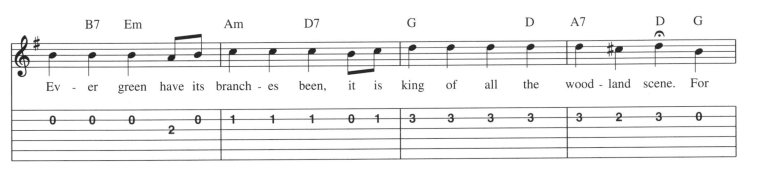

1. Gath - er a - round the Christ - mas tree! Gath - er a - round the Christ - mas tree!
2., 3. *See Additional Lyrics*

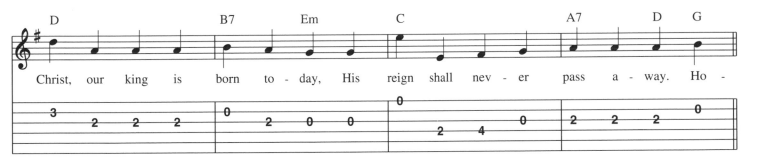

Ev - er green have its branch - es been, it is king of all the wood - land scene. For

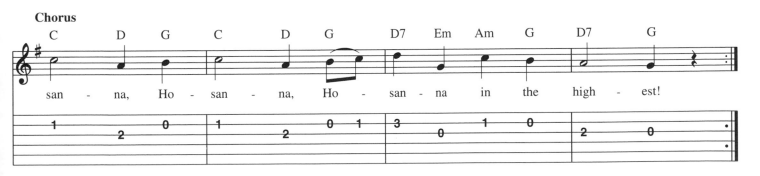

Christ, our king is born to - day, His reign shall nev - er pass a - way. Ho -

Chorus

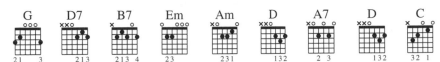

san - na, Ho - san - na, Ho - san - na in the high - est!

Additional Lyrics

2. Gather around the Christmas tree!
   Gather around the Christmas tree!
   Once the pride of the mountainside,
   Now cut down to grace our Christmastide.
   For Christ from heav'n to earth came down
   To gain, through death, a nobler crown.

3. Gather around the Christmas tree!
   Gather around the Christmas tree!
   Ev'ry bough has a burden now,
   They are gifts of love for us, we trow.
   For Christ is born, his love to show
   And give good gifts to men below.

Glad Christmas Bells

Traditional American Carol

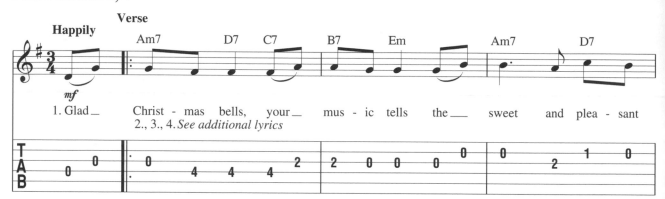

Strum Pattern: 8, 9
Pick Pattern: 8, 9

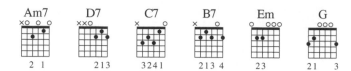

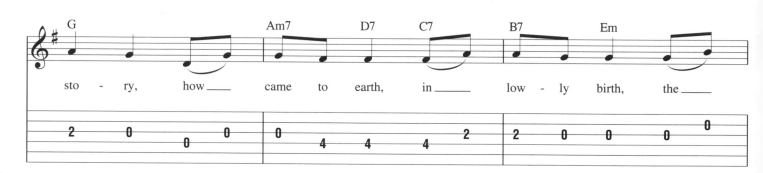

1. Glad __ Christ - mas bells, your __ mus - ic tells the __ sweet and plea - sant
2., 3., 4. *See additional lyrics*

sto - ry, how __ came to earth, in __ low - ly birth, the __

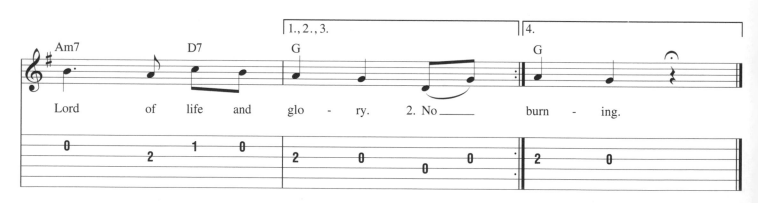

Lord of life and glo - ry. 2. No __ burn - ing.

Additional Lyrics

2. No palace hall, its ceiling tall;
   His kingly head spread over.
   There only stood a table rude
   The heav'nly Babe to cover.

3. Nor raiment gay as there He lay,
   Adorn'd the infant stranger;
   Poor humble child of mother mild,
   She laid Him in a manger.

4. But from afar, a splendid star
   The wise men westward turning;
   The livelong night saw pure and bright,
   Above His birthplace burning.

Glad Tidings
(Shalom Chaverim)

English Lyrics and New Music Arranged by Ronnie Gilbert, Lee Hays, Fred Hellerman and Pete Seeger

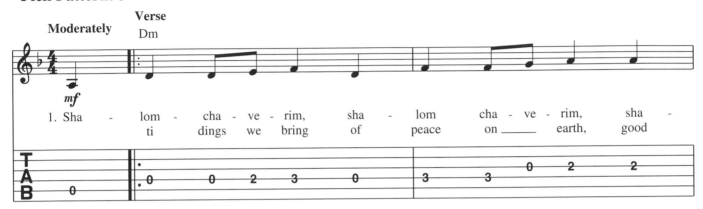

Strum Pattern: 4
Pick Pattern: 3

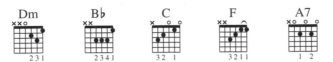

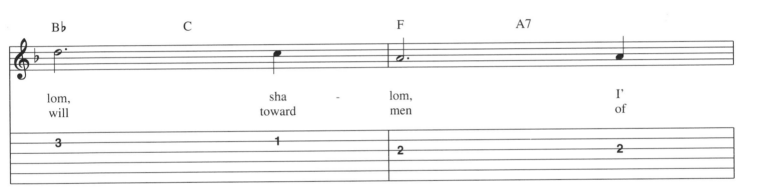

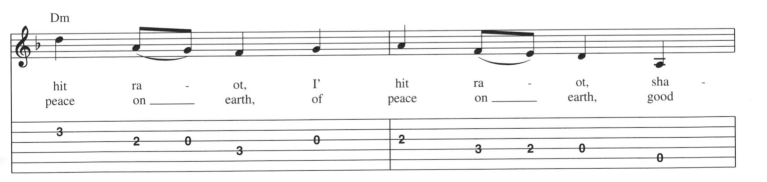

Go Tell It on the Mountain

African-American Spiritual
Verses by John W. Work, Jr.

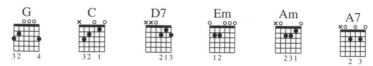

Strum Pattern: 4
Pick Pattern: 5

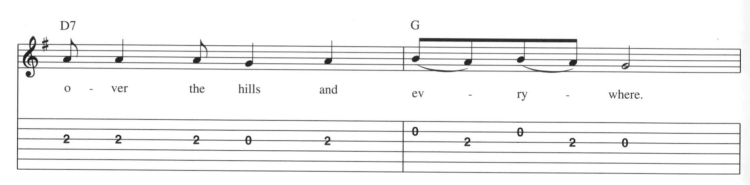

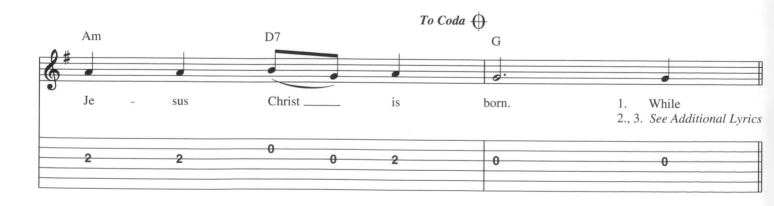

Verse

shep - herds kept their watch - ing o'er si - lent flocks by

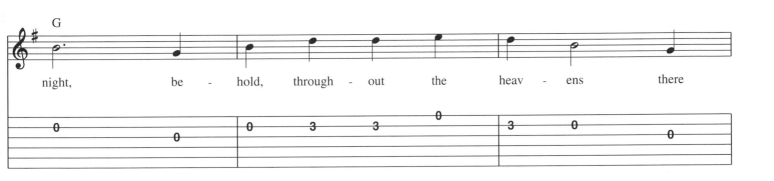

night, be - hold, through - out the heav - ens there

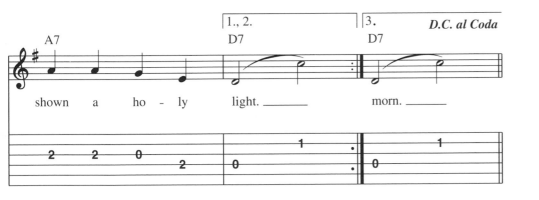

shown a ho - ly light. _____ morn. _____

D.C. al Coda

⊕ *Coda*

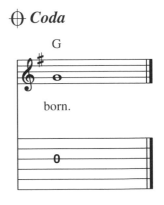

born.

Additional Lyrics

2. The shepherds feared and trembled
   When, lo! above the earth
   Rang out the angel chorus
   That hailed our Savior's birth.

3. Down in a lowly manger
   Our humble Christ was born.
   And God sent us salvation
   That blessed Christmas morn.

God Rest Ye Merry, Gentlemen

19th Century English Carol

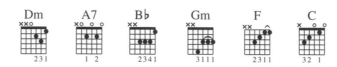

Strum Pattern: 3, 5
Pick Pattern: 3, 4

1. God rest ye mer - ry, gen tle - men, let
2. *See Additional Lyrics*

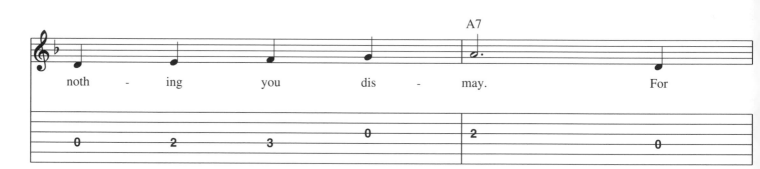

noth - ing you dis - may. For

Je - sus Christ our Sav - ior was

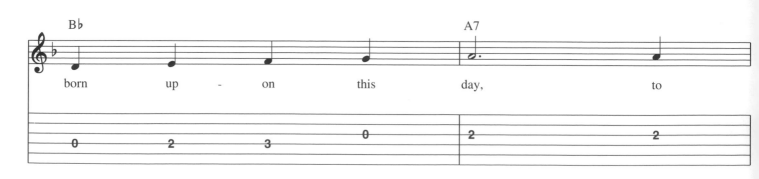

born up - on this day, to

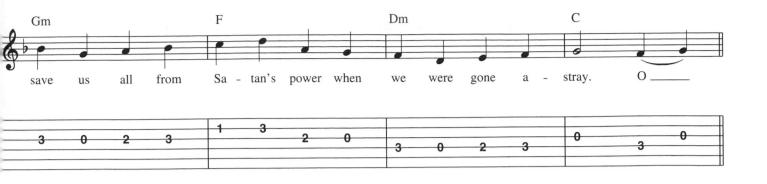

save us all from Sa - tan's power when we were gone a - stray. O _____

Chorus

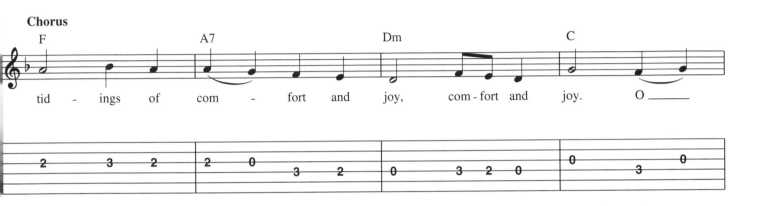

tid - ings of com - fort and joy, com - fort and joy. O _____

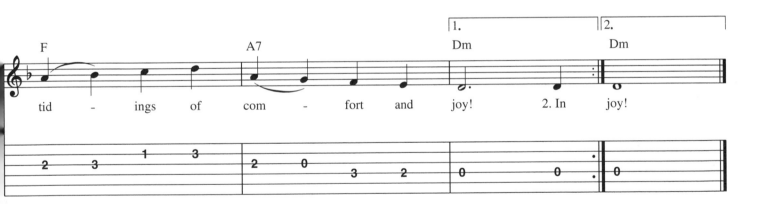

tid - ings of com - fort and joy! 2. In joy!

Additional Lyrics

2. In Bethlehem, in Jewry
   This blessed babe was born
   And laid within a manger
   Upon this blessed morn
   To which His mother Mary
   Did nothing take in scorn.

Good Christian Men, Rejoice

14th Century Latin Text

Translated by John Mason Neale

14th Century German Melody

Strum Pattern: 9
Pick Pattern: 7

Verse
With Spirit

1. Good Chris - tian men, re - joice with heart and soul and voice.
2. *See Additional Lyrics*

Give ye heed to what we say: Je - sus Christ is born to - day!

Ox and ass be - fore Him bow, and He is in the man - ger now.

Christ is born to - day! Christ is born to - day. 2. Good this!

Additional Lyrics

2. Good Christian men, rejoice
With heart and soul and voice.
Now ye hear of endless bliss:
Jesus Christ was born for this.
He hath op'd the heavenly door,
And man is blessed evermore.
Christ was born for this!
Christ was born for this!

Grandma Got Run Over by a Reindeer

Words and Music by Randy Brooks

Strum Pattern: 3
Pick Pattern: 3

Chorus
Moderately Bright

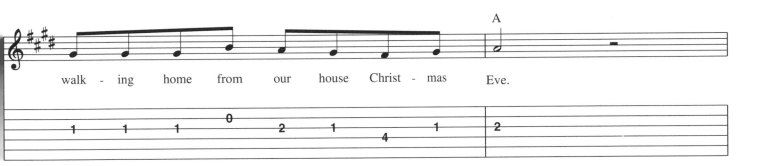

Grand - ma got run o - ver by a rein - deer

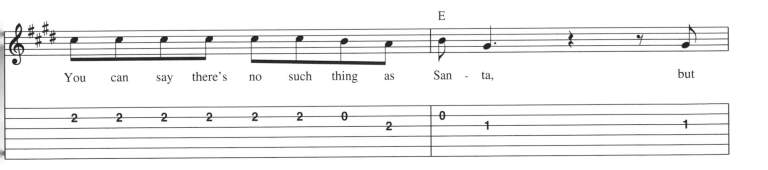

walk - ing home from our house Christ - mas Eve.

You can say there's no such thing as San - ta, but

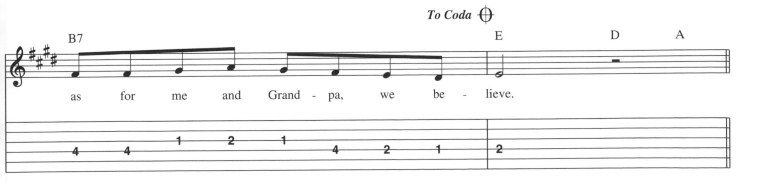

To Coda

as for me and Grand - pa, we be - lieve.

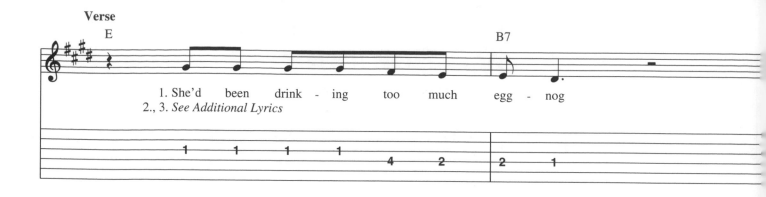

1. She'd been drink - ing too much egg - nog
2., 3. *See Additional Lyrics*

and we begged her not to go.

But she for - got her med - i - ca - tion, and she stag - gered out the door in - to the

snow. When we found her Christ - mas morn - ing

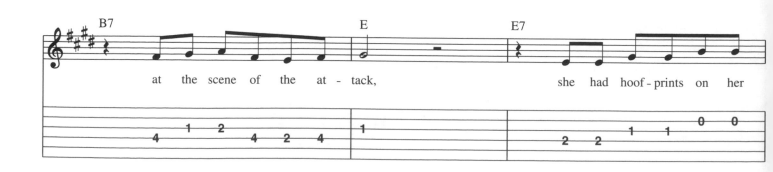

at the scene of the at - tack, she had hoof - prints on her

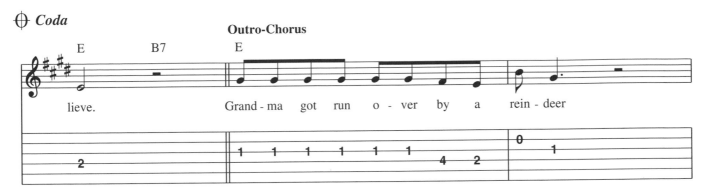

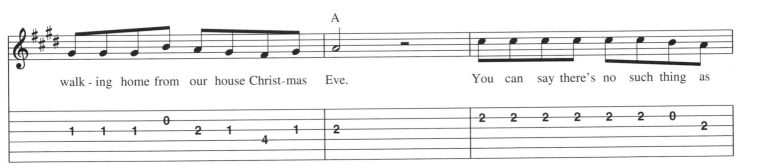

Additional Lyrics

2. Now we're all so proud of Grandpa.
   He's been taking it so well.
   See him in there watching football,
   Drinking beer and playing cards with Cousin Mel.
   It's not Christmas without Grandma.
   All the family's dressed in black,
   And we just can't help but wonder:
   Should we open up her gifts or send them back?

3. Now the goose is on the table,
   And the pudding made of fig.
   And the blue and silver candles,
   That would just have matched the hair in Grandma's wig.
   I've warned all my friends and neighbors.
   Better watch out for yourselves.
   They should never give a license
   To a man who drives a sleigh and plays with elves.

Good King Wenceslas

Words by John M. Neale
Music from Piae Cantiones

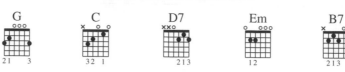

Strum Pattern: 4, 3
Pick Pattern: 5, 3

Verse
With Spirit

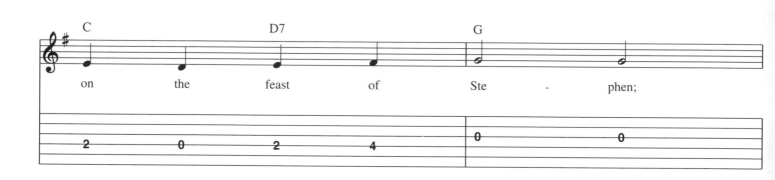

1. Good King Wen - ces - las looked out
2.-5. *See Additional Lyrics*

on the feast of Ste - phen;

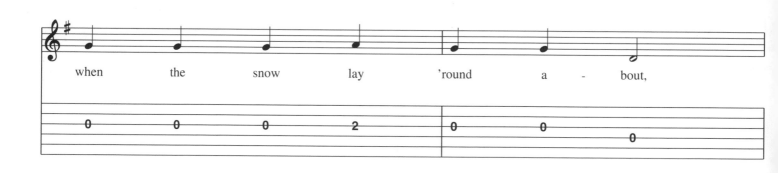

when the snow lay 'round a - bout,

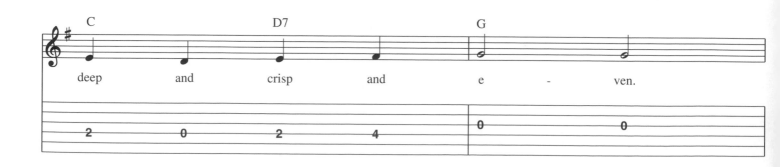

deep and crisp and e - ven.

Bright - ly shone the moon that night,

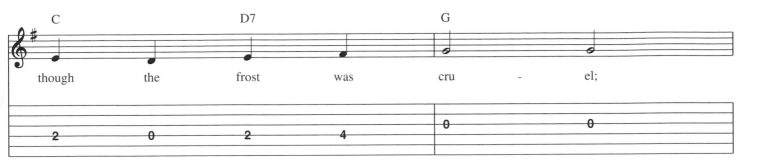

though the frost was cru - el;

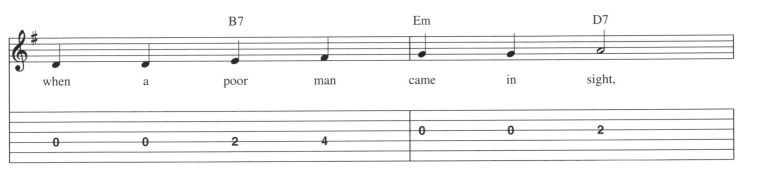

when a poor man came in sight,

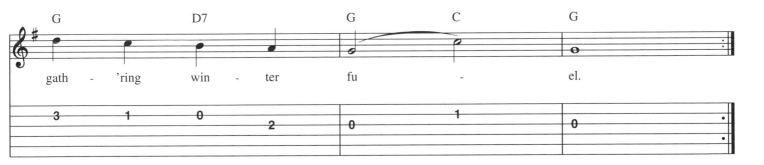

gath - 'ring win - ter fu - el.

Additional Lyrics

2. "Hither page, and stand by me,
   If thou know'st it, telling;
   Yonder peasant, who is he?
   Where and what his dwelling?"
   "Sire, he lives a good league hence,
   Underneath the mountain;
   Right against the forest fence,
   By Saint Agnes' fountain."

3. "Bring me flesh, and bring me wine,
   Bring me pine-logs hither;
   Thou and I will see him dine,
   When we bear them thither."
   Page and monarch forth they went,
   Forth they went together;
   Through the rude winds wild lament,
   And the bitter weather.

4. "Sire, the night is darker now,
   And the wind blows stronger;
   Fails my heart, I know not how,
   I can go not longer."
   "Mark my footsteps, my good page,
   Tread thou in them boldly:
   Thou shalt find the winter's rage
   Freeze thy blood less coldly."

5. In his master's steps he trod,
   Where the snow lay dinted;
   Heat was in the very sod
   Which the saint has printed.
   Therefore, Christian men, be sure,
   Wealth or rank possessing;
   Ye who now will bless the poor,
   Shall yourselves find blessing.

Greenwillow Christmas

from GREENWILLOW

By Frank Loesser

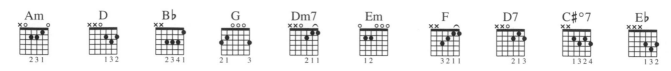

Strum Pattern: 4
Pick Pattern: 3

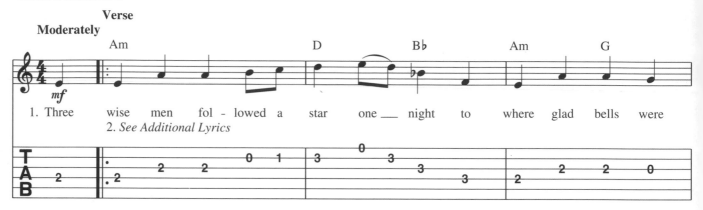

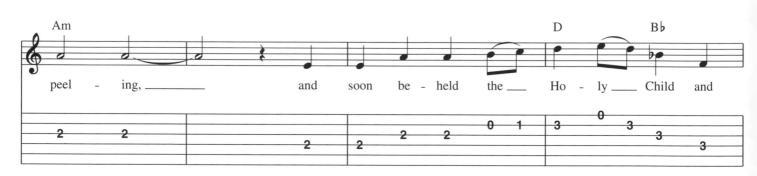

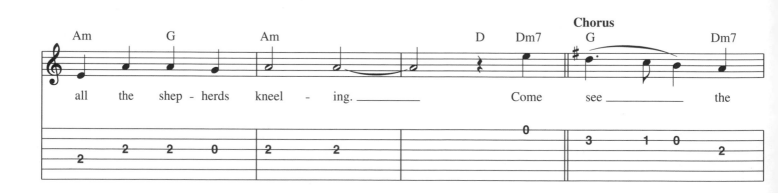

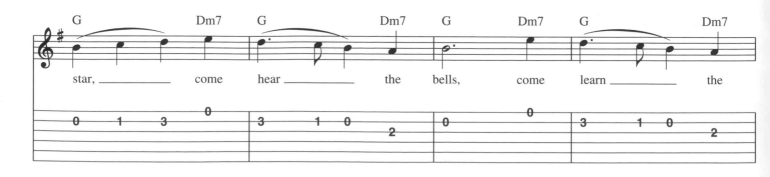

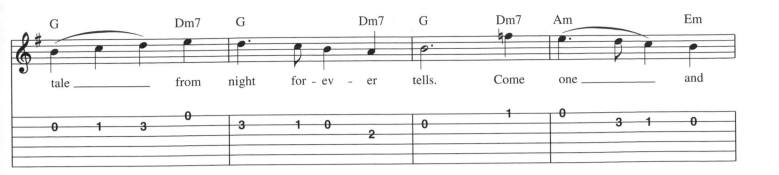

tale _____ from night for - ev - er tells. Come one _____ and

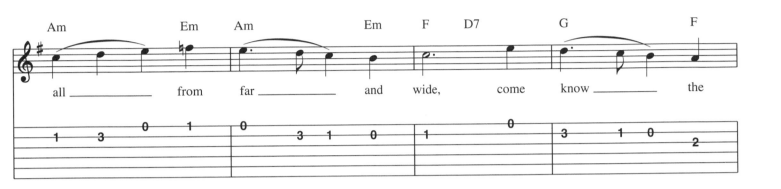

all _____ from far _____ and wide, come know _____ the

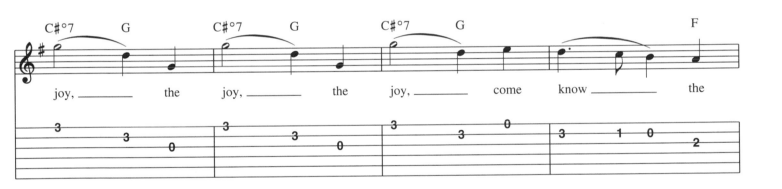

joy, _____ the joy, _____ the joy, _____ come know _____ the

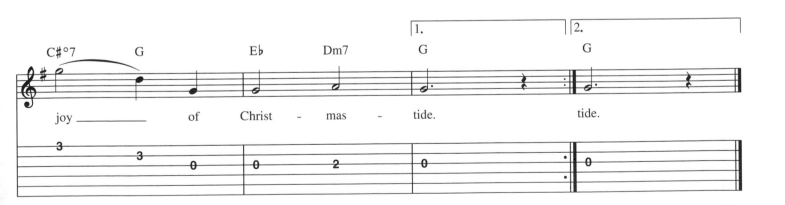

joy _____ of Christ - mas - tide. tide.

Additional Lyrics

2. 'Twas long ago in Bethlehem
   Yet ever live the glory,
   And hearts all glow and voices rise
   A-caroling the story.

The Happy Christmas Comes Once More

Words by Nicolai F.S. Grundtvig
Music by C. Balle

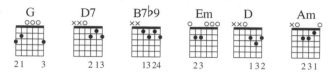

Strum Pattern: 8, 9
Pick Pattern: 8, 9

Verse

Flowing Waltz

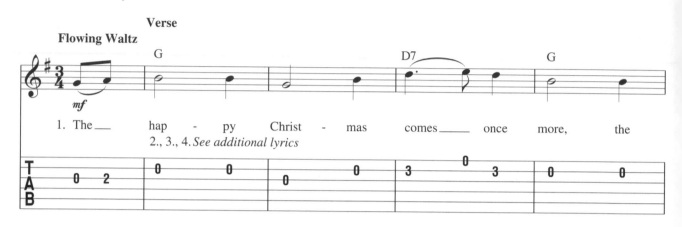

1. The __ hap - py Christ - mas comes __ once more, the
2., 3., 4. *See additional lyrics*

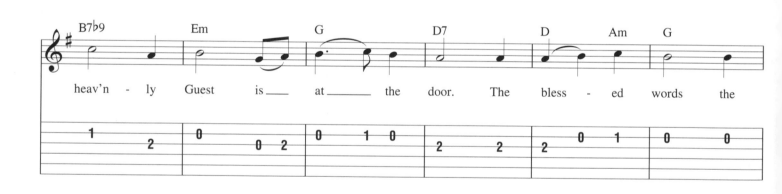

heav'n - ly Guest is __ at __ the door. The bless - ed words the

shep - herds thrill, the joy - ous ti - dings, peace, good __ will.

Additional Lyrics

2. To David's city let us fly,
   Where angels sing beneath the sky;
   Through plain and village pressing near,
   And news from God with shepherds hear.

3. O, let us go with quiet mind,
   The gentle Babe with shepherds find.
   To gaze on Him who gladdens them,
   The loveliest flow'r on Jesse's stem.

4. Come, Jesus, glorious heav'nly guest,
   Keep Thine own Christmas in our brea
   Then David's harp-string, hushed so lo
   Shall swell our jubilee of song.

Happy Holiday

from the Motion Picture Irving Berlin's HOLIDAY INN

Words and Music by Irving Berlin

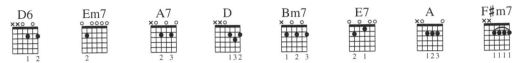

Strum Pattern: 3, 2
Pick Pattern: 3, 4

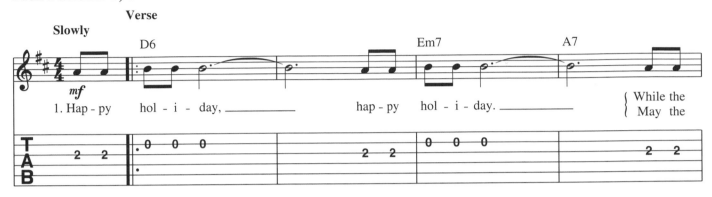

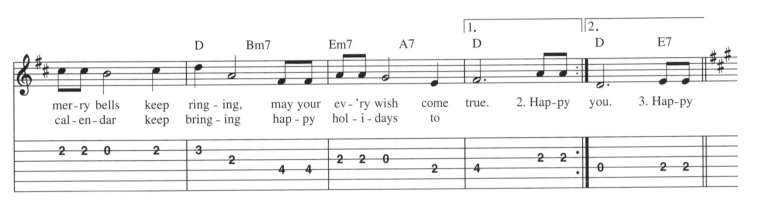

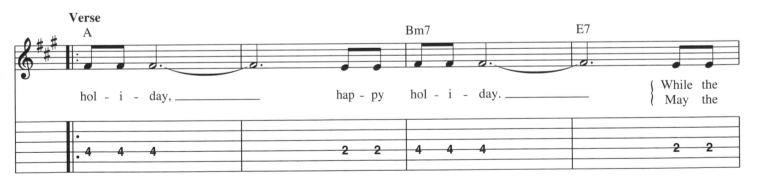

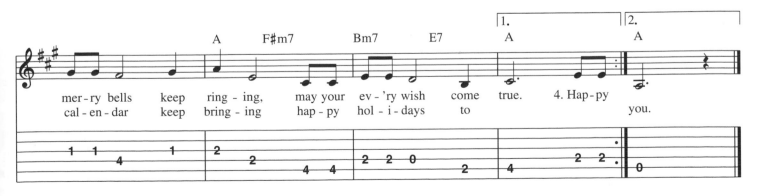

Happy Xmas (War Is Over)

Words and Music by John Lennon and Yoko Ono

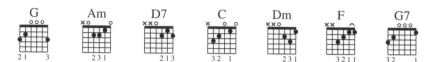

Strum Pattern: 8
Pick Pattern: 8

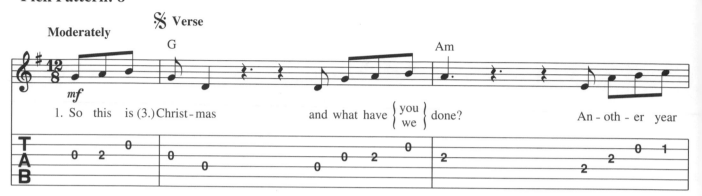

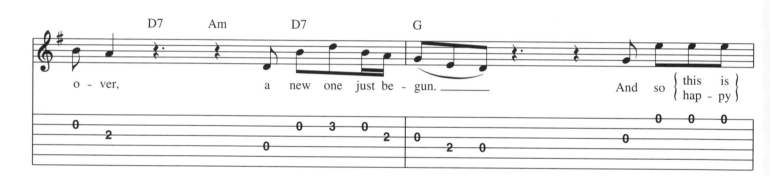

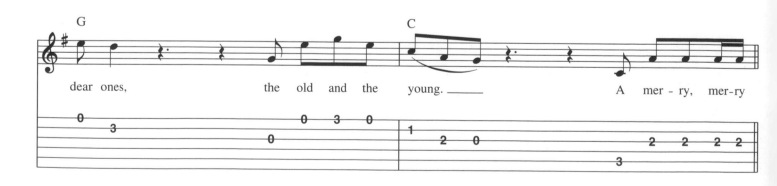

Chorus

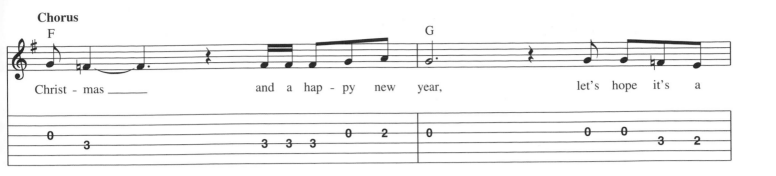

Christ - mas _____ and a hap - py new year, let's hope it's a

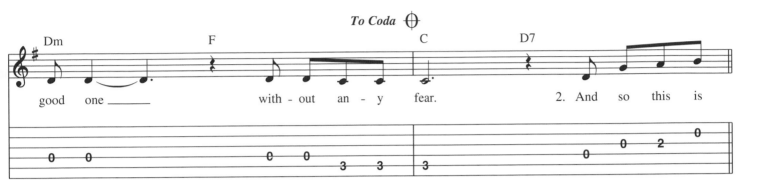

To Coda

good one _____ with - out an - y fear. 2. And so this is

Verse

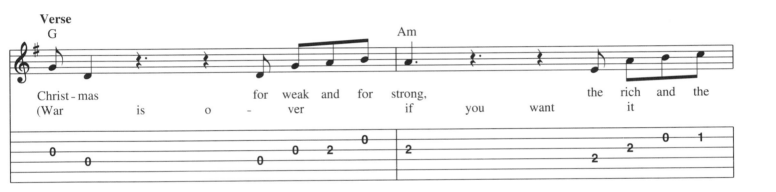

Christ - mas for weak and for strong, the rich and the
(War is o - ver if you want it

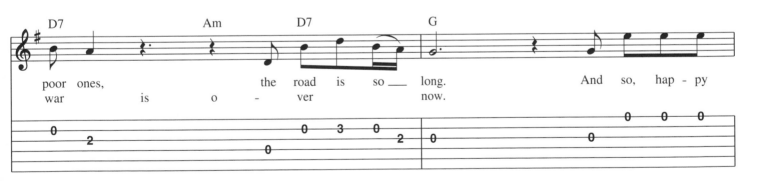

poor ones, the road is so _____ long. And so, hap - py
war is o - ver now.

Christ - mas for black and for white, for the yel - low and
War is o - ver if you want it

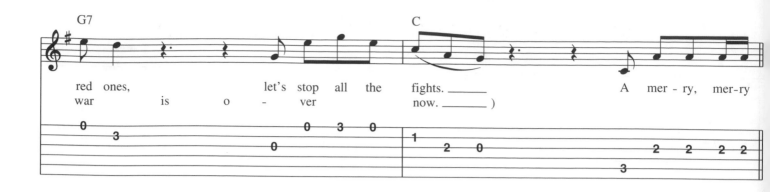

red ones,   let's stop all the   fights. _____   A mer-ry, mer-ry
war   is   o   -   ver   now. _____)

Chorus

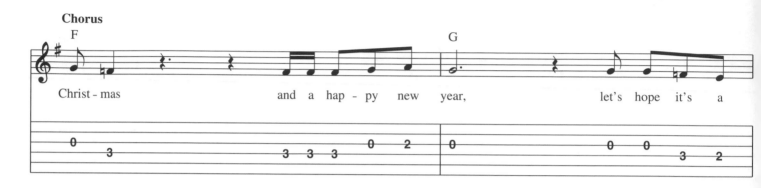

Christ - mas   and a hap - py new   year,   let's hope it's a

D.S. al Coda

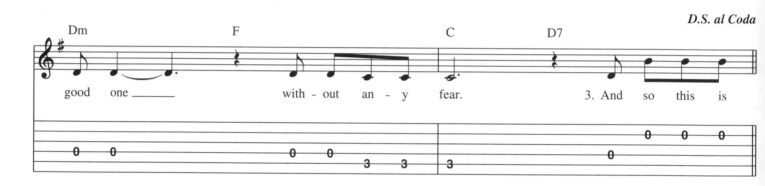

good   one _____   with - out an - y   fear.   3. And so this is

⊕ *Coda*

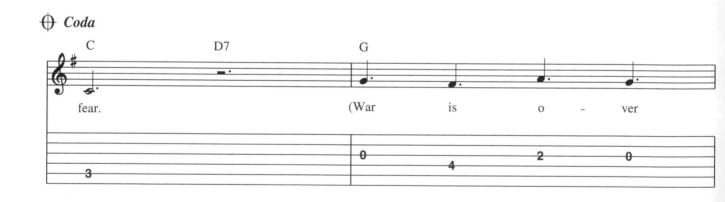

fear.   (War   is   o   -   ver

if   you   want   it   war   is   o   -   ver   now. _____)

Hark! The Herald Angels Sing

Words by Charles Wesley
Altered by George Whitefield
Music by Felix Mendelssohn-Bartholdy
Arranged by William H. Cummings

Strum Pattern: 2, 3
Pick Pattern: 3, 4

Verse
Joyfully

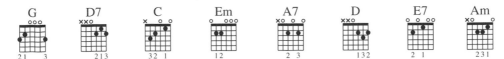

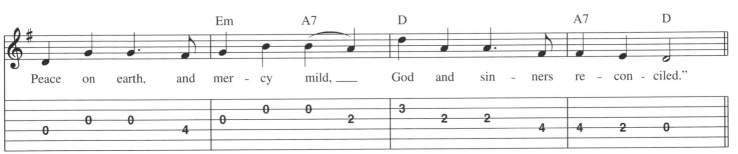

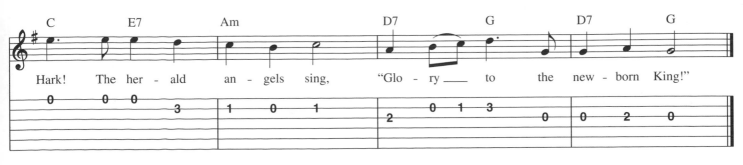

Hear Them Bells

Words and Music by D.S. McCosh

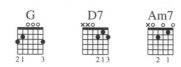

Strum Pattern: 3
Pick Pattern: 3

Verse
Brightly

Hear them bells, _____ mer - ry Christ - mas bells! _____ They are

ring - ing out the e - vil of the sword. _____

Hear them bells, _____ mer - ry Christ - mas bells! _____ They are

ring - ing in the glo - ry of the Lord! _____

The Holly and the Ivy

18th Century English Carol

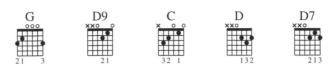

Strum Pattern: 8
Pick Pattern: 8

Verse
Moderately Slow

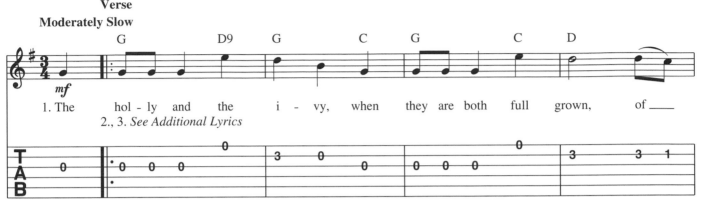

1. The hol - ly and the i - vy, when they are both full grown, of ___
2., 3. *See Additional Lyrics*

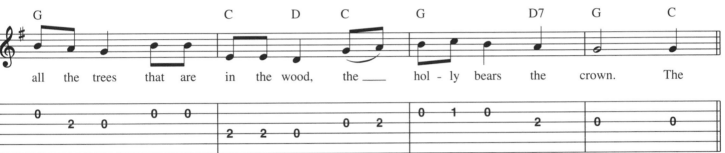

all the trees that are in the wood, the ___ hol - ly bears the crown. The

Refrain

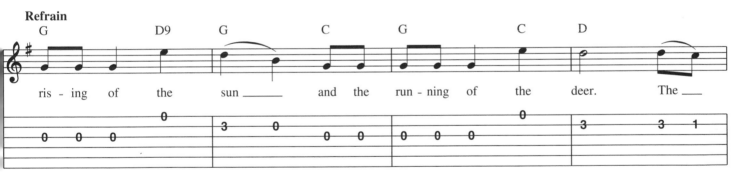

ris - ing of the sun ___ and the run - ning of the deer. The ___

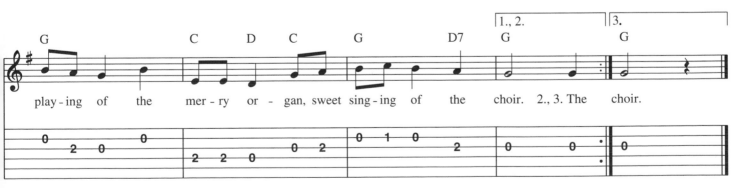

play - ing of the mer - ry or - gan, sweet sing - ing of the choir. 2., 3. The choir.

Additional Lyrics

2. The holly bears a blossom,
   As white as lily flow'r,
   And Mary bore sweet Jesus Christ,
   To be our sweet Saviour.

3. The holly bears a berry,
   As red as any blood,
   And Mary bore sweet Jesus Christ,
   To do poor sinners good.

Here We Come A-Wassailing

Traditional

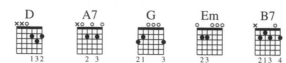

Strum Pattern: 7, 9
Pick Pattern: 7, 9

Verse
Brightly

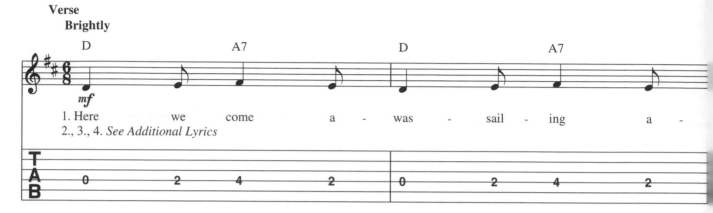

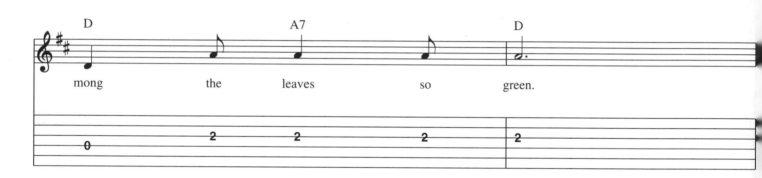

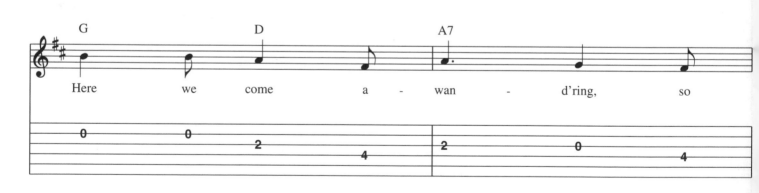

Strum Pattern: 3
Pick Pattern: 3

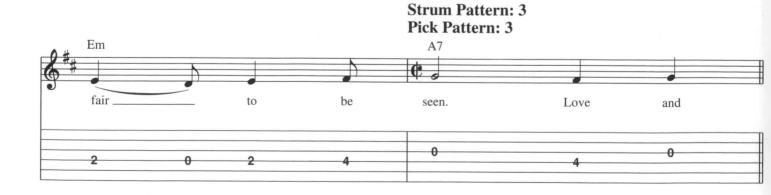

Chorus

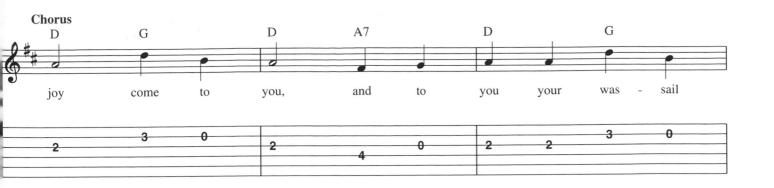

joy   come   to   you,   and   to   you   your   was - sail   too.

too.   And   God   bless   you   and   send _____   you   a   hap -

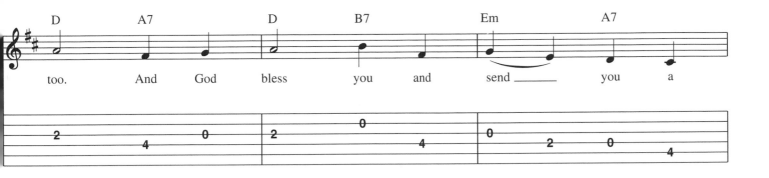

hap - py   New   Year.   And   God   send   you   a

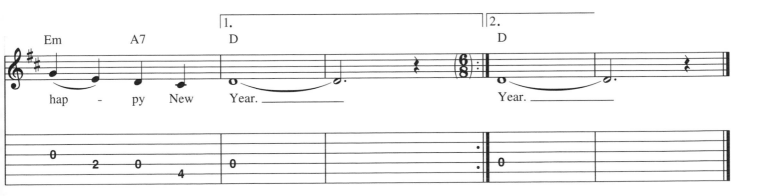

hap - py   New   Year. _____   Year. _____

Additional Lyrics

2. We are not daily beggars
   That beg from door to door.
   But we are neighbor children
   Whom you have seen before.

3. We have got a little purse
   Of stretching leather skin.
   We want a little money
   To line it well within:

4. God bless the master of this house,
   Likewise the mistress too;
   And all the little children
   That round the table go:

A Holly Jolly Christmas

Music and Lyrics by Johnny Marks

Strum Pattern: 2, 3
Pick Pattern: 3, 4

Verse

Brightly

1. Have a (4.) hol - ly jol - ly Christ - mas, it's the best time of the year.

I don't know if there'll be snow but have a cup of cheer. 2., 5. Have a

Verse

hol - ly jol - ly Christ - mas, and when you walk down the street,

say hel - lo to friends you know and ev - 'ry - one you meet.

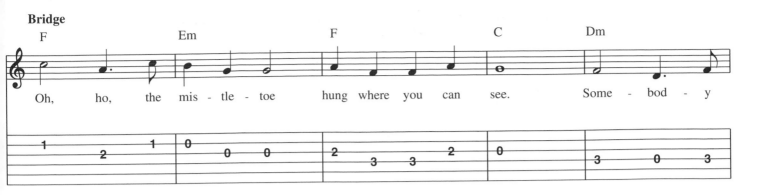

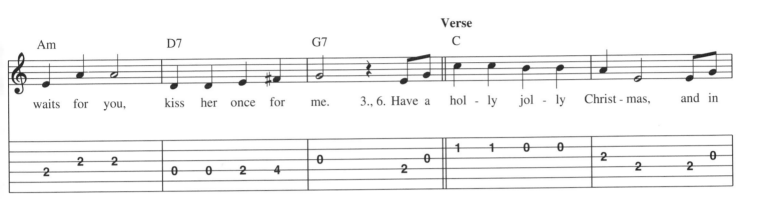

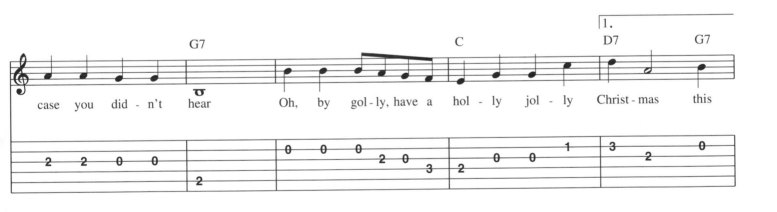

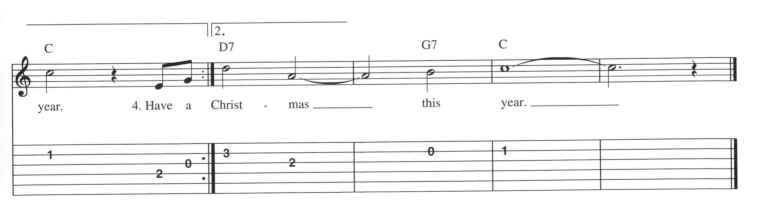

How Brightly Beams the Morning Star

Words and Music by Philipp Nicolai
Translated by William Mercer
Harmonized by J.S. Bach

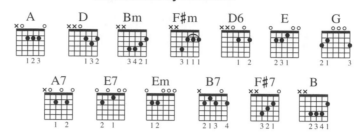

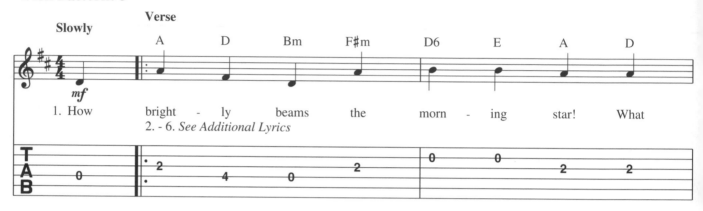

Strum Pattern: 4
Pick Pattern: 3

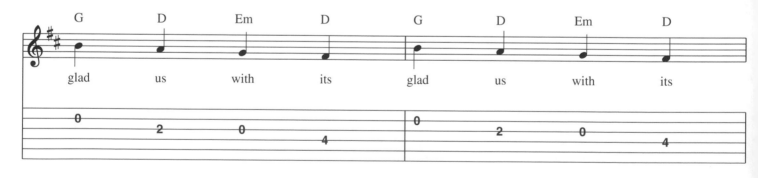

1. How bright - ly beams the morn - ing star! What
2. - 6. *See Additional Lyrics*

sud - den ra - diance from a - far doth

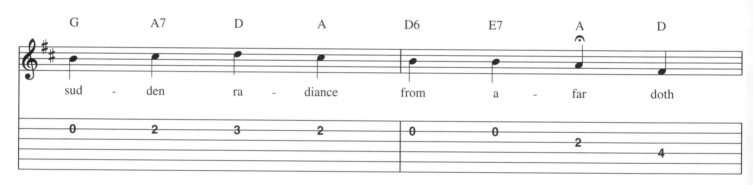

glad us with its glad us with its

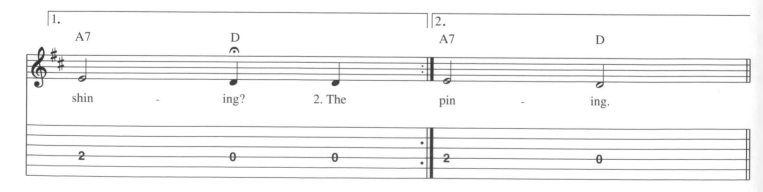

shin - ing? 2. The pin - ing.

Chorus

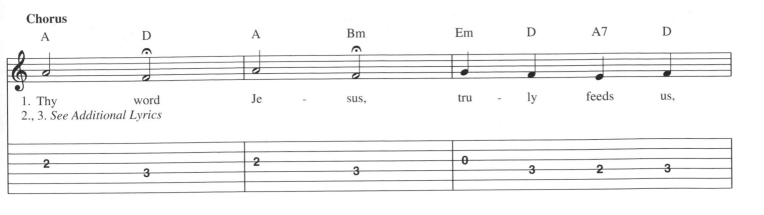

1. Thy word Je - sus, tru - ly feeds us,
2., 3. *See Additional Lyrics*

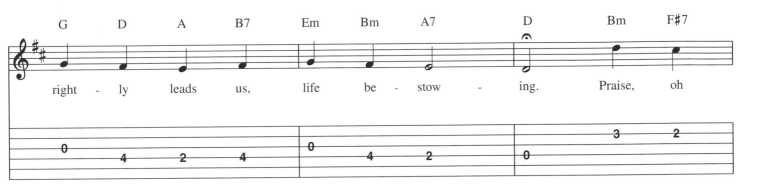

right - ly leads us, life be - stow - ing. Praise, oh

To Coda ⊕

1st time, D.S.
(take repeat)

2nd time, D.S. al Coda
(take repeat)

⊕ *Coda*

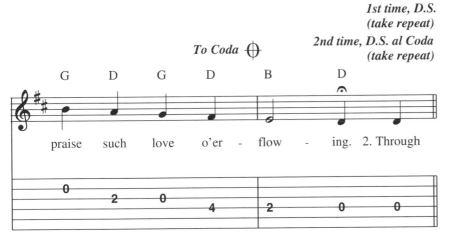

praise such love o'er - flow - ing. 2. Through

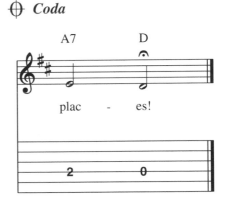

plac - es!

Additional Lyrics

2. The ray of God that breaks our night.
   And fills the darkened souls with light,
   Who long for truth were pining.

3. Through thee alone can we be blest;
   Then deep be on our hearts imprest
   The love that thou hast borne us.

4. So make us ready to fulfill
   With burning zeal thy holy will,
   Though men may vex or scorn us.

Chorus 2. Saviour, let us never lose thee,
   For we choose thee,
   Thirst to know thee
   All we are and have we owe thee!

5. O praise to him who came to save,
   Who conquer'd death and burst the grave.
   Each day new praise resoundeth.

6. To him the Lamb who once was slain,
   The friend whom none shall trust in vain,
   Whose grace for ay aboundeth.

Chorus 3. Sing, ye heavens, tell the story
   Of his glory,
   Till his praises
   Flood with light earth's darkest places!

I Heard the Bells on Christmas Day

Words by Henry Wadsworth Longfellow
Adapted by Johnny Marks
Music by Johnny Marks

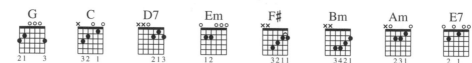

Strum Pattern: 4
Pick Pattern: 5

Additional Lyrics

2. I thought as now this day had come,
The belfries of all Christendom
Had rung so long the unbroken song
Of peace on earth, good will to men.

3. And in despair I bowed my head;
"There is no peace on earth," I said,
"For hate is strong, and mocks the song
Of peace on earth, good will to men."

4. Then pealed the bells more loud and deep;
"God is not dead, nor noth He sleep.
The wrong shall fail, the right prevail
With peace on earth good will to men."

I Saw Three Ships

Traditional English Carol

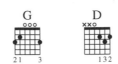

Strum Pattern: 8, 7
Pick Pattern: 8, 9

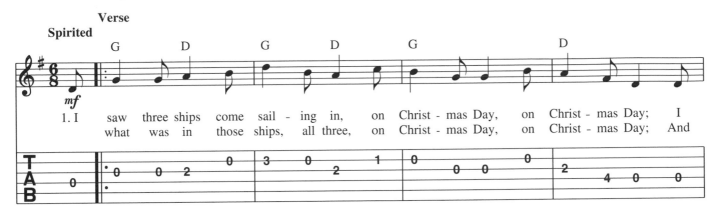

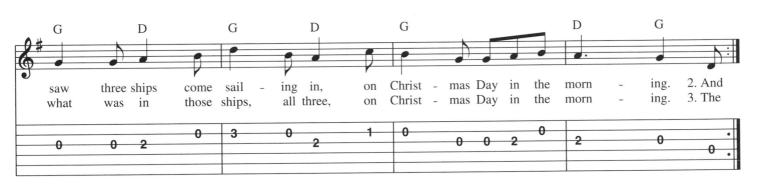

I Saw Mommy Kissing Santa Claus

Words and Music by Tommie Connor

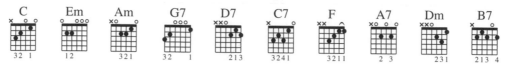

Strum Pattern: 2, 3
Pick Pattern: 3, 4

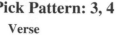

Moderately

thought that I was tucked up in my bed - room fast a - sleep. Then

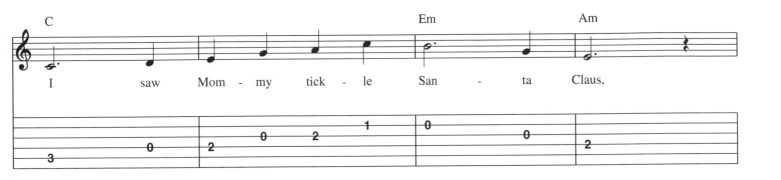

I saw Mom - my tick - le San - ta Claus,

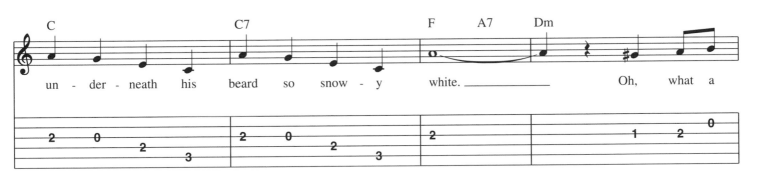

un - der - neath his beard so snow - y white. _____ Oh, what a

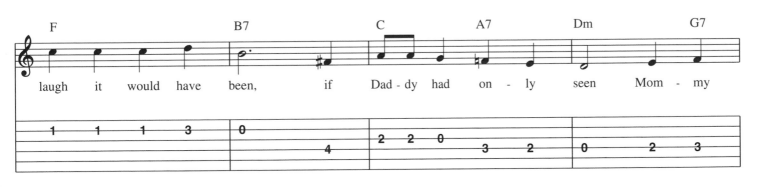

laugh it would have been, if Dad - dy had on - ly seen Mom - my

kiss - ing San - ta Claus last night. night. _____

I Wonder As I Wander

By John Jacob Niles

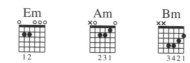

Strum Pattern: 8
Pick Pattern: 8

Verse
Slowly

1. I won-der as I wan-der, our un-der the sky, how
2. *See Additional Lyrics*

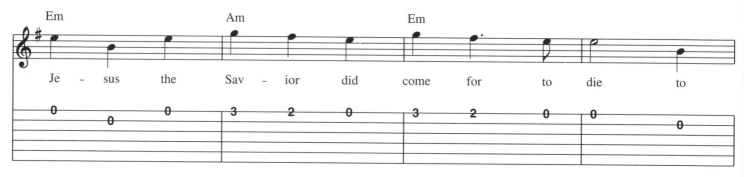

Je - sus the Sav - ior did come for to die to

save low - ly peo - ple like you and like I, I

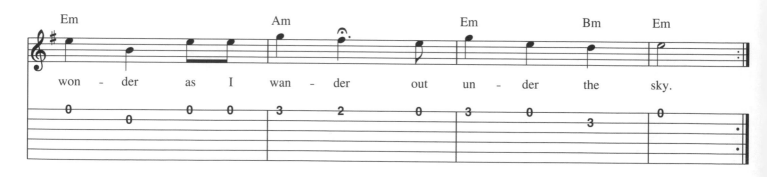

won - der as I wan - der out un - der the sky.

Additional Lyrics

2. When Jesus was born, it was in a cow's stall,
   With shepherds and wise men and angels and all.
   The blessings of Christmas from heaven did fall
   And the weary world woke to the Savior's call.

Infant Holy, Infant Lowly

Traditional Polish Carol
Paraphrased by Edith M.G. Reed

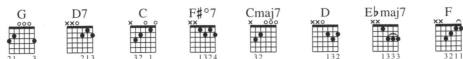

Strum Pattern: 7, 9
Pick Pattern: 7, 9

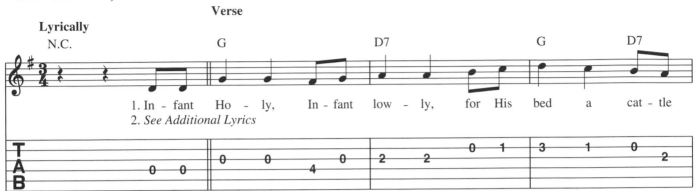

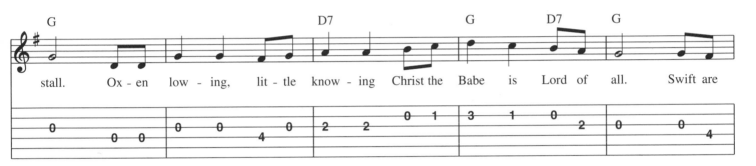

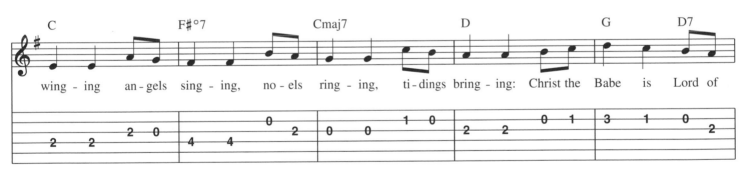

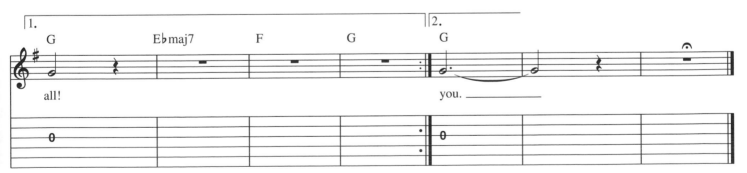

Additional Lyrics

2. Flocks are sleeping, shepherds keeping
   Vigil 'til the morning new.
   Saw the glory, heard the story,
   Tidings of a Gospel true.
   Thus rejoicing, free from sorrow,
   Praises voicing, greet the morrow:
   Christ the Babe was born for you.

I'll Be Home for Christmas

Words and Music by Kim Gannon and Walter Kent

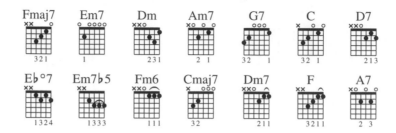

Strum Pattern: 4, 3
Pick Pattern: 4, 3

Verse
Moderately Slow

I'm dream-ing to-night of a place I love, e-ven more than I u-sual-ly

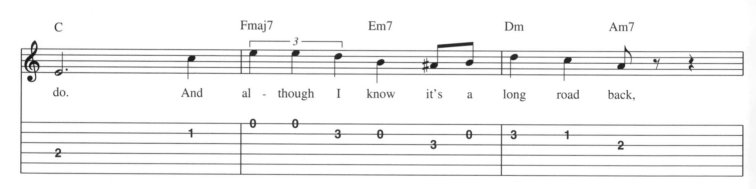

do. And al-though I know it's a long road back,

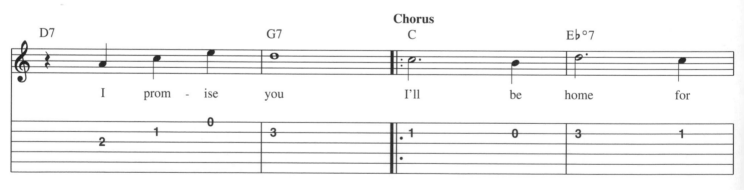

Chorus

I prom-ise you I'll be home for

Christ-mas, _____ you can count on

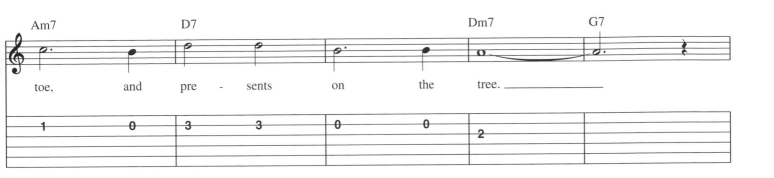

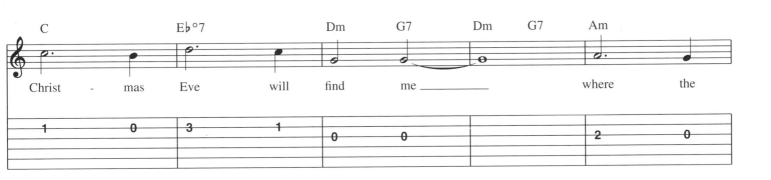

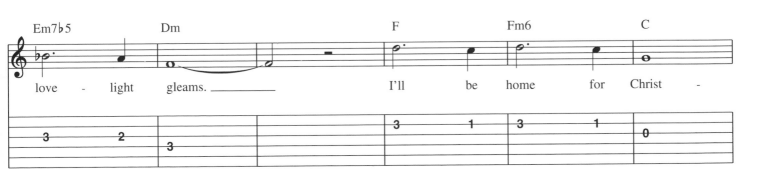

I'm Spending Christmas With You

Words and Music by Tom Occhipinti

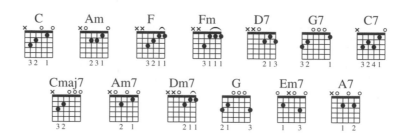

Strum Pattern: 7
Pick Pattern: 7

Verse
Moderately Slow

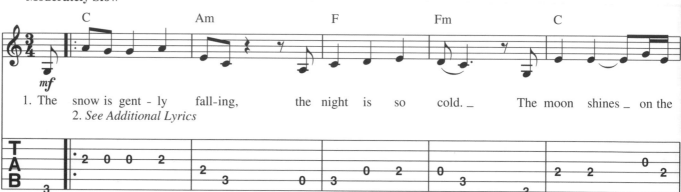

1. The snow is gent - ly fall-ing, the night is so cold. _ The moon shines _ on the
2. *See Additional Lyrics*

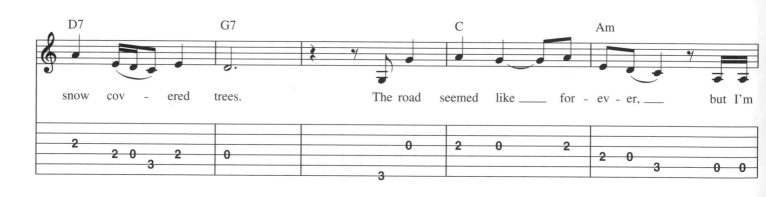

snow cov - ered trees. The road seemed like ____ for - ev - er, ___ but I'm

fi - nal - ly home. _ We're a - lone on this Christ - mas Eve.

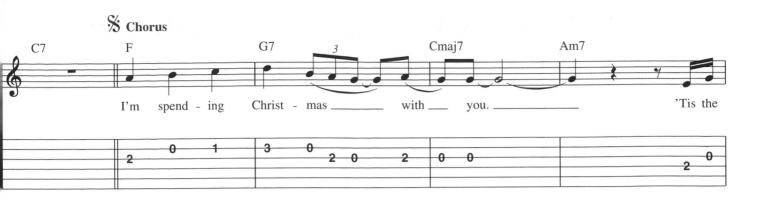

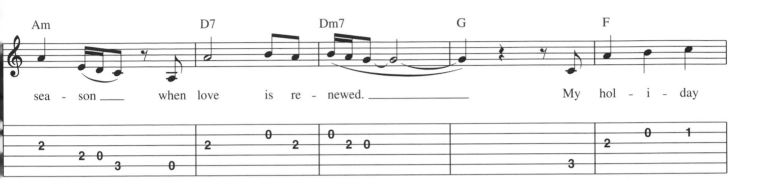

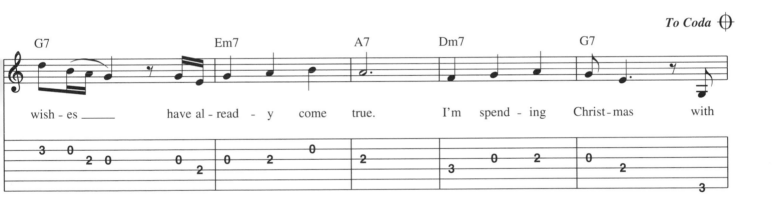

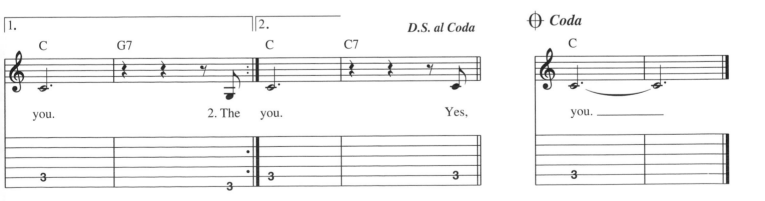

Additional Lyrics

2. The fireplace is burning and your hands feel so warm.
   We're hanging popcorn on the tree.
   I take you in my arms, your lips touch mine.
   It feels like our first Christmas Eve.

In Field With Flocks Abiding

Traditional

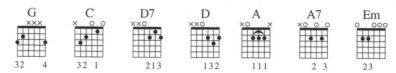

Strum Pattern: 2, 3
Pick Pattern: 2, 3

Moderately

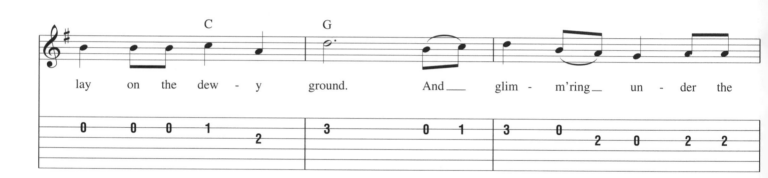

In the field with their flocks a - bid - ing, they ___

lay on the dew - y ground. And ___ glim - m'ring ___ un - der the

star - light, the ___ sheep lay white a - round. When the

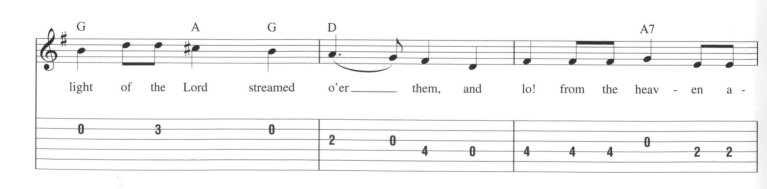

light of the Lord streamed o'er ___ them, and lo! from the heav - en a-

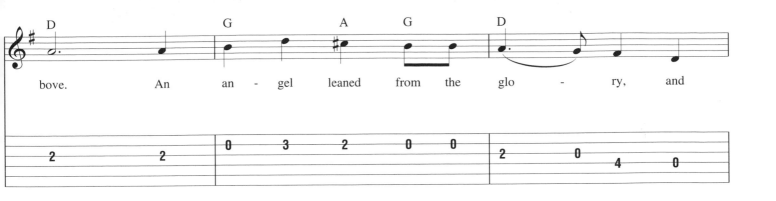

bove.   An   an - gel   leaned   from   the   glo -   ry,   and

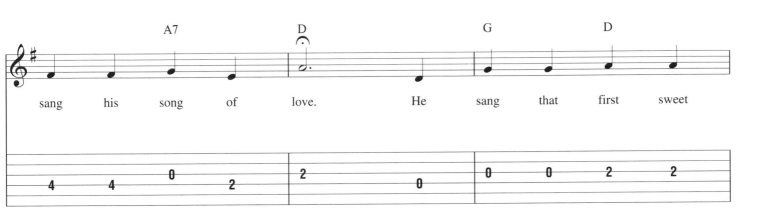

sang   his   song   of   love.   He   sang   that   first   sweet

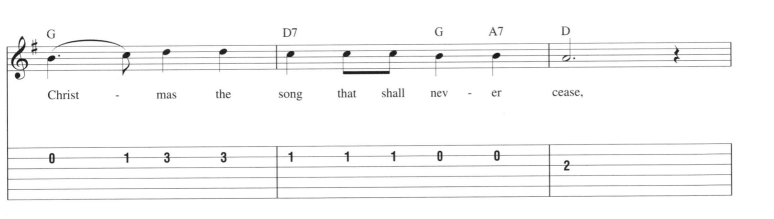

Christ - mas   the   song   that   shall   nev - er   cease,

glo - ry   to   God   in   the   high - est,   on   earth   good   will   and   peace.

It Came Upon the Midnight Clear

Words by Edmund Hamilton Sears
Music by Richard Storrs Willis

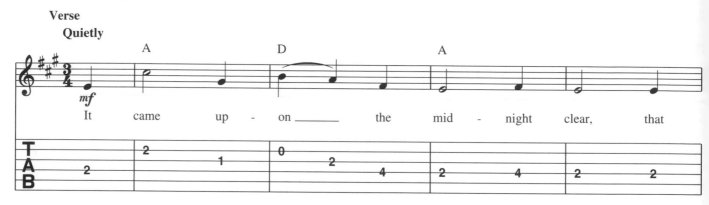

Strum Pattern: 8, 7
Pick Pattern: 8, 9

Verse
Quietly

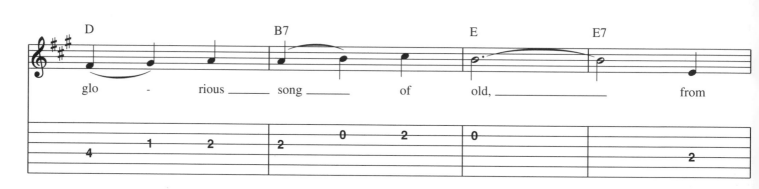

It came up - on _____ the mid - night clear, that

glo - rious _____ song _____ of old, _____ from

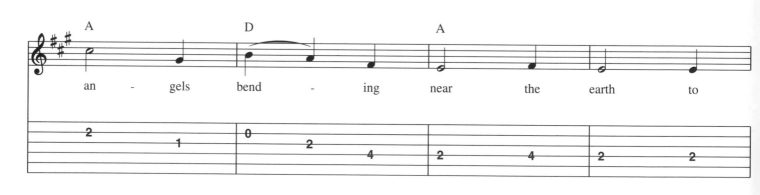

an - gels bend - ing near the earth to

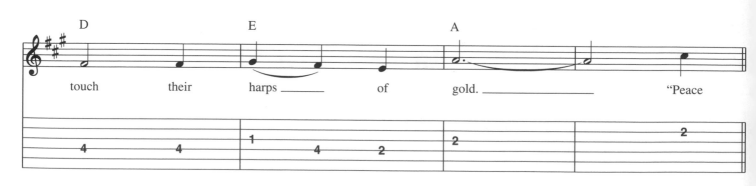

touch their harps _____ of gold. _____ "Peace

Chorus

on the earth, _____ good will to men, from

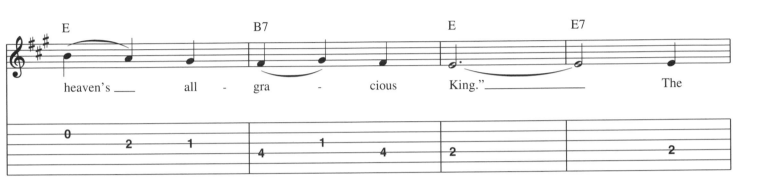

heaven's _____ all - gra - cious King." _____ The

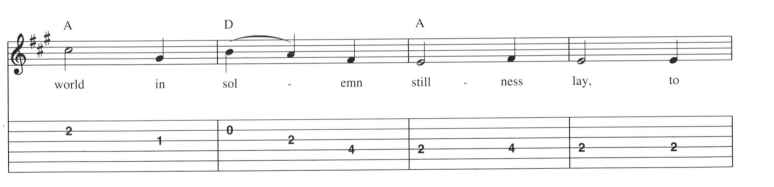

world in sol - emn still - ness lay, to

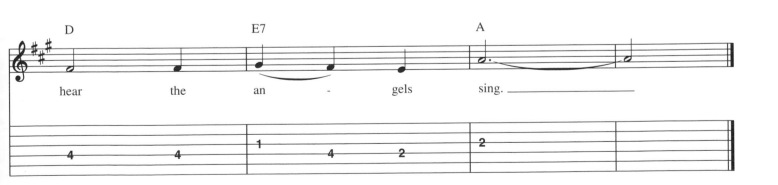

hear the an - gels sing. _____

It's Beginning to Look Like Christmas

By Meredith Willson

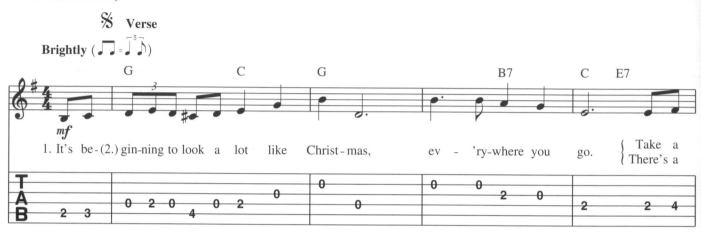

Strum Pattern: 2, 3
Pick Pattern: 3, 4

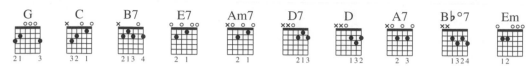

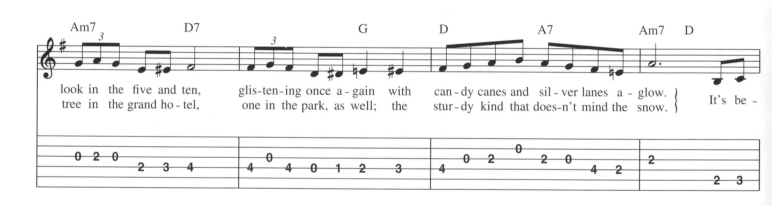

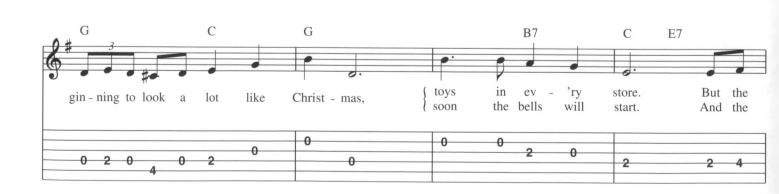

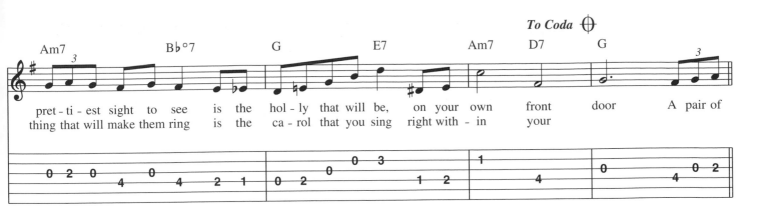
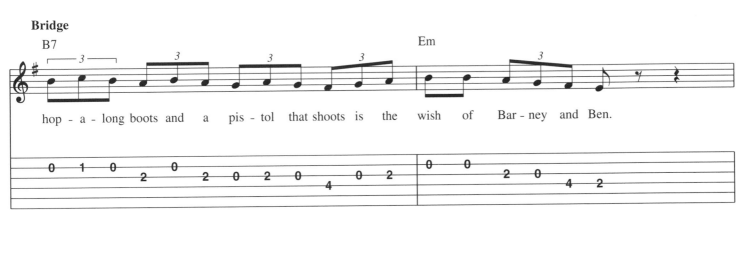

Jesu, Joy of Man's Desiring

By Johann Sebastian Bach

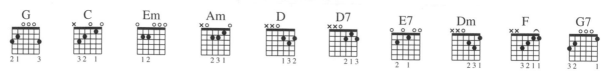

Strum Pattern: 8
Pick Pattern: 8

Intro
Moderately

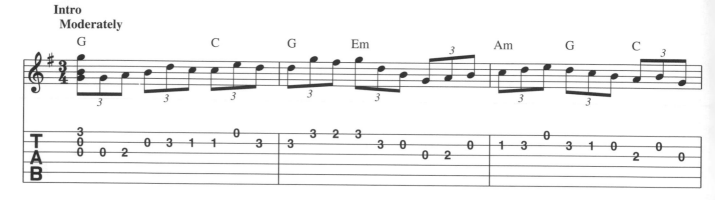

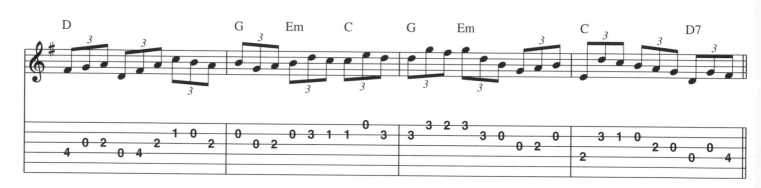

Verse

1. Je - su, joy of man's de -
2. *See Additional Lyrics*

sir - ing,   ho - ly wis - dom,

Striv - ing still to Truth un - known,

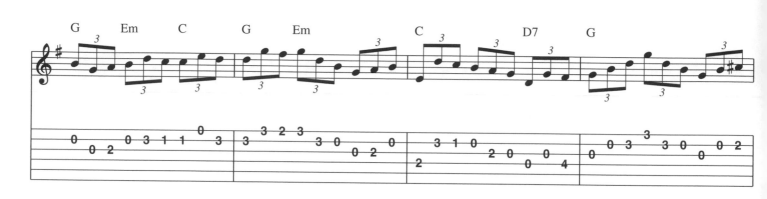

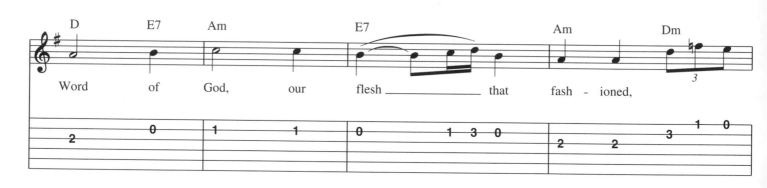

Word of God, our flesh _____ that fash - ioned,

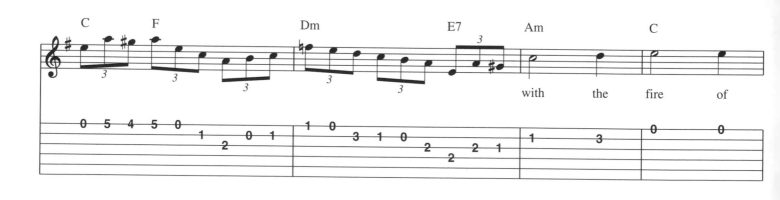

with the fire of

life _____ im - pas - sioned.

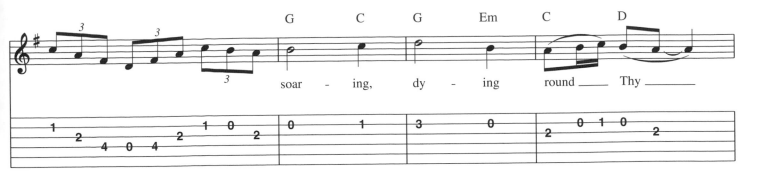

soar - ing, dy - ing round _____ Thy _____

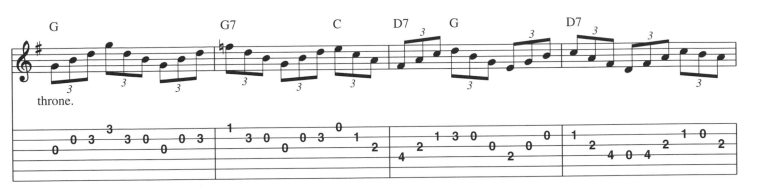

throne.

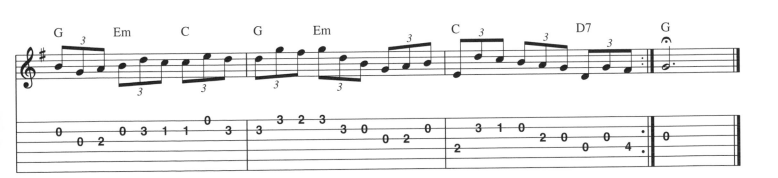

Additional Lyrics

2. Through the way where hope is guiding.
   Hark, what peaceful music rings!
   Where the flock in Thee confiding,
   Drink of joy from deathless springs.
   Their's is beauty's fairest pleasure.
   Their's is wisdom's holiest treasure.
   Thou dost ever lead Thine own,
   In the love of joys unknown.

Jesus Is Born

Words and Music by Steve Green, Phil Naish and Colleen Green

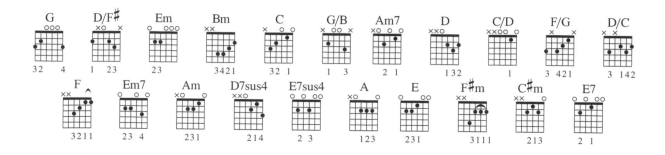

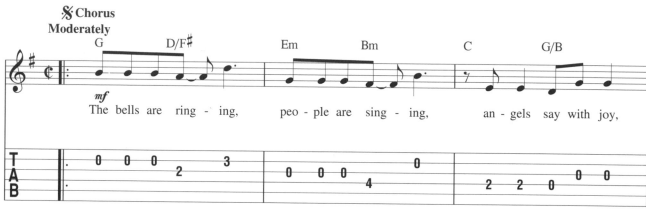

*Strum Pattern: 2
*Pick Pattern: 4

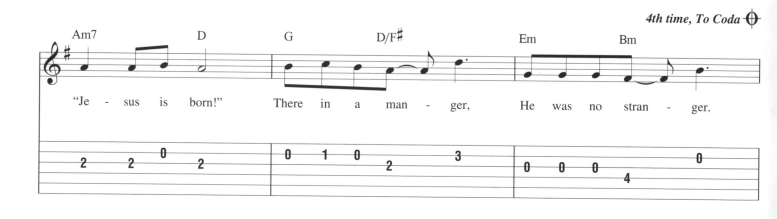

*Use Pattern 10 for 2/4 meas.

Bridge

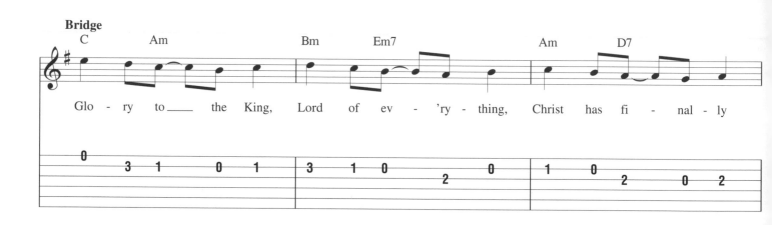

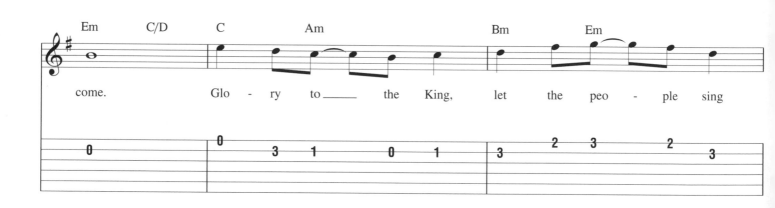

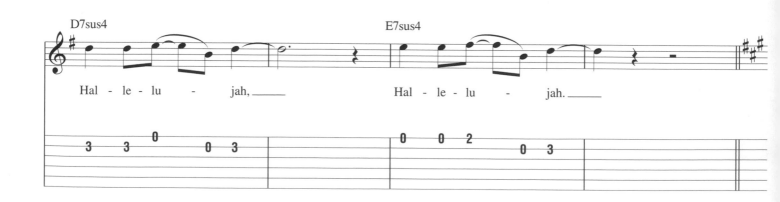

Outro-Chorus

Jingle-Bell Rock

Words and Music by Joe Beal and Jim Boothe

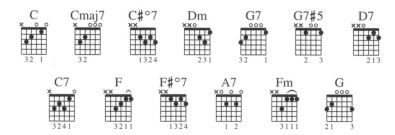

Strum Pattern: 1, 3
Pick Pattern: 2, 3

Verse
Moderate Rock

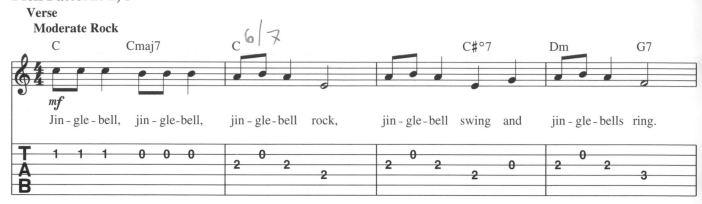

Jin - gle-bell, jin - gle-bell, jin - gle-bell rock, jin - gle-bell swing and jin - gle-bells ring.

Snow - in' and blow - in' up bush-els of fun, now the jin - gle-hop has be - gun.

Jin - gle-bell, jin - gle-bell, jin - gle-bell rock, jin - gle-bells chime in jin - gle-bell time.

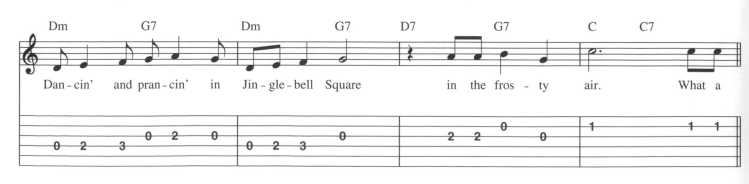

Dan - cin' and pran - cin' in Jin - gle-bell Square in the fros - ty air. What a

Bridge

bright time, it's the right time to rock the night a - way. Jin - gle -

bell time is a swell time to go gli - din' in a one horse sleigh.

Gid - dy - ap, jin - gle horse pick up your feet, jin - gle a - round the clock.

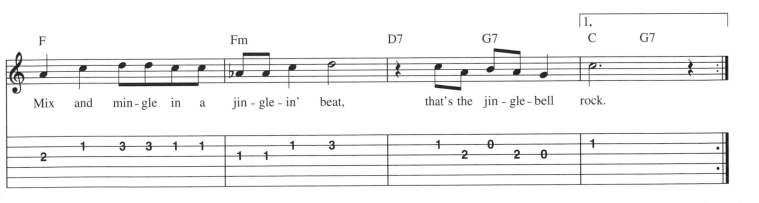

Mix and min - gle in a jin - gle - in' beat, that's the jin - gle - bell rock.

1.

2.

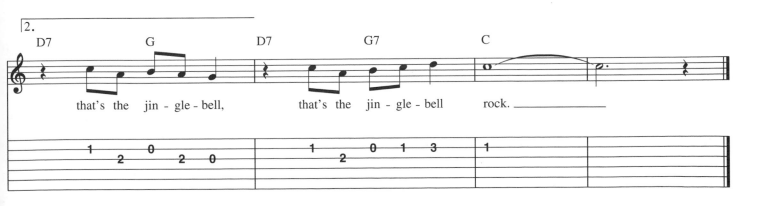

that's the jin - gle - bell, that's the jin - gle - bell rock. _____

Jingle Bells

Words and Music by J. Pierpont

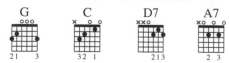

Strum Pattern: 2, 3
Pick Pattern: 3, 4

Verse
Brightly

1. Dash - ing through the snow, in a one horse o - pen sleigh.
2., 3. *See Additional Lyrics*

O'er the fields we go, laugh - ing all the way.

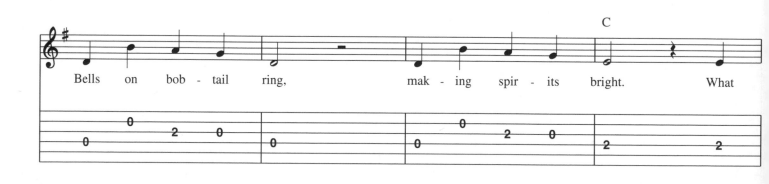

Bells on bob - tail ring, mak - ing spir - its bright. What

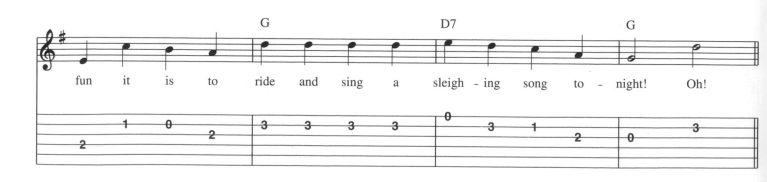

fun it is to ride and sing a sleigh - ing song to - night! Oh!

Chorus

Jin - gle bells, jin - gle bells, jin - gle all the way.

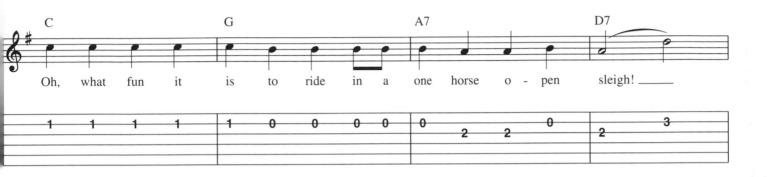

Oh, what fun it is to ride in a one horse o - pen sleigh! _____

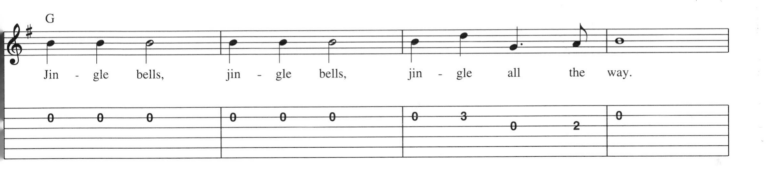

Jin - gle bells, jin - gle bells, jin - gle all the way.

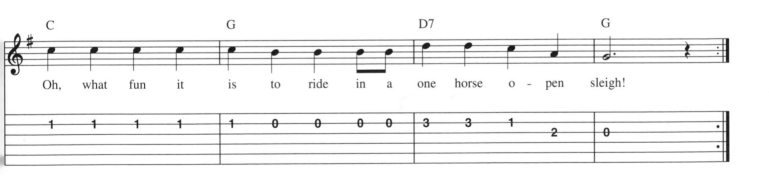

Oh, what fun it is to ride in a one horse o - pen sleigh!

Additional Lyrics

2. A day or two ago, I thought I'd take a ride,
   And soon Miss Fannie Bright was sitting by my side.
   The horse was lean and lank,
   Misfortune seemed his lot.
   He got into a drifted bank and we, we got upshot! Oh!

3. Now the ground is white, go it while you're young.
   Take the girls tonight and sing this sleighing song.
   Just get a bobtail bay,
   Two-forty for his speed.
   Then hitch him to an open sleigh and
   Crack, you'll take the lead! Oh

Jingle, Jingle, Jingle

Music and Lyrics by Johnny Marks

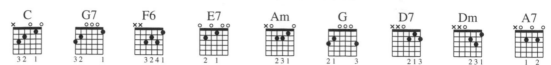

Strum Pattern: 4
Pick Pattern: 4

Verse
Moderately

1., 2. Jin - gle, jin - gle, jin - gle, you will hear {my his} sleigh bells ring.

{I am Jol - ly} old Kris Krin - gle, {I'm is} the King of jin - gl - ing.

Jin - gle, jin - gle rein - deer, through the frost - y air they'll go.

They are not just plain deer, they're the fast - est deer I know. *(Ho! Ho!)* You

Bridge

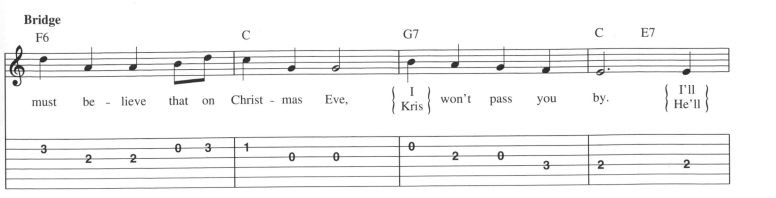

must be - lieve that on Christ - mas Eve, { I / Kris } won't pass you by. { I'll / He'll }

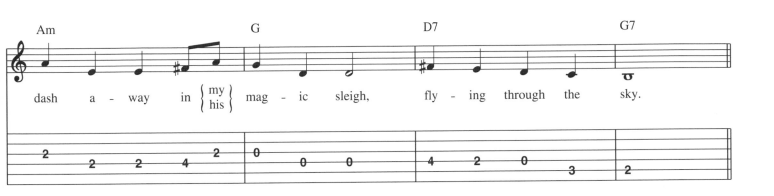

dash a - way in { my / his } mag - ic sleigh, fly - ing through the sky.

Verse

Jin - gle, jin - gle rein - deer, through the frost - y air they'll go.

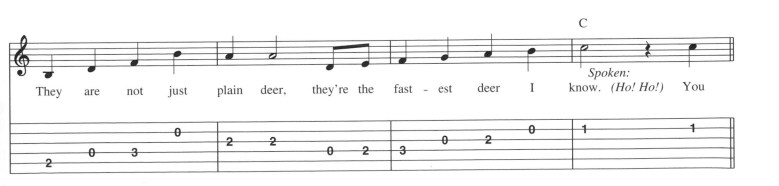

They are not just plain deer, they're the fast - est deer I know. *(Ho! Ho!)* You

Spoken:

Bridge

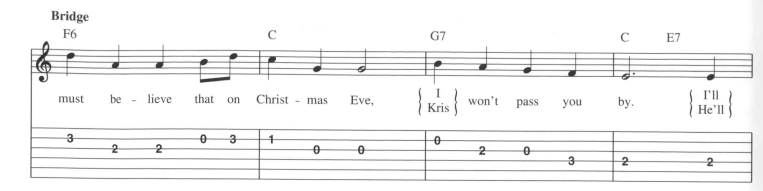

must be - lieve that on Christ - mas Eve, {I/Kris} won't pass you by. {I'll/He'll}

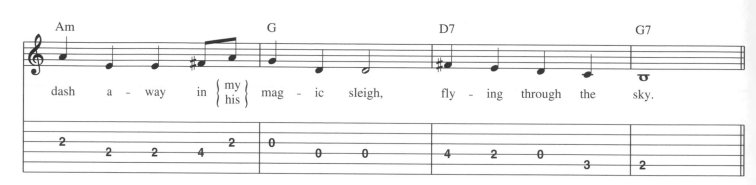

dash a - way in {my/his} mag - ic sleigh, fly - ing through the sky.

Outro-Verse

Jin - gle, jin - gle, jin - gle, you will hear {my/his} sleigh bells ring.

1.

{I/Jol - ly} am old Kris Krin - gle; I'm the King of jin - gl - ing. *(Ho! Ho!)*
old Kris Krin - gle is the

2.

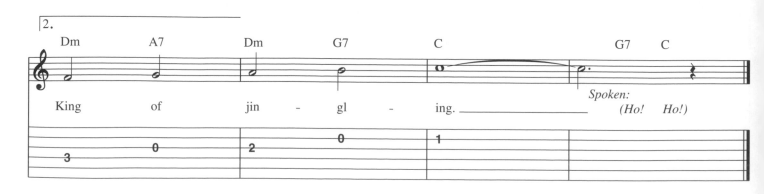

King of jin - gl - ing. _____ *(Ho! Ho!)*

Jolly Old St. Nicholas

Traditional 19th Century American Carol

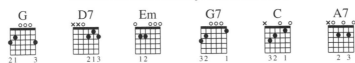

Strum Pattern: 10
Pick Pattern: 10

Additional Lyrics

2. When the clock is striking twelve, when I'm fast asleep.
   Down the chimney broad and black, with your pack you'll creep.
   All the stockings you will find hanging in a row.
   Mine will be the shortest one, you'll be sure to know.

3. Johnny wants a pair of skates; Susy wants a sled.
   Nellie wants a picture book, yellow, blue and red.
   Now I think I'll leave to you what to give the rest.
   Choose for me, dear Santa Claus.
   You will know the best.

Joy to the World

Words by Isaac Watts
Music by George Frideric Handel
Arranged by Lowell Mason

Strum Pattern: 3
Pick Pattern: 3

Verse

With Spirit

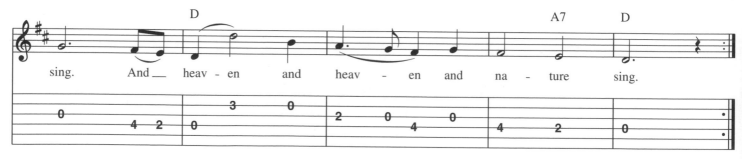

Additional Lyrics

2. He rules the world with truth and grace
And makes the nations prove
The glories of His righteousness
And wonders of His love,
And wonders of His love.
And wonders, wonders of His love.

Joyous Christmas

Music and Lyrics by Johnny Marks

Strum Pattern: 4
Pick Pattern: 3

Verse
Moderately Slow

1. Have a Joy - ous Christ - mas, Joy - ous Christ - mas, fill your heart with good cheer. Thank the
2., 3. *See Additional Lyrics*

Lord a - bove for all the love you have from those you hold dear.

Chorus

Let the Christ - mas bells ring out, pro - claim - ing loud and clear: Have a

Joy - ous Christ - mas, Joy - ous Christ - mas and __ a hap - py New Year. 2. Have a Year.

Additional Lyrics

2. Have a Joyous Christmas, Joyous Christmas,
   But don't fail to recall
   That a tiny stranger
   In a manger was the start of it all.

3. Have a Joyous Christmas, Joyous Christmas,
   Sing it loudly and then
   Pray to all your worth for peace
   On earth and for good will to men.

The Last Month of the Year
(What Month Was Jesus Born In?)

Words and Music by Vera Hall
Adapted and Arranged by Ruby Pickens Tartt and Alan Lomax

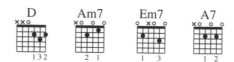

Strum Pattern: 6
Pick Pattern: 3

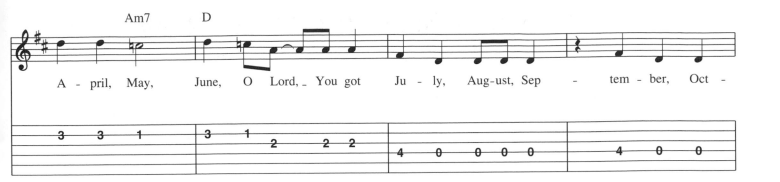

A - pril, May, June, O Lord, _ You got Ju - ly, Aug-ust, Sep - tem - ber, Oct -

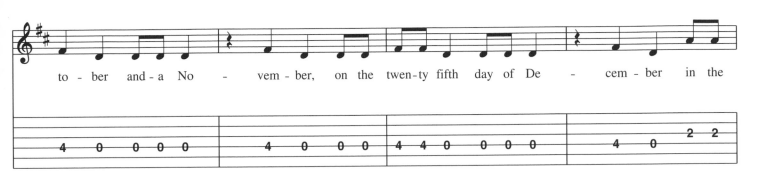

to - ber and - a No - vem - ber, on the twen-ty fifth day of De - cem - ber in the

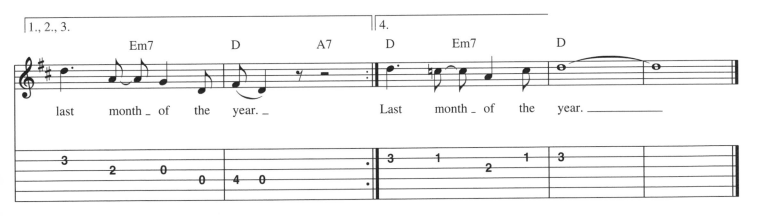

last month _ of the year. _ Last month _ of the year. _____

Additional Lyrics

2. Well, they laid Him in the manger,
Last month of the year!
Well, they laid Him in the manger,
Last month of the year!

3. Wrapped Him up in swaddling clothing,
Last month of the year!
Wrapped Him up in swaddling clothing,
Last month of the year!

4. He was born of the Virgin Mary,
Last month of the year!
He was born of the Virgin Mary,
Last month of the year!

Let It Snow! Let It Snow! Let It Snow!

Words by Sammy Cahn
Music by Jule Styne

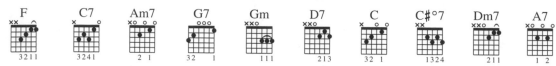

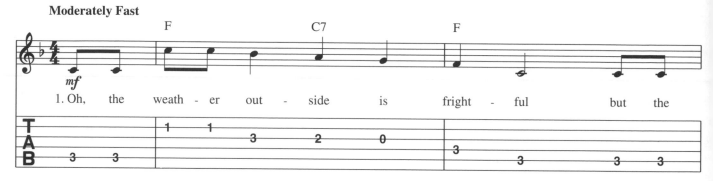

Strum Pattern: 2
Pick Pattern: 4

Verse

Moderately Fast

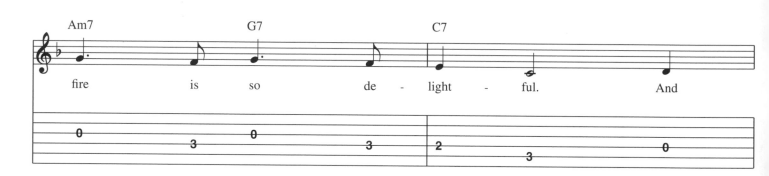

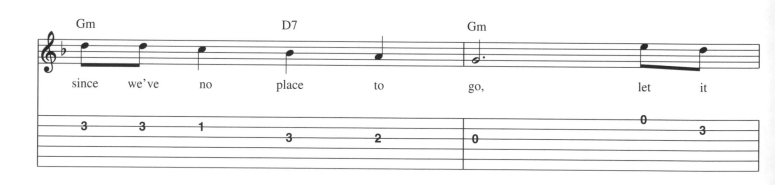

%

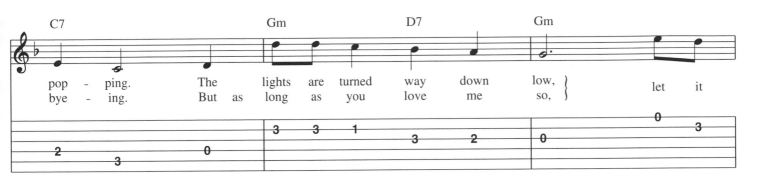

Little Saint Nick

Words and Music by Brian Wilson and Mike Love

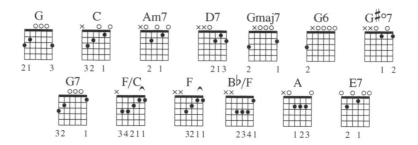

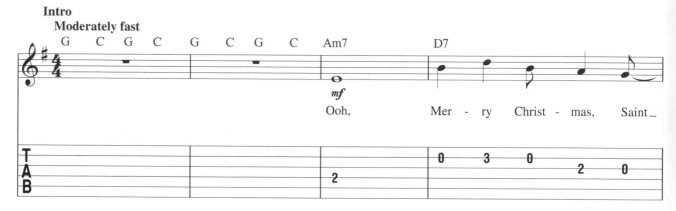

Strum Pattern: 3, 4
Pick Pattern: 1, 3

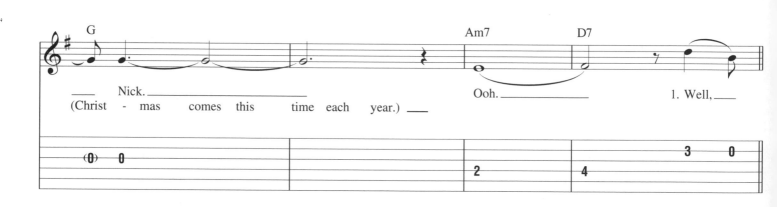

Intro
Moderately fast

Ooh, Mer - ry Christ - mas, Saint __

__ Nick. (Christ - mas comes this time each year.) __ Ooh. __ 1. Well, __

Verse

way up north where the air gets cold, __ there's a tale a - bout Christ-mas that you've

2., 3. See additional lyrics

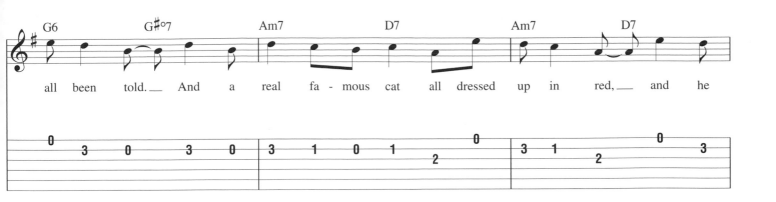

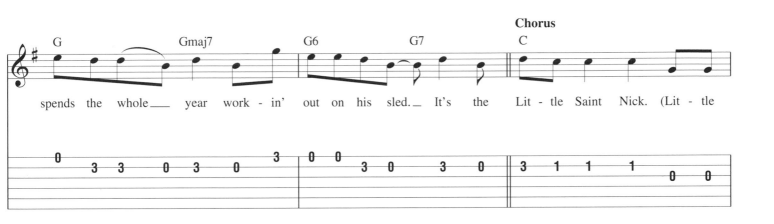

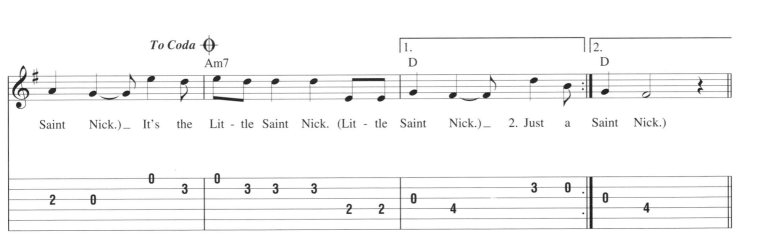

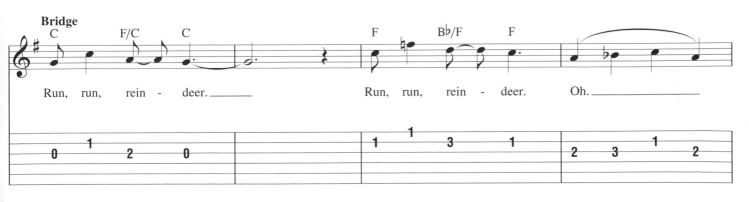

Run, run, rein - deer._____ Run, run, rein - deer. He don't miss no one. 3. And

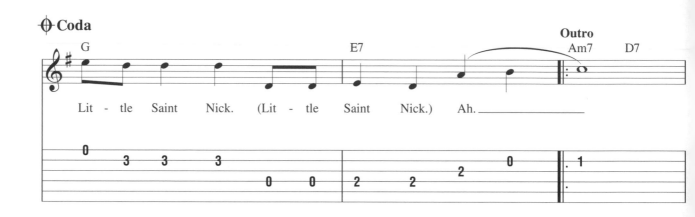

Coda

Lit - tle Saint Nick. (Lit - tle Saint Nick.) Ah._____

Outro

Repeat and fade

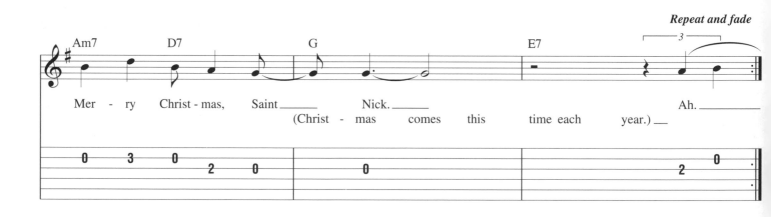

Mer - ry Christ - mas, Saint_____ Nick._____ Ah._____
(Christ - mas comes this time each year.)__

Lo, How a Rose E'er Blooming

15th Century German Carol
Translated by Theodore Baker
Music from *Alte Catholische Geistliche Kirchengesang*

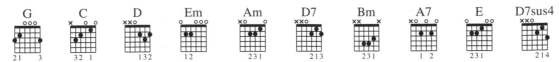

Strum Pattern: 3, 4
Pick Pattern: 4, 5

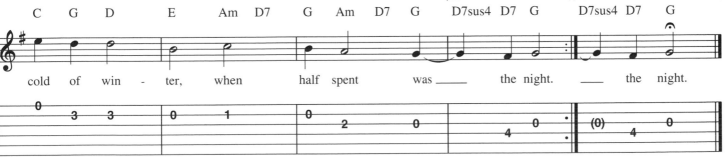

Additional Lyrics

2. Isaiah 'twas foretold it,
The rose I have in mind.
With Mary we behold it,
The Virgin Mother kind.
To show God's love aright.
She bore to men a Savior
When half spent was the night.

139

March of the Three Kings

Words by M.L. Hohman
Traditional French Melody

Am   Dm   E7   C   D#°7   E7sus4

Strum Pattern: 10
Pick Pattern: 10

Chorus
March Tempo

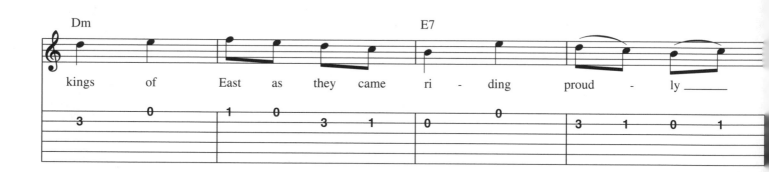

Verse

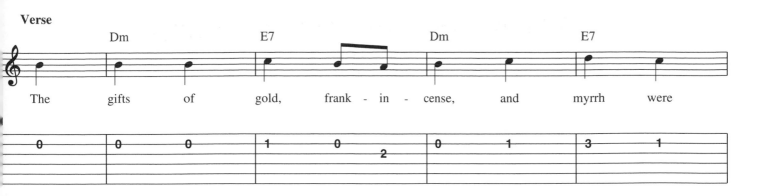

The gifts of gold, frank - in - cense, and myrrh were

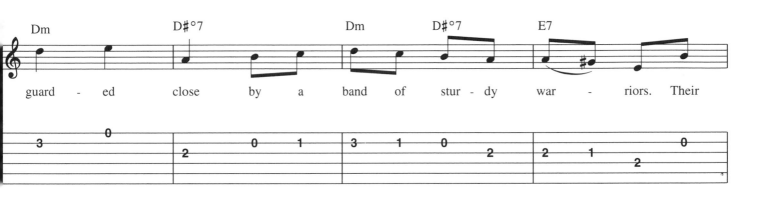

guard - ed close by a band of stur - dy war - riors. Their

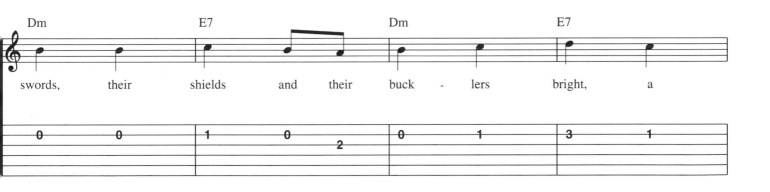

swords, their shields and their buck - lers bright, a

D.C. al Fine

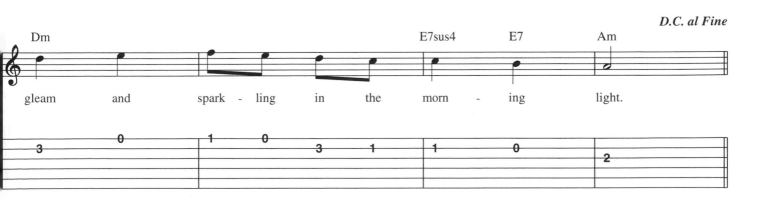

gleam and spark - ling in the morn - ing light.

A Marshmallow World

Words by Carl Sigman
Music by Peter De Rose

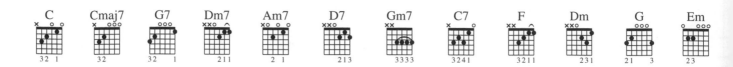

Strum Pattern: 3
Pick Pattern: 3

Intro
Brightly

1. It's a

%S **Verse**

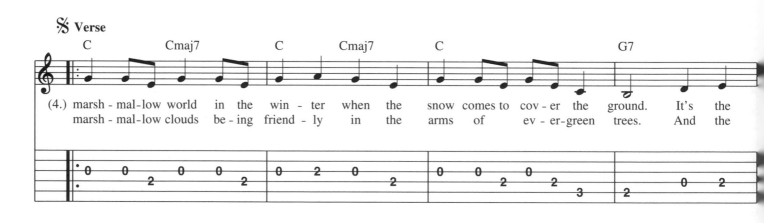

(4.) marsh - mal-low world   in the   win - ter   when   the   snow comes to cov - er the   ground.   It's   the
marsh - mal-low clouds   be - ing   friend - ly   in   the   arms   of   ev - er-green   trees.   And   the

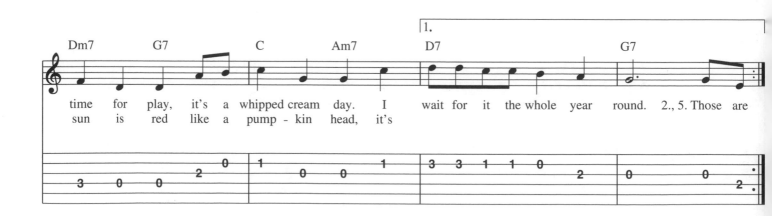

time   for   play,   it's a   whipped cream   day.   I   wait   for   it   the whole   year   round.   2., 5. Those   are
sun   is   red   like a   pump - kin   head,   it's

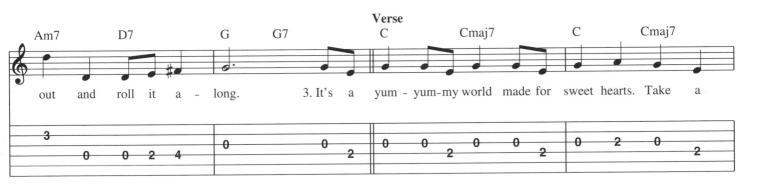

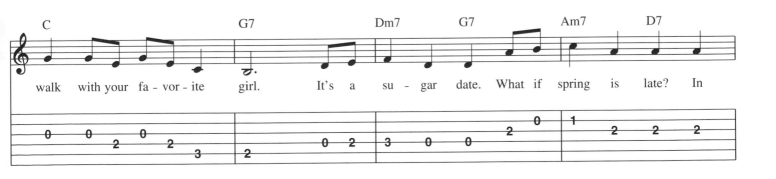

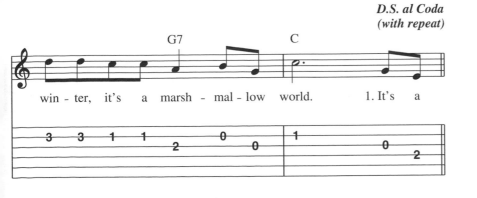

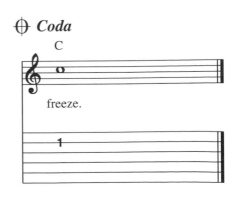

Mary Had a Baby

African-American Spiritual

Strum Pattern: 1, 3
Pick Pattern: 1, 3

Verse
Moderately

1. Mar - y had a ba - by,
2. What __ did she name Him?
3.-7. *See Additional Lyrics*

Oh, Lord; __

Mar - y had a ba - by,
What __ did she name Him?

Oh, my __ Lord;

Mar - y had a ba - by,
What __ did she name Him?

Oh, Lord; __ The

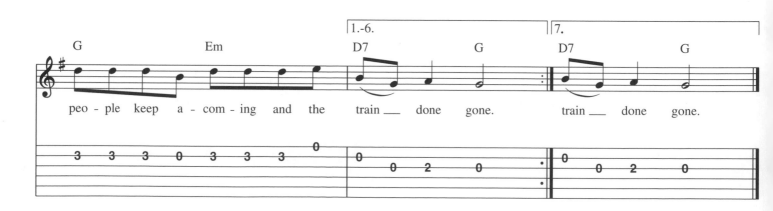

peo - ple keep a - com - ing and the train __ done gone.

train __ done gone.

Additional Lyrics

3. She called Him Jesus,
4. Where was He born?
5. Born in a stable,
6. Where did they lay Him?
7. Laid Him in a manger,

Merry Christmas, Darling

Words and Music by Richard Carpenter and Frank Pooler

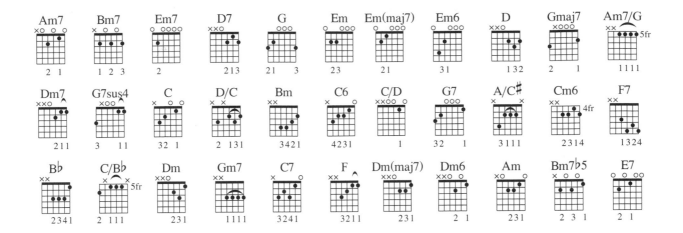

Strum Pattern: 4
Pick Pattern: 6

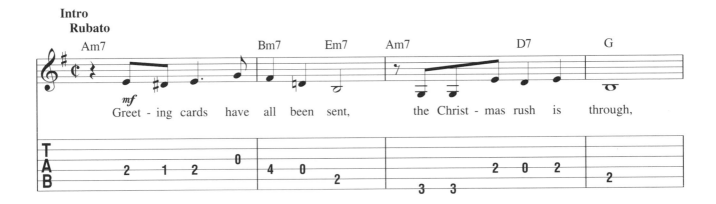

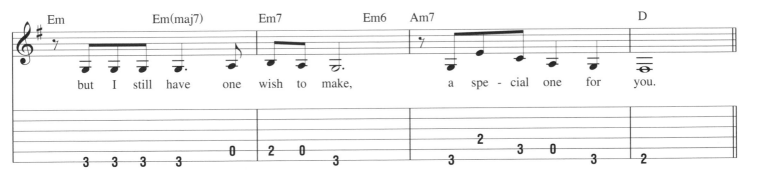

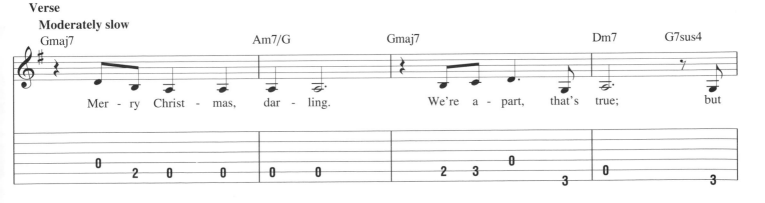

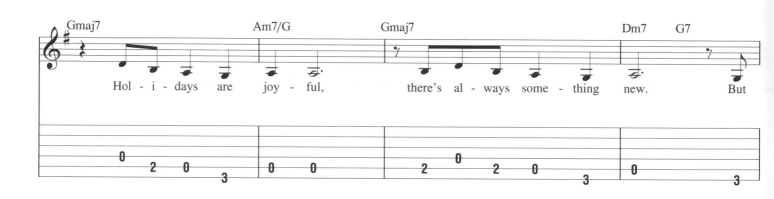

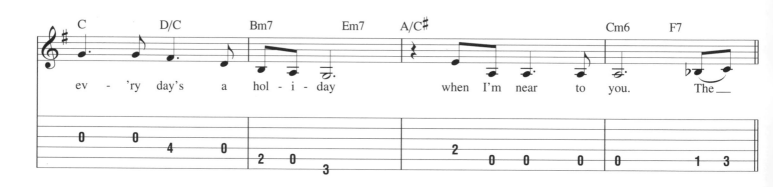

𝄋 **Bridge**

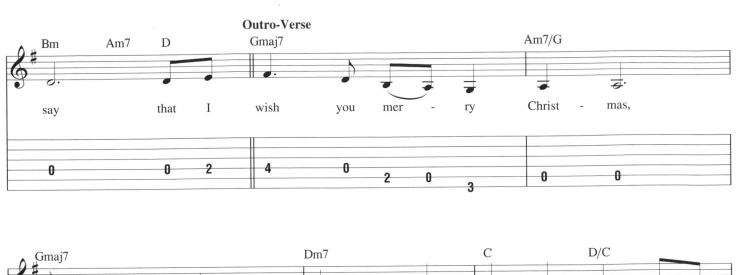

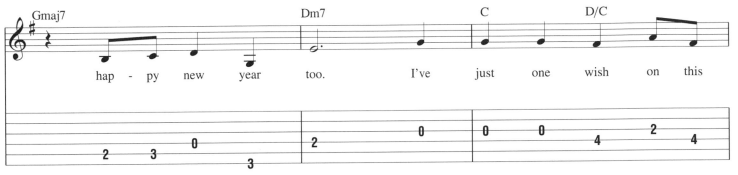

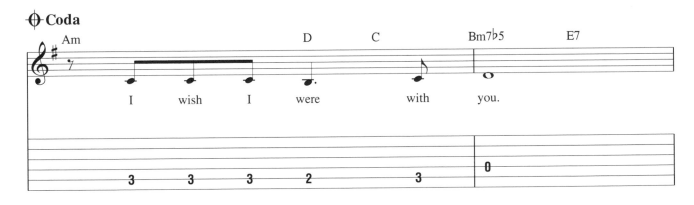

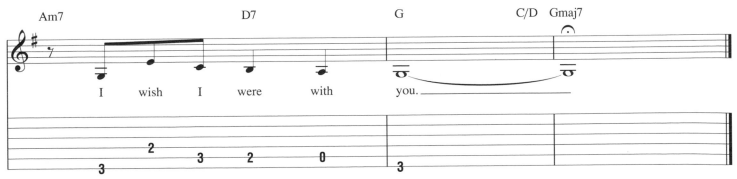

Mary's Little Boy Child

Words and Music by Jester Hairston

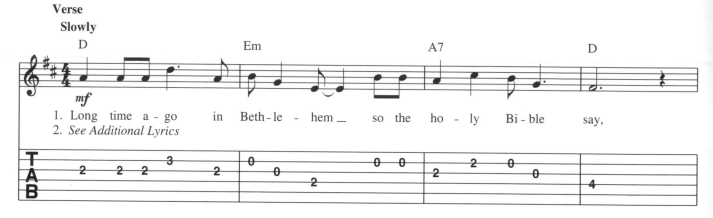

Strum Pattern: 4
Pick Pattern: 3

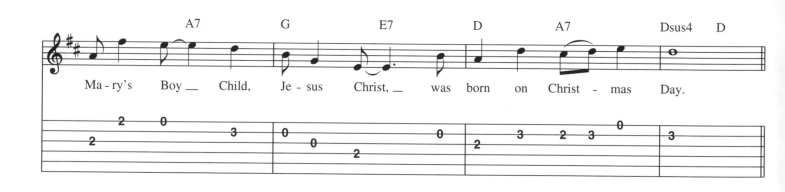

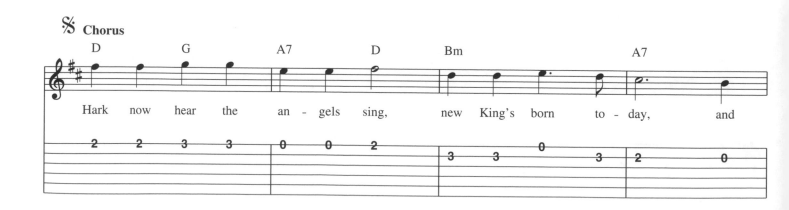

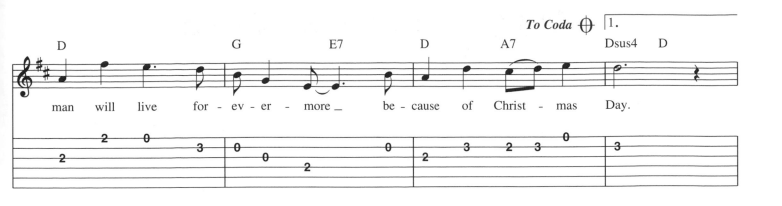

man will live for - ev - er - more _ be - cause of Christ - mas Day.

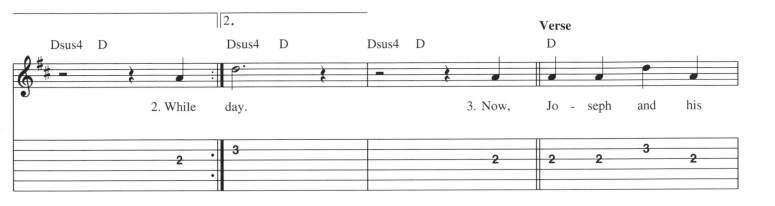

2. While day.

Verse

3. Now, Jo - seph and his

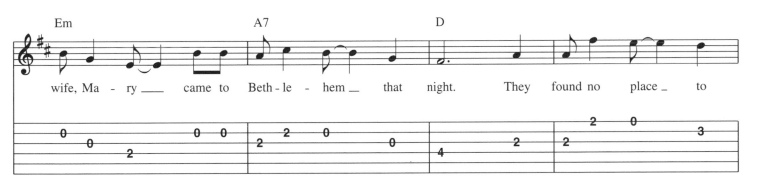

wife, Ma - ry ___ came to Beth - le - hem _ that night. They found no place _ to

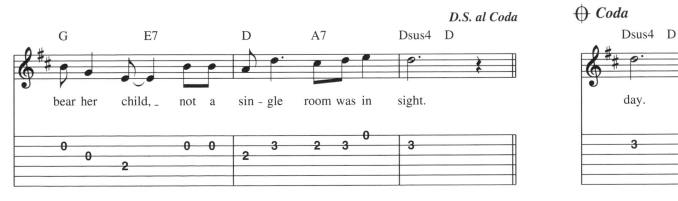

D.S. al Coda

Coda

bear her child, _ not a sin - gle room was in sight.

day.

Additional Lyrics

2. While shepherds watched their flocks by night
They saw a bright, new, shining star.
Heard a choir from Heaven sing.
The music came from afar.

The Merry Christmas Polka

Words by Paul Francis Webster

Music by Sonny Burke

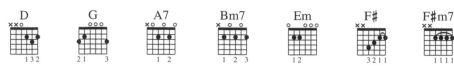

Strum Pattern: 4
Pick Pattern: 3

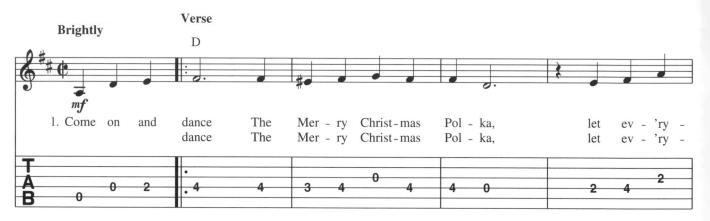

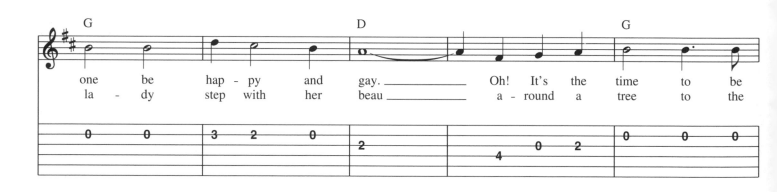

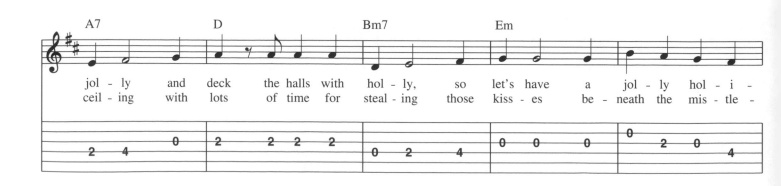

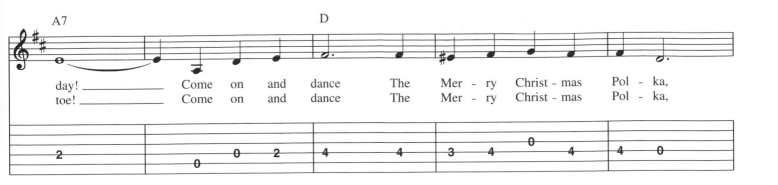

day! _____ Come on and dance The Mer - ry Christ - mas Pol - ka,
toe! _____ Come on and dance The Mer - ry Christ - mas Pol - ka,

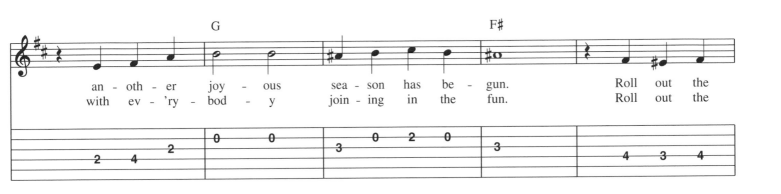

an - oth - er joy - ous sea - son has be - gun. Roll out the
with ev - 'ry - bod - y join - ing in the fun. Roll out the

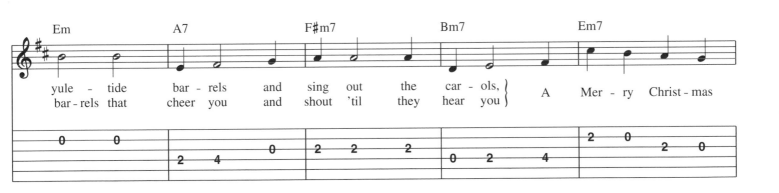

yule - tide bar - rels and sing out the car - ols, } A Mer - ry Christ - mas
bar - rels that cheer you and shout 'til they hear you }

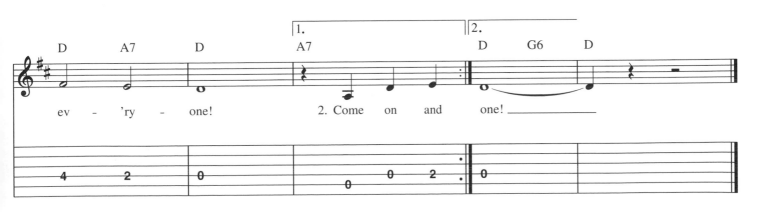

ev - 'ry - one! 2. Come on and one! _____

Mister Santa

Words and Music by Pat Ballard

Strum Pattern: 4
Pick Pattern: 3

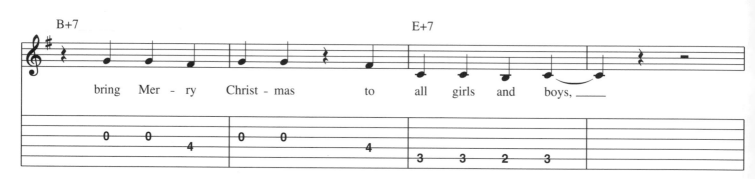

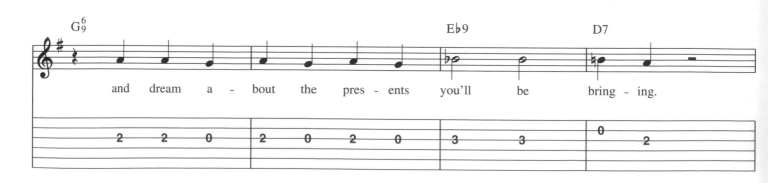

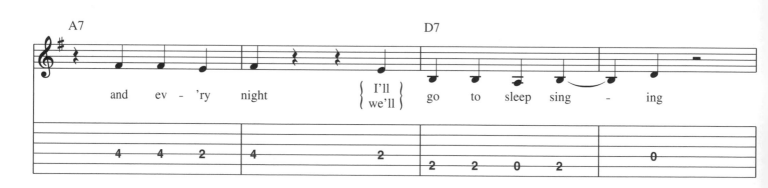

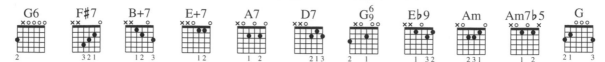

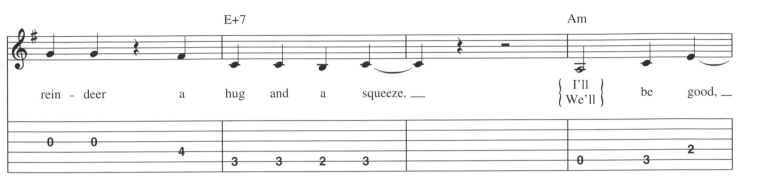

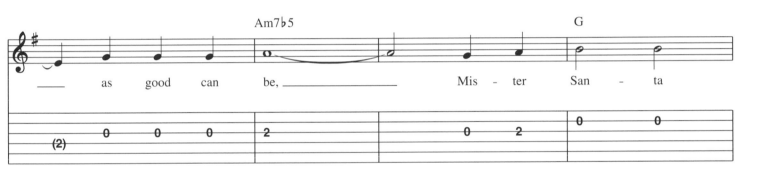

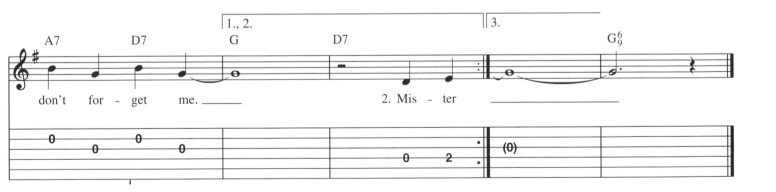

Additional Lyrics

2. Mister Santa, dear old Saint Nick
Be awful careful and please don't get sick.
Put on your coat when breezes are blowin'
And when you cross the street look where you're goin'.
Santa, we (I) love you so,
We (I) hope you never get lost in the snow.
Take your time when you unpack,
Mister Santa don't hurry back.

3. Mister Santa, we've been so good.
We've washed the dishes and done what we should.
Made up the beds and scrubbed up our toesies.
We've used a kleenex when we've blown our nosesies.
Santa look at our ears, they're clean as whistles.
We're sharper than shears.
Now we've put you on the spot,
Mister Santa bring us a lot.

The Most Wonderful Day of the Year

Music and Lyrics by Johnny Marks

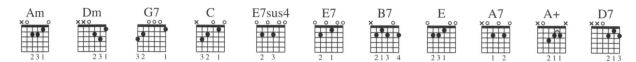

Strum Pattern: 7
Pick Pattern: 7

Intro
Freely

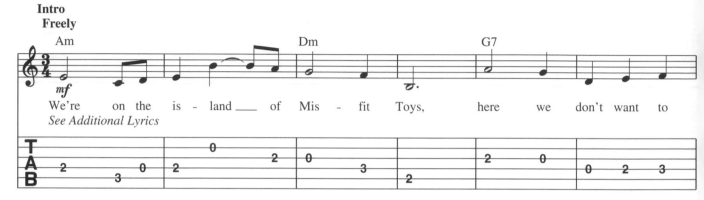

We're on the is-land ___ of Mis-fit Toys, here we don't want to
See Additional Lyrics

stay. ___ We want to trav-el ___ with San-ta Claus, in his

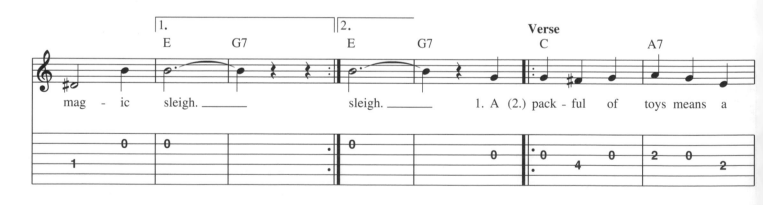

mag-ic sleigh. ___ sleigh. ___ 1. A (2.) pack-ful of toys means a

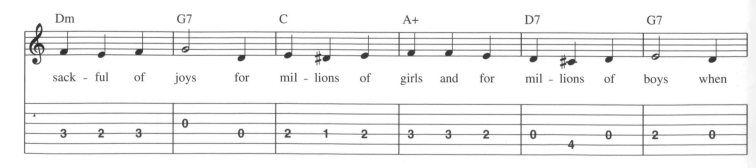

sack-ful of joys for mil-lions of girls and for mil-lions of boys when

Christ - mas Day is here. _____ The most won - der - ful day of the

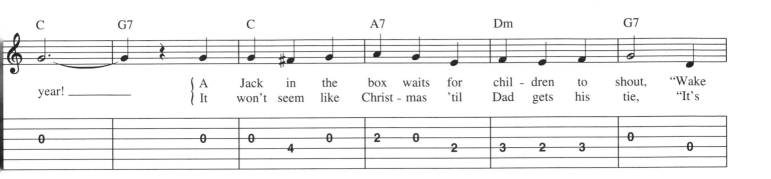

year! _____ { A Jack in the box waits for chil - dren to shout, "Wake
It won't seem like Christ - mas 'til Dad gets his tie, "It's

Chorus

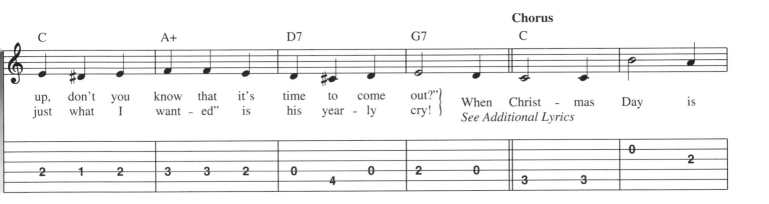

up, don't you know that it's time to come out?"} When Christ - mas Day is
just what I want - ed" is his year - ly cry! } *See Additional Lyrics*

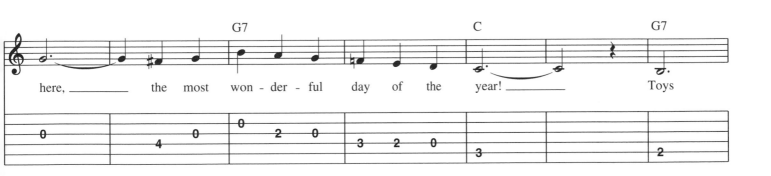

here, _____ the most won - der - ful day of the year! _____ Toys

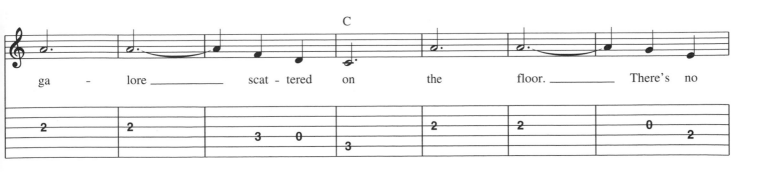

ga - lore _____ scat - tered on the floor. _____ There's no

Additional Lyrics

Intro Up at the North Pole they have their laws,
Elves must work ev'ry day.
Making the toys that Old Santa Claus
Leads upon his sleigh.

Chorus When Christmas Day is here,
The most wonderful day of the year!
Spirits gay; ev'ryone will say, "Happy Holiday!
And the best to you all the whole year through."
An electric train hidden high on a shelf
That Daddy gives David but then runs himself.
When Christmas Day is here,
The most wonderful, wonderful, wonderful,
Wonderful, wonderful day of the year!

The Most Wonderful Time of the Year

Words and Music by Eddie Pola and George Wyle

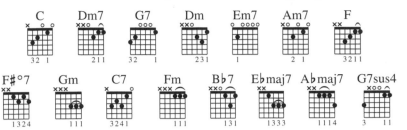

Strum Pattern: 7
Pick Pattern: 8

𝄋 **Verse**

Brightly

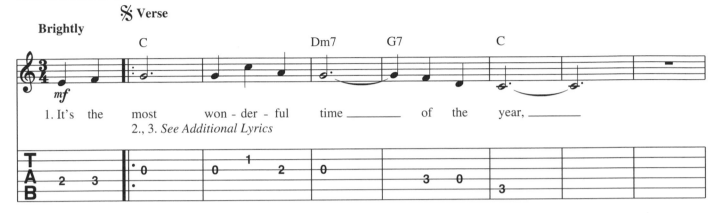

1. It's the most won-der-ful time _____ of the year, _____
2., 3. *See Additional Lyrics*

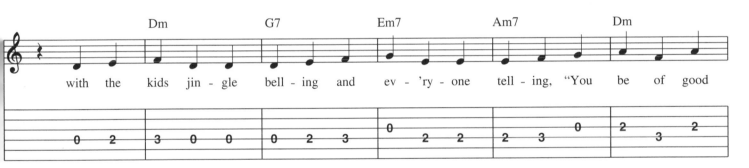

with the kids jin-gle bell-ing and ev-'ry-one tell-ing, "You be of good

To Coda ⊕ |1.

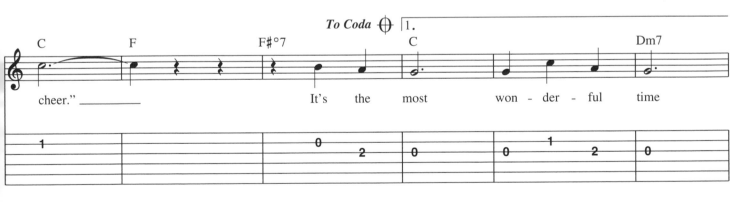

cheer." _____ It's the most won-der-ful time

|2.

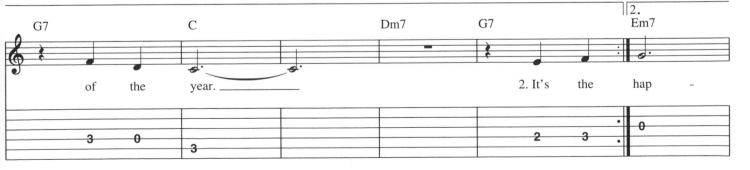

of the year. _____   2. It's the hap -

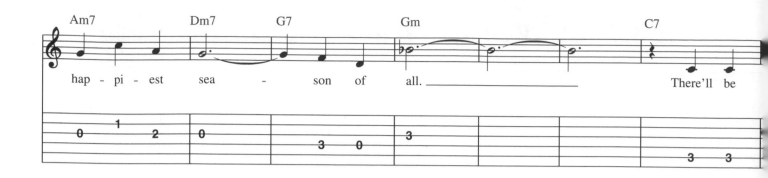

hap - pi - est sea - son of all. _____ There'll be

Bridge

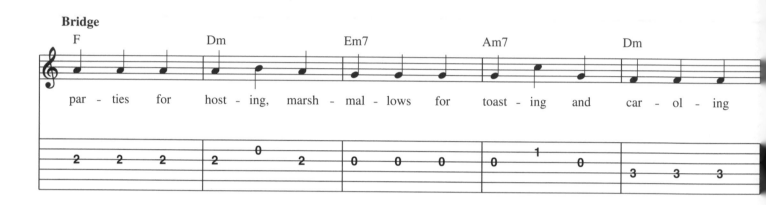

par - ties for host - ing, marsh - mal - lows for toast - ing and car - ol - ing

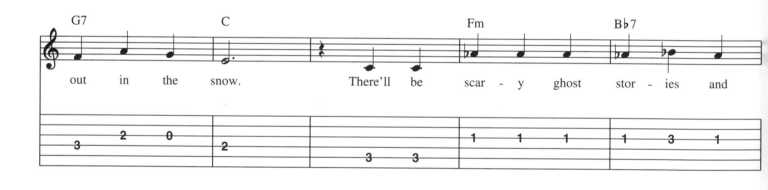

out in the snow. There'll be scar - y ghost stor - ies and

D.S. al Coda

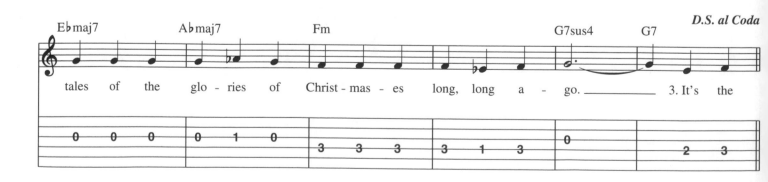

tales of the glo - ries of Christ - mas - es long, long a - go. _____ 3. It's the

Coda

most won - der - ful time, it's the most won - der - ful

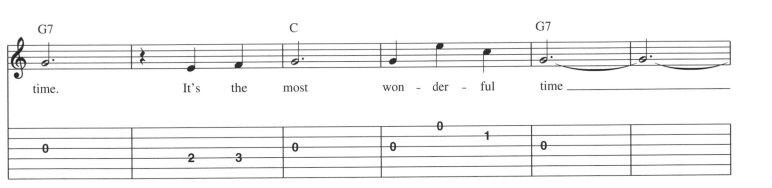

time. It's the most won - der - ful time _____

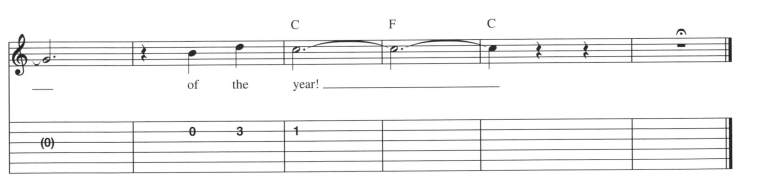

_____ of the year! _____

Additional Lyrics

2. It's the hap-happiest season of all,
   With those holiday greetings
   And gay happy meetings
   When friends come to call.
   It's the hap-happiest season of all.

3. It's the most wonderful time of the year.
   There'll be much mistletoeing
   And hearts will be glowing
   When loved ones are near.
   It's the most wonderful time of the year.

My Favorite Things

from THE SOUND OF MUSIC

Lyrics by Oscar Hammerstein II
Music by Richard Rodgers

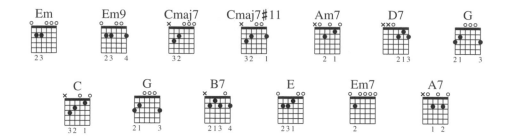

Strum Pattern: 8
Pick Pattern: 8

Verse
Lively, With Spirit

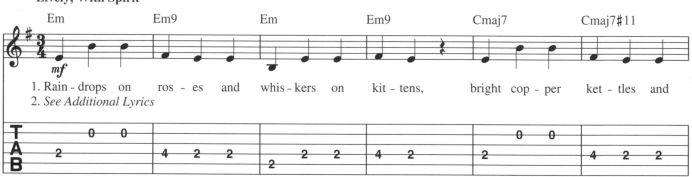

1. Rain - drops on ros - es and whis - kers on kit - tens, bright cop - per ket - tles and
2. *See Additional Lyrics*

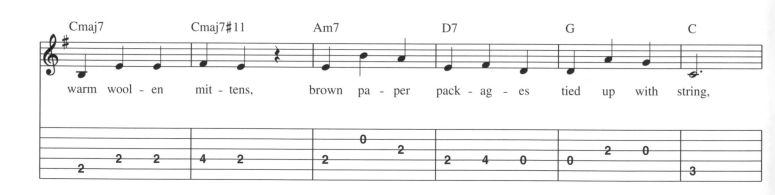

warm wool - en mit - tens, brown pa - per pack - ag - es tied up with string,

these are a few of my fa - vor - ite things.

Bridge

When the dog bites, when the bee stings, when I'm feel - ing

sad, _____ I sim - ply re - mem - ber my fa - vor - ite things and

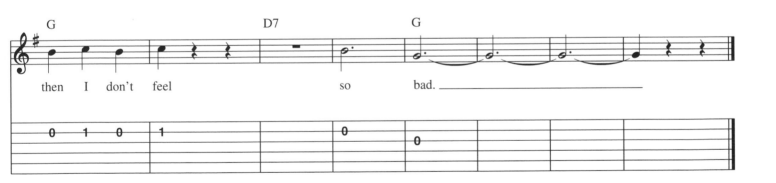

then I don't feel so bad. _____

Additional Lyrics

2. Cream colored ponies and crisp apple strudles,
   Doorbells and sleigh bells and schnitzel with noodles,
   Wild geese that fly with the moon on their wings,
   These are a few of my favorite things.

The Night Before Christmas Song

Music by Johnny Marks
Lyrics adapted by Johnny Marks from Clement Moore's Poem

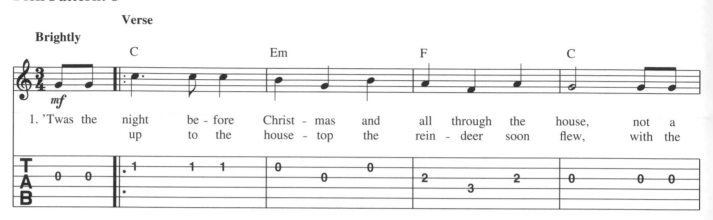

Strum Pattern: 8
Pick Pattern: 8

Brightly

Verse

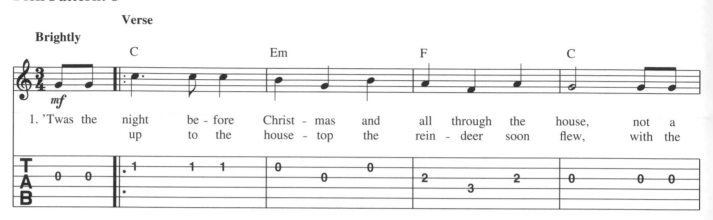

1. 'Twas the night be-fore Christ-mas and all through the house, not a
up to the house - top the rein - deer soon flew, with the

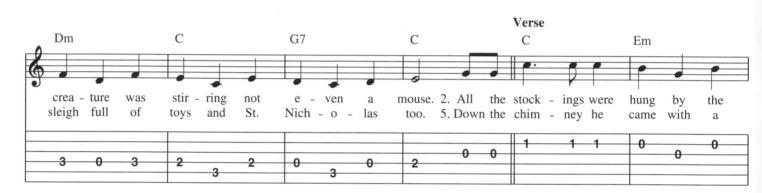

crea-ture was stir-ring not e - ven a mouse. 2. All the stock-ings were hung by the
sleigh full of toys and St. Nich - o - las too. 5. Down the chim - ney he came with a

Verse

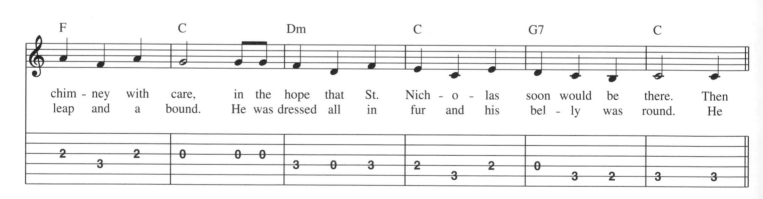

chim - ney with care, in the hope that St. Nich - o - las soon would be there. Then
leap and a bound. He was dressed all in fur and his bel - ly was round. He

Bridge

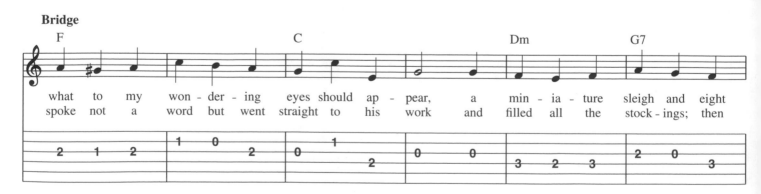

what to my won - der - ing eyes should ap - pear, a min - ia - ture sleigh and eight
spoke not a word but went straight to his work and filled all the stock - ings; then

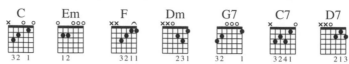

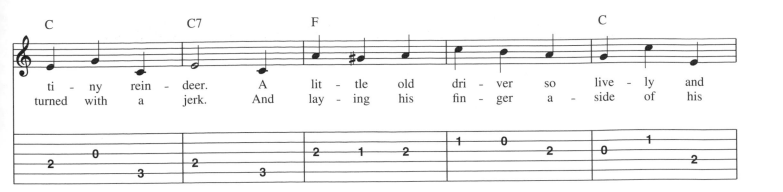

ti - ny rein - deer. A lit - tle old dri - ver so live - ly and
turned with a jerk. And lay - ing his fin - ger a - side of his

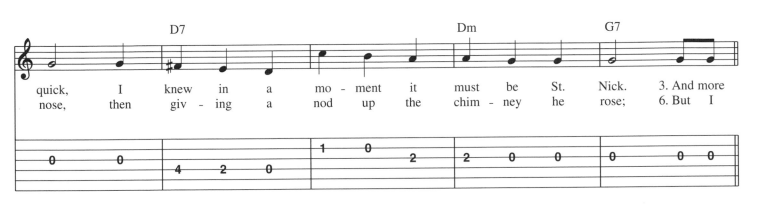

quick, I knew in a mo - ment it must be St. Nick. 3. And more
nose, then giv - ing a nod up the chim - ney he rose; 6. But I

Verse

rap - id than ea - gles his rein - deer all came, And he shout - ed "On Dash - er" and
heard him ex - claim as he drove out of sight, "Mer - ry Christ - mas to all and to

each rein - deer's name.   4. And so all a good night!"

Noël! Noël!

French-English Carol

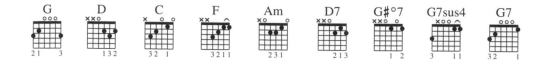

Strum Pattern: 4
Pick Pattern: 3

Verse
Rubato

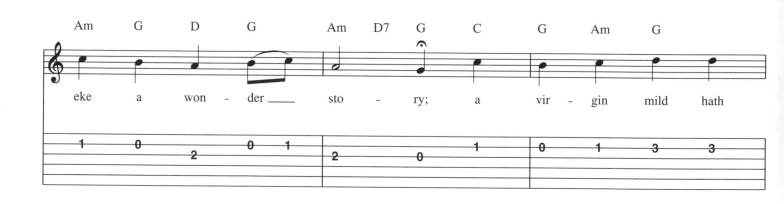

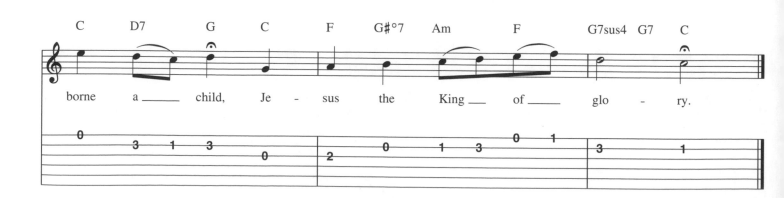

O Bethlehem

Traditional Spanish

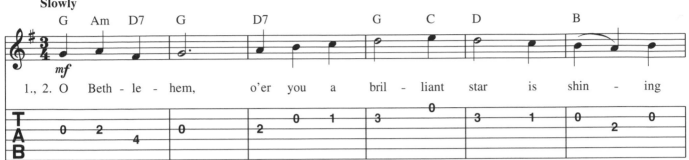

Strum Pattern: 7
Pick Pattern: 7

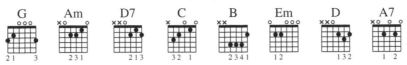

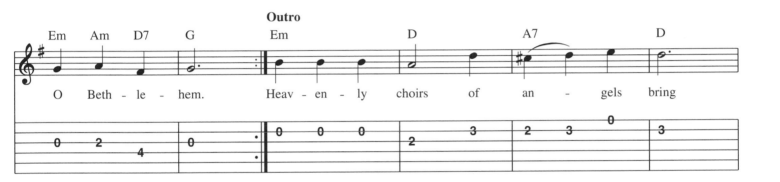

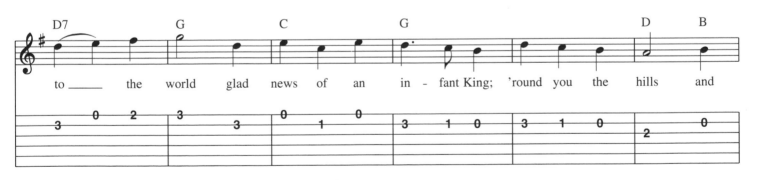

Nuttin' for Christmas

Words and Music by Roy Bennett and Sid Tepper

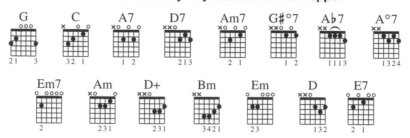

Strum Pattern: 4
Pick Pattern: 5

Verse

Brightly

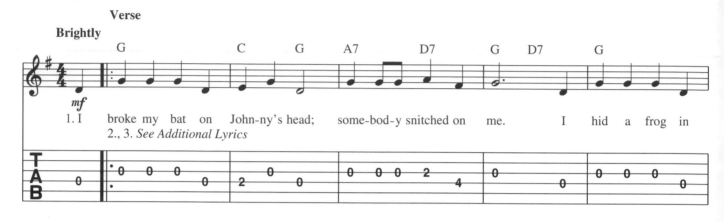

1. I broke my bat on John-ny's head; some-bod-y snitched on me. I hid a frog in
2., 3. *See Additional Lyrics*

sis-ter's bed; some-bod-y snitched on me. I spilled some ink on Mom-my's rug, I made Tom-my

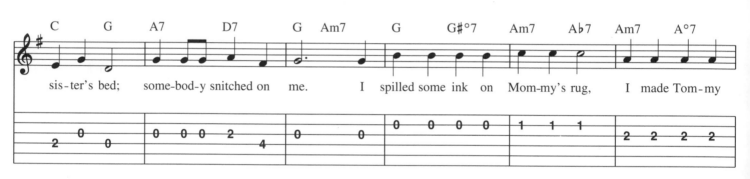

eat a bug, bought some gum with a pen-ny slug; some-bod-y snitched on me. Oh,

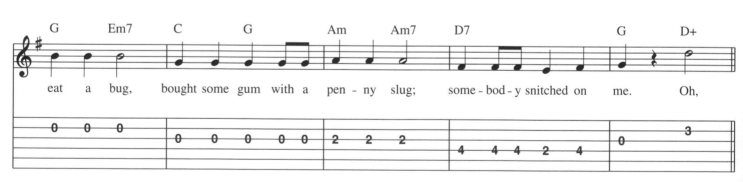

Chorus

I'm get-tin' nut-tin' for Christ-mas. Mom-my and Dad-dy are

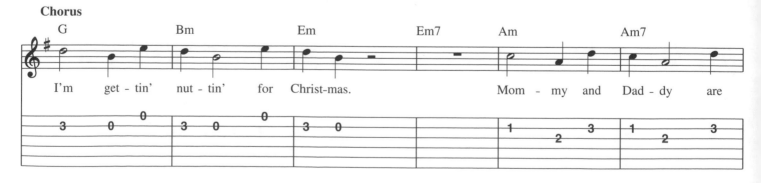

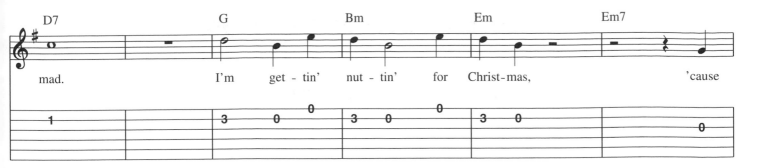

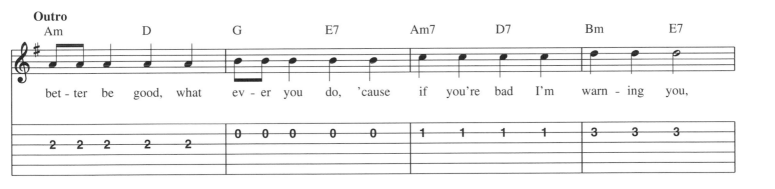

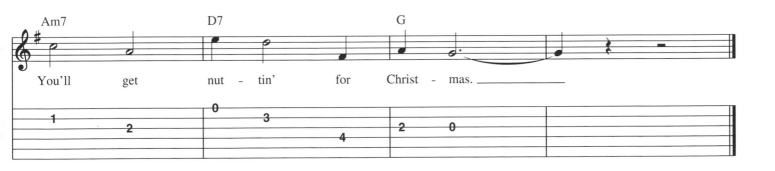

Additional Lyrics

2. I put a tack on teacher's chair;
   Somebody snitched on me.
   I tied a knot in Susie's hair;
   Somebody snitched on me.
   I did a dance on Mommy's plants,
   Climbed a tree and tore my pants.
   Filled the sugar bowl with ants;
   Somebody snitched on me.

3. I won't be seeing Santa Claus;
   Somebody snitched on me.
   He won't come visit me because
   Somebody snitched on me.
   Next year, I'll be going straight.
   Next year, I'll be good, just wait.
   I'd start now but it's too late;
   Somebody snitched on me, Oh,

O Christmas Tree

Traditional German Carol

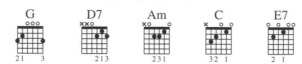

Strum Pattern: 8, 7
Pick Pattern: 8, 9

Verse
Moderately

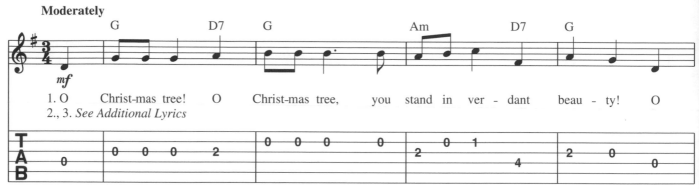

1. O Christ-mas tree! O Christ-mas tree, you stand in ver - dant beau - ty! O
2., 3. *See Additional Lyrics*

Christ-mas tree, O Christ-mas tree, you stand in ver - dant beau - ty! Your

boughs are green in sum-mer's glow, and do not fade in win - ter's snow. O

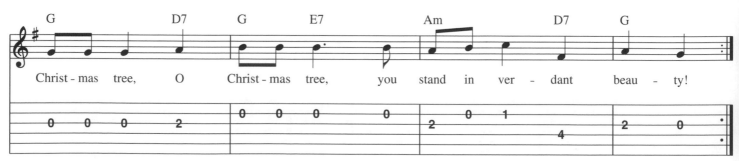

Christ - mas tree, O Christ - mas tree, you stand in ver - dant beau - ty!

Additional Lyrics

2. O, Christmas tree! O, Christmas tree,
Much pleasure doth thou bring me!
O, Christmas tree! O, Christmas tree,
Much pleasure does thou bring me!
For every year the Christmas tree
Brings to us all both joy and glee.
O, Christmas tree, O, Christmas tree,
Much pleasure doth thou bring me!

3. O, Christmas tree! O, Christmas tree,
Thy candles shine out brightly!
O, Christmas Tree, O, Christmas tree,
Thy candles shine out brightly!
Each bough doth hold its tiny light
That makes each toy to sparkle bright.
O, Christmas tree, O Christmas tree,
Thy candles shine out brightly.

O Come Rejoicing

Traditional Polish Carol

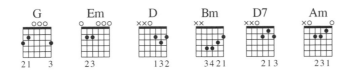

Strum Pattern: 8, 9
Pick Pattern: 8, 9

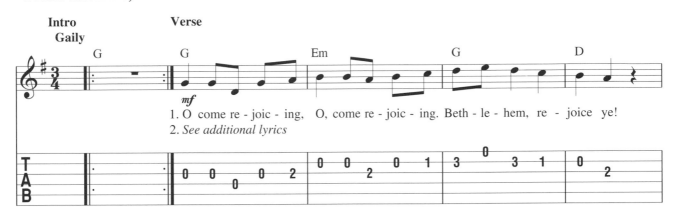

1. O come re - joic - ing, O, come re - joic - ing. Beth - le - hem, re - joice ye!
2. *See additional lyrics*

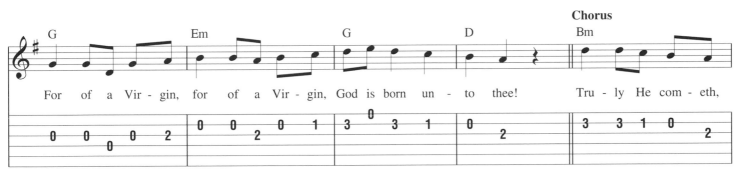

For of a Vir - gin, for of a Vir - gin, God is born un - to thee! Tru - ly He com - eth,

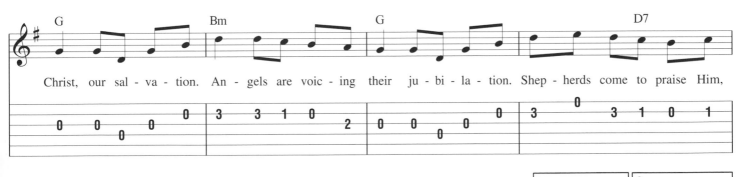

Christ, our sal - va - tion. An - gels are voic - ing their ju - bi - la - tion. Shep - herds come to praise Him,

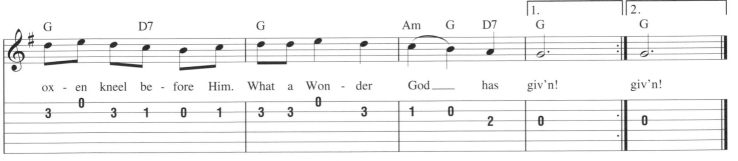

ox - en kneel be - fore Him. What a Won - der God___ has giv'n! giv'n!

Additional Lyrics

2. Mary is singing, Mary is singing,
   Songs for Thee, dear Jesus.
   Joseph is watching, Joseph is watching
   O'er the Son so glorious.

O Come, All Ye Faithful
(Adeste Fideles)

Words and Music by John Francis Wade
Latin Words translated by Frederick Oakeley

Strum Pattern: 4
Pick Pattern: 5

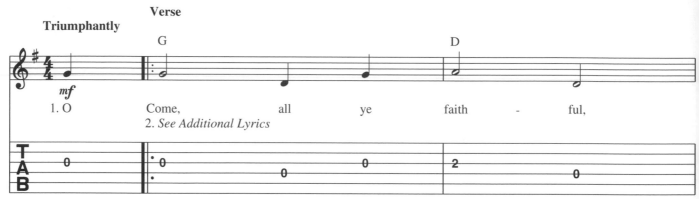

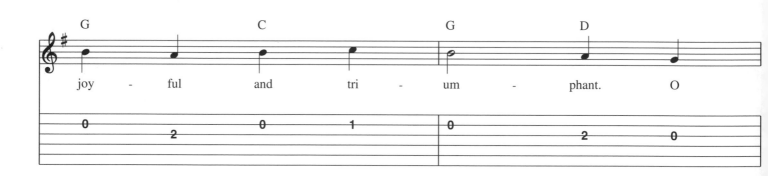

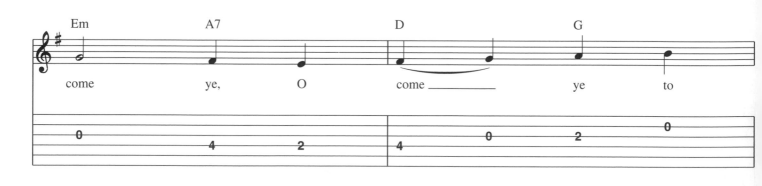

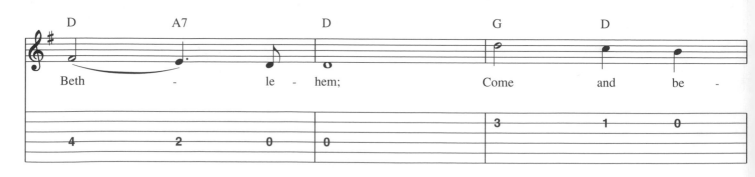

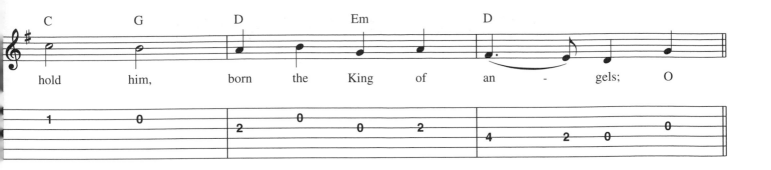

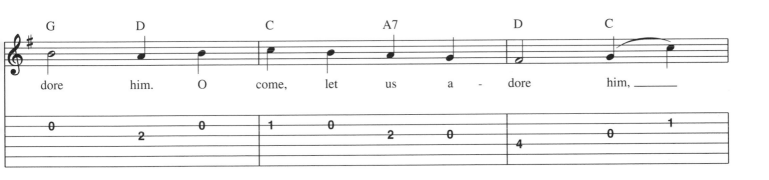

Additional Lyrics

2. Sing choirs of angels, sing in exultation.
   O sing all ye citizens of heaven above.
   Glory to God in the highest.

O Come, Little Children

Words by C. von Schmidt
Music by J.P.A. Schulz

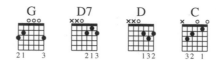

Strum Pattern: 10
Pick Pattern: 10

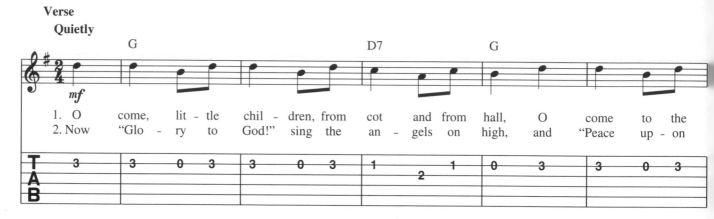

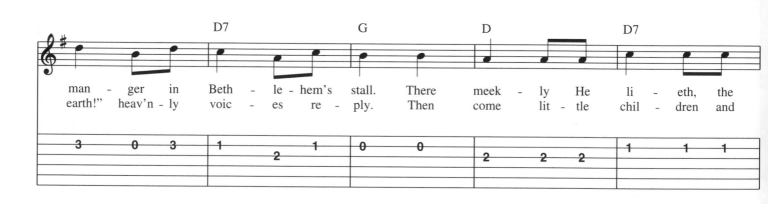

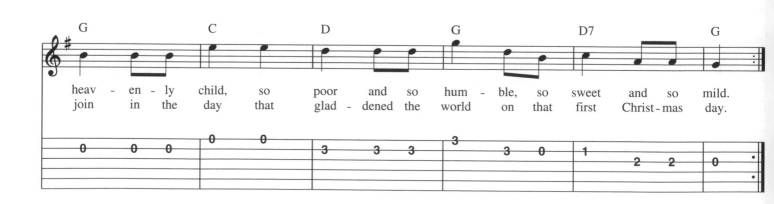

O Come, O Come Immanuel

Plainsong, 13th Century

Words translated by John M. Neale and Henry S. Coffin

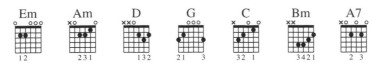

Strum Pattern: 4
Pick Pattern: 5

Verse

Slowly And Expressively

1. O come, O come Im - man - u - el, and ran - som cap - tive
2. *See Additional Lyrics*

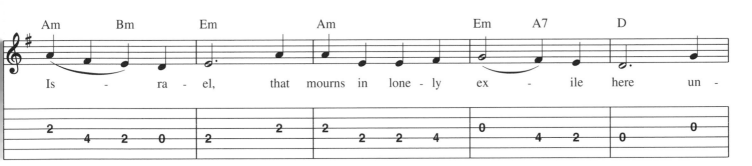

Is - ra - el, that mourns in lone - ly ex - ile here un -

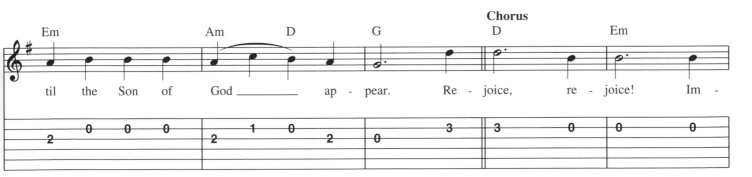

Chorus

til the Son of God ap - pear. Re - joice, re - joice! Im -

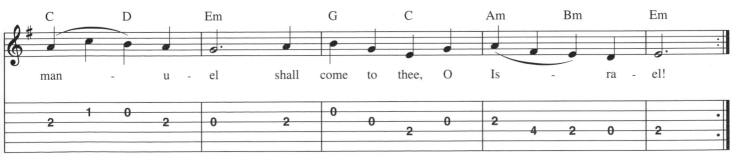

man - u - el shall come to thee, O Is - ra - el!

Additional Lyrics

2. O come, Thou Key Of David, come
And open wide our heav'nly home.
Make safe the way that leads on high
And close the path to misery.

O Hearken Ye

Lyric by Wihla Hutson
Music by Alfred Burt

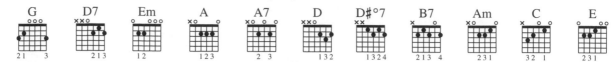

Strum Pattern: 4
Pick Pattern: 3

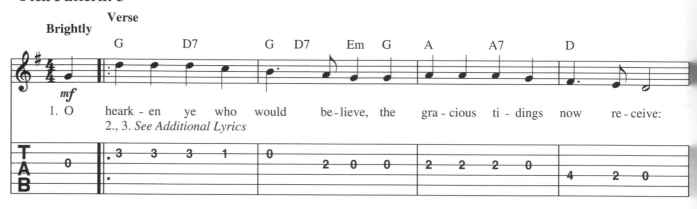

Brightly / Verse

1. O heark-en ye who would be-lieve, the gra-cious ti-dings now re-ceive:
2., 3. *See Additional Lyrics*

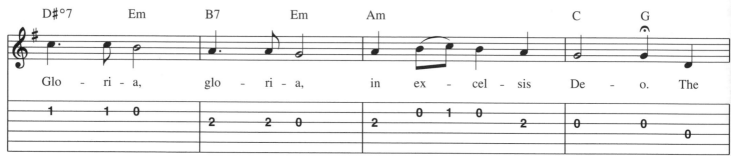

Glo - ri - a, glo - ri - a, in ex - cel - sis De - o. The

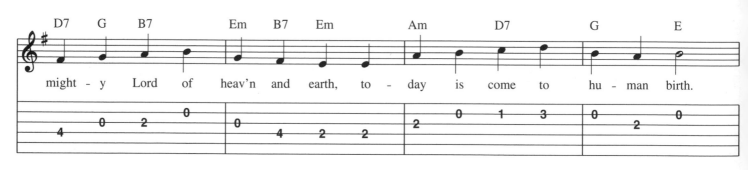

might - y Lord of heav'n and earth, to - day is come to hu - man birth.

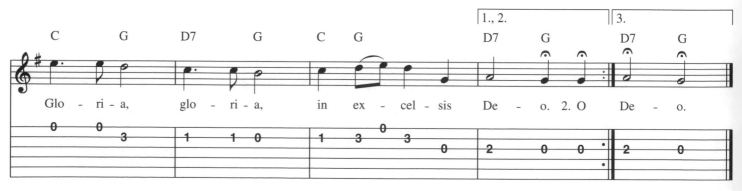

Glo - ri - a, glo - ri - a, in ex - cel - sis De - o. 2. O De - o.

Additional Lyrics

2. O hearken, ye who long for peace,
   Your troubled searching now may cease.
   Gloria, gloria, in excelsis Deo.
   For at his cradle you shall find
   God's healing grace for all mankind.
   Gloria, gloria, in excelsis Deo.

3. O hearken, ye who long for love,
   And turn your hearts to God above.
   Gloria, gloria, in excelsis Deo.
   The angel's song the wonder tells:
   New Love Incarnate with us dwells.
   Gloria, gloria, in excelsis Deo.

O Holy Night

French Words by Placide Cappeau
English Words by John S. Dwight
Music by Adolphe Adam

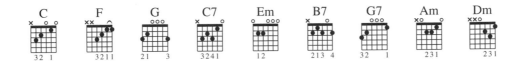

Strum Pattern: 7, 9
Pick Pattern: 7, 9

Verse
Slow And Flowing

1. O Ho - ly night _____ the stars are bright - ly shin - ing, it is the
2. Tru - ly He taught us to love _____ one an - oth - er. His law is

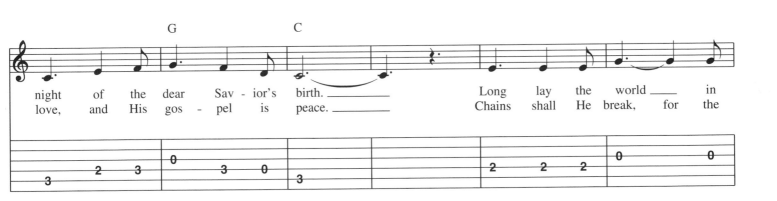

night of the dear Sav - ior's birth. _____ Long lay the world _____ in
love, and His gos - pel is peace. _____ Chains shall He break, for the

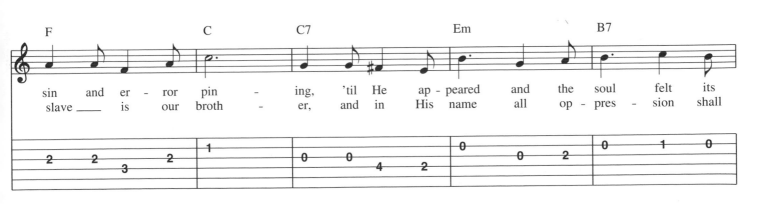

sin and er - ror pin - ing, 'til He ap - peared and the soul felt its
slave _____ is our broth - er, and in His name all op - pres - sion shall

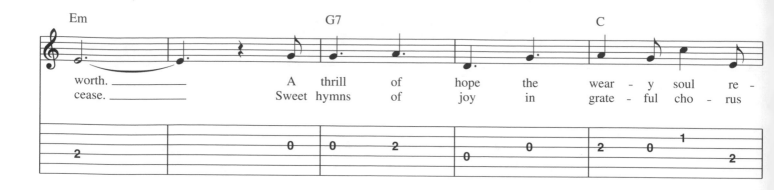

worth. _____ A thrill of hope the wear - y soul re -
cease. _____ Sweet hymns of joy in grate - ful cho - rus

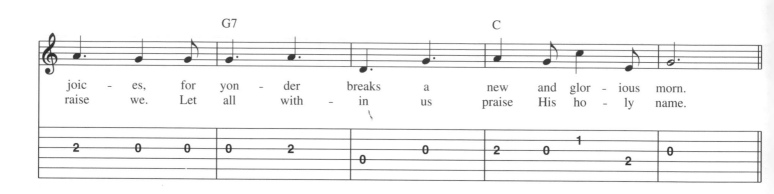

joic - es, for yon - der breaks a new and glor - ious morn.
raise we. Let all with - in us praise His ho - ly name.

Chorus

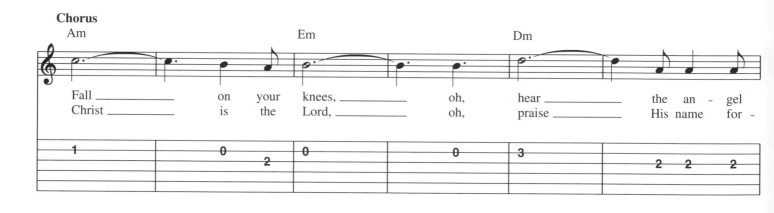

Fall _____ on your knees, _____ oh, hear _____ the an - gel
Christ _____ is the Lord, _____ oh, praise _____ His name for -

voic - es! O night _____ di - vine, _____ O
ev - er! His pow'r _____ and glo - ry

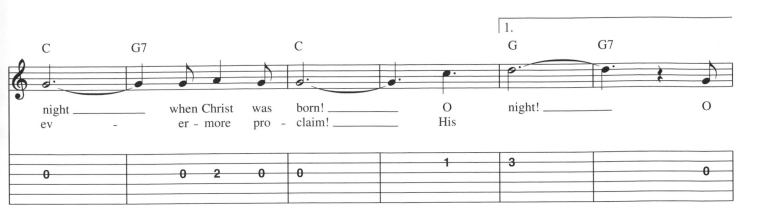

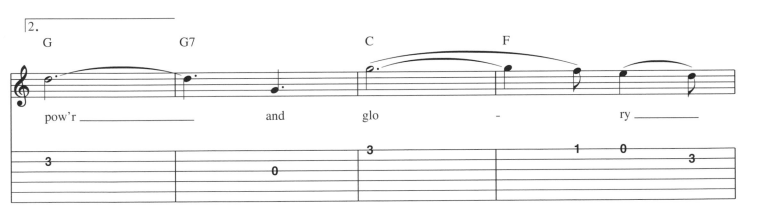

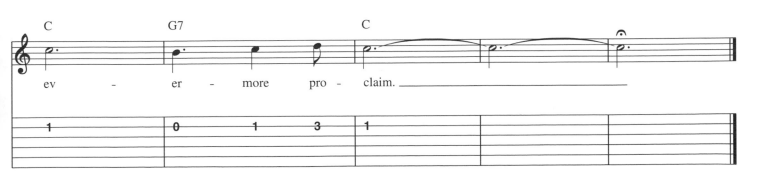

O Little Town of Bethlehem

Words by Phillips Brooks
Music by Lewis H. Redner

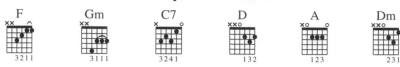

Strum Pattern: 4
Pick Pattern: 5

Verse
Quietly

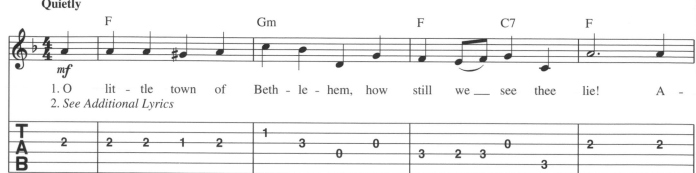

1. O lit - tle town of Beth - le - hem, how still we __ see thee lie! A -
2. *See Additional Lyrics*

bove thy deep and dream - less sleep, the si - lent __ stars go by; yet

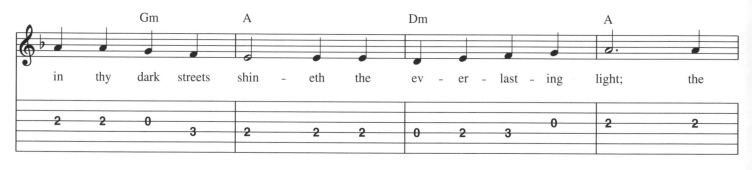

in thy dark streets shin - eth the ev - er - last - ing light; the

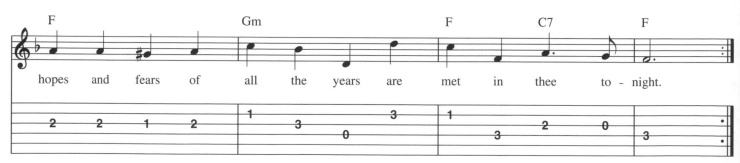

hopes and fears of all the years are met in thee to - night.

Additional Lyrics

2. For Christ is born of Mary, and gathered all above.
While mortals sleep the angels keep
Their watch of wond'ring love.
O morning stars, together proclaim the holy birth!
And praises sing to God the King,
And peace to men on earth!

O Sanctissima

Sicilian Carol

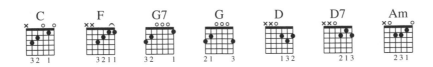

Strum Pattern: 4
Pick Pattern: 3

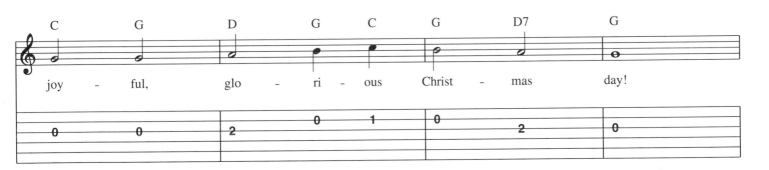

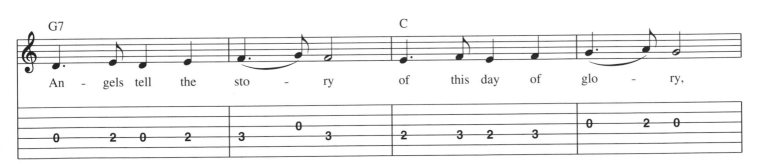

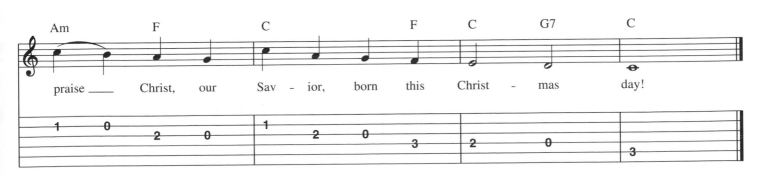

Old Toy Trains

Words and Music by Roger Miller

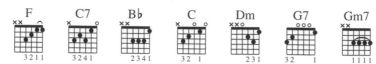

Strum Pattern: 3
Pick Pattern: 3

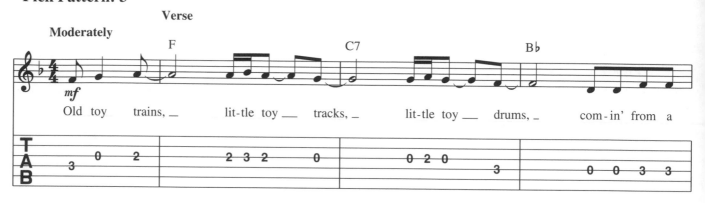

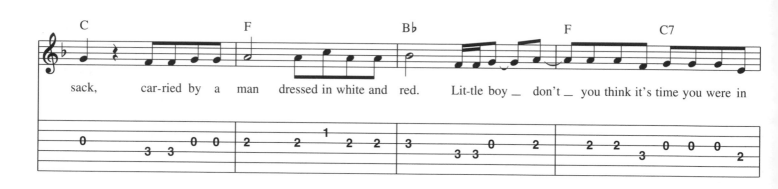

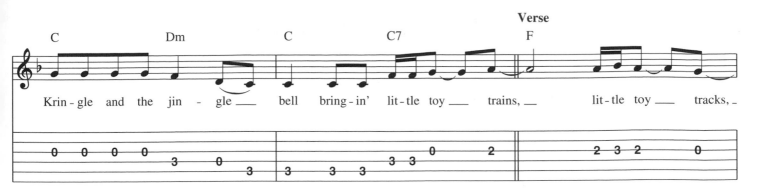

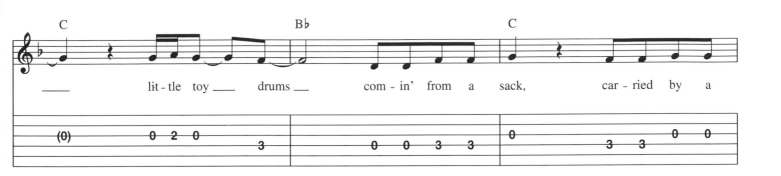

On Christmas Night

Sussex Carol

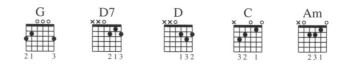

Strum Pattern: 8
Pick Pattern: 8

Verse
Moderately Slow

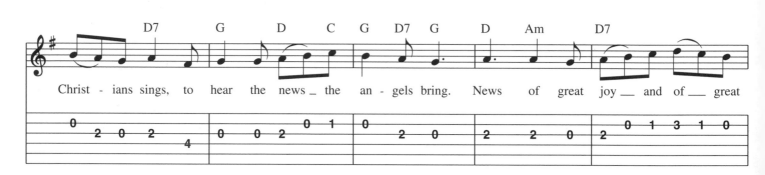

1. On Christ-mas Night, true Christ - ians sings, to hear the news __ the an - gels bring. Christ-mas Night, true
2., 3., 4. *See Additional Lyrics*

Christ - ians sings, to hear the news __ the an - gels bring. News of great joy __ and of __ great

mirth, ti - dings of our dear Sav - ior's birth. _____

Additional Lyrics

2. The King of Kings to us is giv'n,
   The Lord of earth and King of heav'n;
   The King of Kings to us is giv'n,
   The Lord of earth and King of Heav'n;
   Angels and men with joy may sing
   Of blest Jesus, their newborn King.

3. So how on earth can men be sad,
   When Jesus comes to make us glad?
   So how on earth can man be sad,
   When Jesus comes to make us glad?
   From all our sins to set us free,
   Buying for us our liberty.

4. From out the darkness have we light,
   Which makes the angels sing this night.
   From out the darkness have we light,
   Which makes the angels sing this night.
   "Glory to God, His peace to men,
   And good will, evermore! Amen."

Once in Royal David's City

Words by Cecil F. Alexander
Music by Henry J. Gauntlett

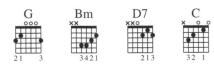

Strum Pattern: 4
Pick Pattern: 5

Verse
Quietly

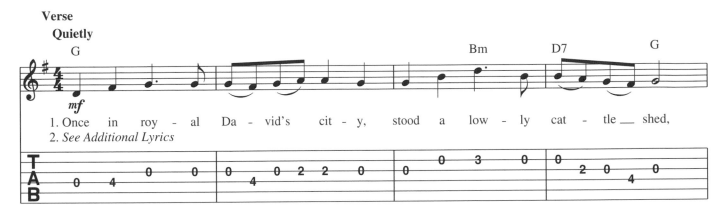

1. Once in roy - al Da - vid's cit - y, stood a low - ly cat - tle __ shed,
2. *See Additional Lyrics*

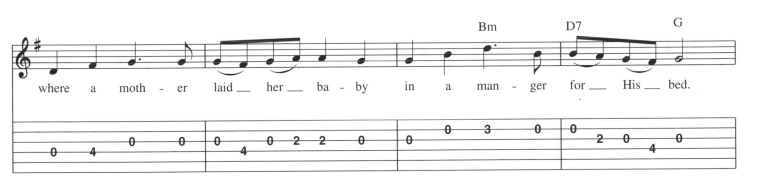

where a moth - er laid __ her __ ba - by in a man - ger for __ His __ bed.

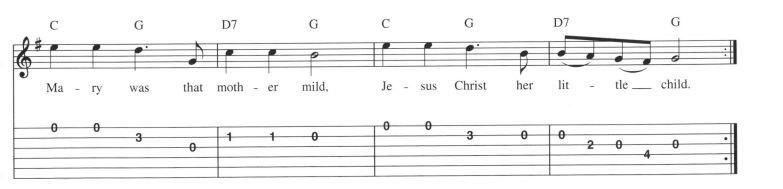

Ma - ry was that moth - er mild, Je - sus Christ her lit - tle __ child.

Additional Lyrics

2. And our eyes at last shall see Him,
   Through His own redeeming love.
   For that child so dear and gentle
   Is our Lord in heav'n above.
   And He leads His children on
   To the place where He is gone.

One for the Little Bitty Baby
(Go Where I Send Thee)

Spiritual Arranged by Ronnie Gilbert, Lee Hays, Fred Hellerman and Pete Seeger

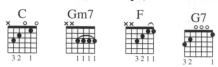

Strum Pattern: 4
Pick Pattern: 3

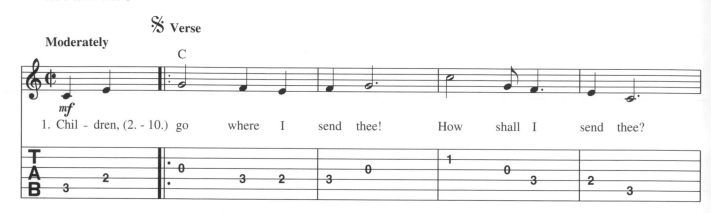

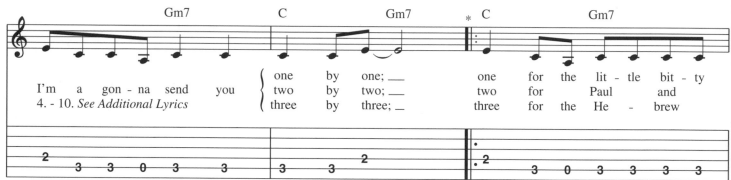

* Repeat as needed, from 2nd verse on, reading up,
until all previous verses have been sung.

Additional Lyrics

4. I'm a-gonna send you four by four;
   four for the four that stood by the door,

5. I'm a-gonna send you five by five;
   five for the gospel preachers,

6. I'm a-gonna send you six by six;
   six for the six that never got fixed,

7. I'm a-gonna send you seven by seven;
   seven for the seven that never got to heaven,

8. I'm a-gonna send you eight by eight;
   eight for the eight that stood at the gate,

9. I'm a-gonna send you nine by nine;
   nine for the nine all dressed so fine,

10. I'm a-gonna send you ten by ten;
    ten for the ten commandments,

Parade of the Wooden Soldiers

English Lyrics by Ballard MacDonald
Music by Leon Jessel

Strum Pattern: 2
Pick Pattern: 3

185

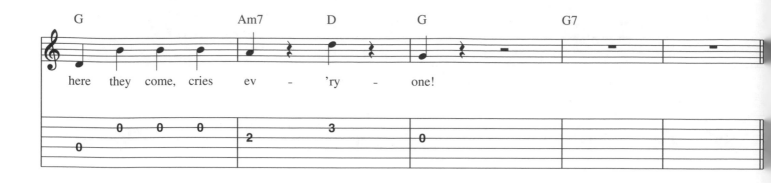

here they come, cries ev - 'ry - one!

Chorus

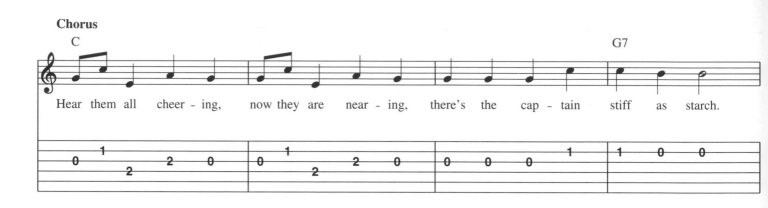

Hear them all cheer - ing, now they are near - ing, there's the cap - tain stiff as starch.

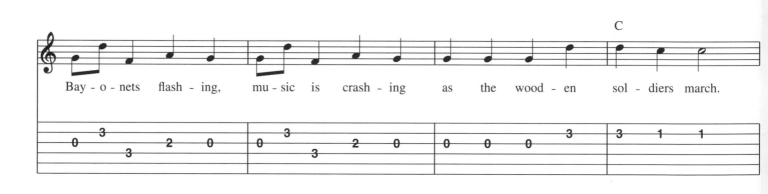

Bay - o - nets flash - ing, mu - sic is crash - ing as the wood - en sol - diers march.

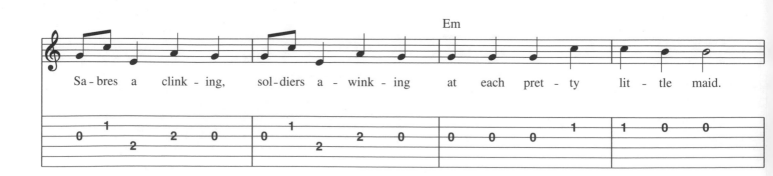

Sa - bres a clink - ing, sol - diers a - wink - ing at each pret - ty lit - tle maid.

Here they come! Here they come! Here they come! Here they come! Wood - en sol-diers on pa - rade.

Day-light is creep - ing, dol - lies are sleep - ing in the toy - shop win - dow fast.

Sol-diers so jol - ly, think of each dol - ly dream - ing of the night that's past.

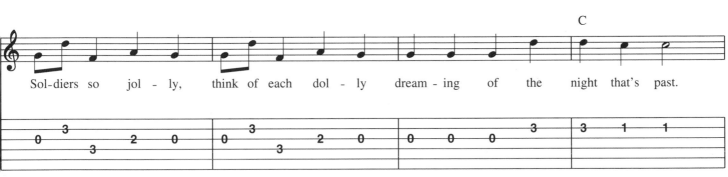

When in the morn - ing, with-out a warn - ing, toy - man pulls the win - dow shade,

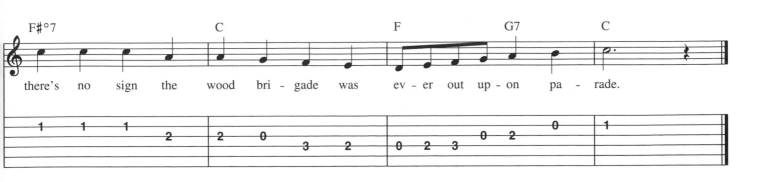

there's no sign the wood bri - gade was ev - er out up - on pa - rade.

Pat-A-Pan
(Willie, Take Your Little Drum)

Words and Music by Bernard de la Monnoye

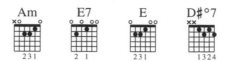

Strum Pattern: 2, 3
Pick Pattern: 2, 3

Verse
Very Fast

1. Wil - lie take your lit - tle drum. Ro - bin, bring your flute, and
2., 3. *See Additional Lyrics*

come. Aren't they fun to play up - on? Tu - re - lu - re - lu, pat - a - pat - a -

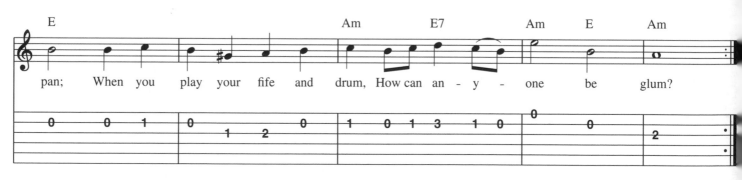

pan; When you play your fife and drum, How can an - y - one be glum?

Additional Lyrics

2. When the men of olden days
   Gave the King of Kings their praise,
   They had pipes to play upon.
   Tu-re-lu-re-lu, pat-a-pat-a-pan.
   And also the drums they'd play.
   Full of joy, on Christmas Day.

3. God and man today become
   Closely joined as flute and drum.
   Let the joyous tune play on!
   Tu-re-lu-re-lu, pat-a-pat-a-pan.
   As the instruments you play,
   We will sing, this Christmas Day.

Poor Little Jesus

Arranged by Ronnie Gilbert, Lee Hays, Fred Hellerman and Pete Seeger

Strum Pattern: 3
Pick Pattern: 4

Moderately

Verse

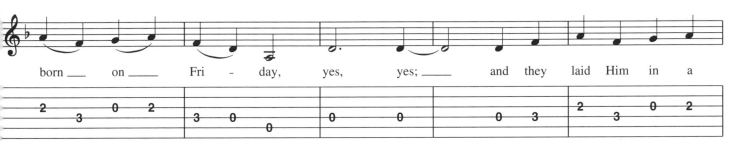

1. It was Poor ___ Lit - tle Je - sus, yes, yes; ___
2., 3., 4. *See Additional Lyrics*

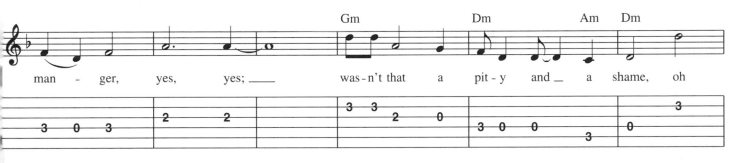

born ___ on ___ Fri - day, yes, yes; ___ and they laid Him in a

man - ger, yes, yes; ___ was - n't that a pit - y and ___ a shame, oh

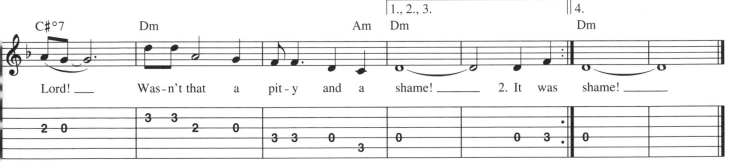

Lord! ___ Was - n't that a pit - y and a shame! ___ 2. It was shame! ___

Additional Lyrics

2. It was Poor Little Jesus, yes, yes;
   Child of Mary, yes, yes;
   Didn't have no shelter, yes, yes;
   Wasn't that a pity and a shame, oh Lord!
   Wasn't that a pity and a shame!

3. It was Poor Little Jesus, yes, yes;
   They whipped Him up a mountain, yes, yes;
   And they hung Him with a robber, yes, yes;
   Wasn't that a pity and a shame, oh Lord!
   Wasn't that a pity and a shame!

4. He was born on Christmas, yes, yes;
   He was born on Christmas, yes, yes;
   Didn't have no cradle, yes, yes;
   Wasn't that a pity and a shame, oh Lord!
   Wasn't that a pity and a shame!

Pretty Paper

Words and Music by Willie Nelson

Strum Pattern: 8, 7
Pick Pattern: 8, 9

Verse
Slowly, With Expression

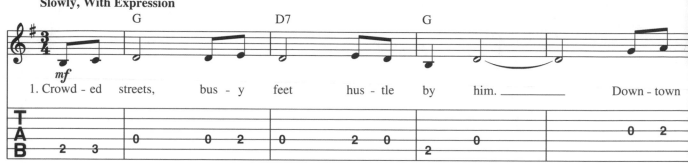

1. Crowd - ed streets, bus - y feet hus - tle by him. _____ Down - town

shop - pers, Christ - mas is nigh. _____ There he sits all a - lone on the

side - walk. _____ Hop - ing that you won't pass him by. _____ 2. Should you

Verse

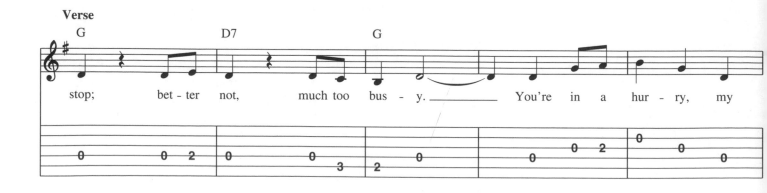

stop; bet - ter not, much too bus - y. _____ You're in a hur - ry, my

how time does fly. _____ In the dis - tance the ring - ing of __ laugh - ter _____

__ and in the midst of the laugh - ter he cries. _____ Pret - ty

Chorus

pa - per, pret - ty rib - bons of blue. _____ Wrap your pres - ents to your dar - ling from

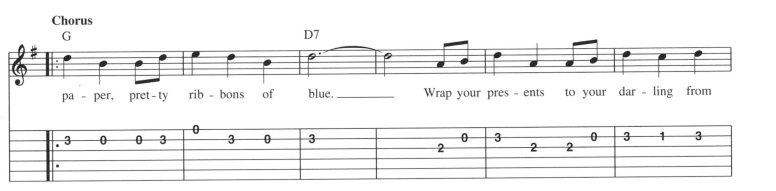

you. _____ Pret - ty pen - cils to write, "I love you." _____ Pret - ty

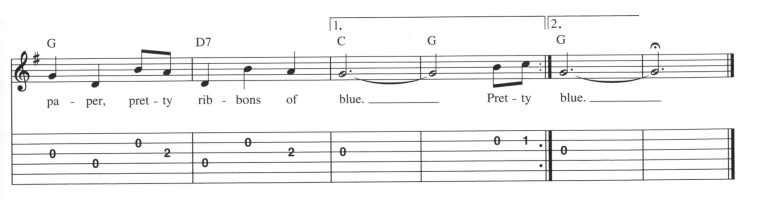

pa - per, pret - ty rib - bons of blue. _____ Pret - ty blue. _____

Rejoice and Be Merry

Gallery Carol

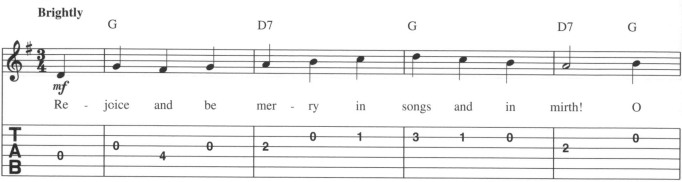

Strum Pattern: 7
Pick Pattern: 7

Verse
Brightly

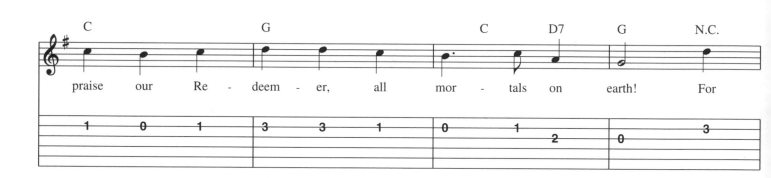

Re - joice and be mer - ry in songs and in mirth! O

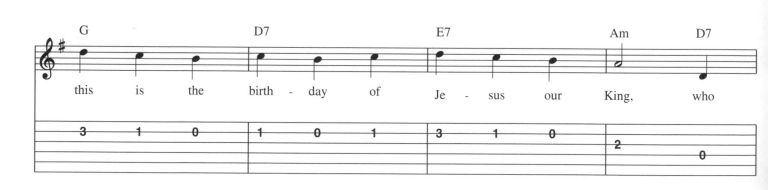

praise our Re - deem - er, all mor - tals on earth! For

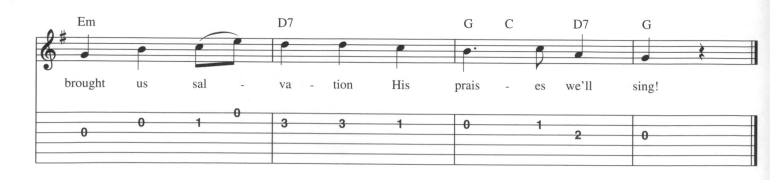

this is the birth - day of Je - sus our King, who

brought us sal - va - tion His prais - es we'll sing!

Rudolph the Red-Nosed Reindeer

Music and Lyrics by Johnny Marks

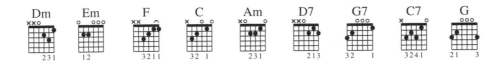

Intro
Freely

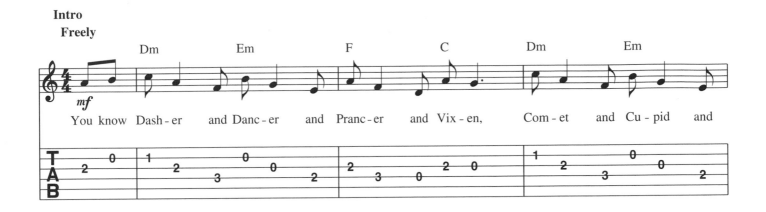

You know Dash-er and Danc-er and Pranc-er and Vix-en, Com-et and Cu-pid and

Don-ner and Blitz-en, but do you re-call the most fa-mous rein-deer of all.

Strum Pattern: 2, 3
Pick Pattern: 2, 3
Verse
Lightly

Ru-dolph, the red-nosed rein-deer had a ver-y shin-y nose,

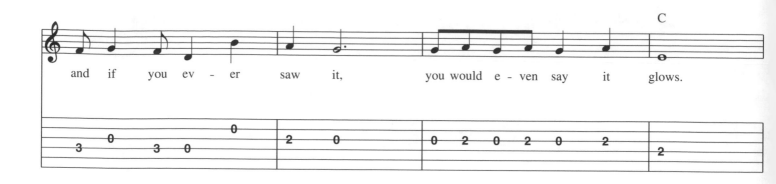

and if you ev - er saw it, you would e - ven say it glows.

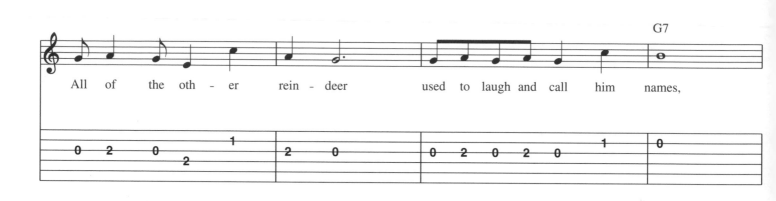

All of the oth - er rein - deer used to laugh and call him names,

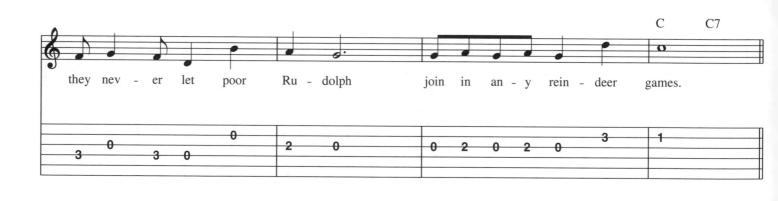

they nev - er let poor Ru - dolph join in an - y rein - deer games.

Bridge

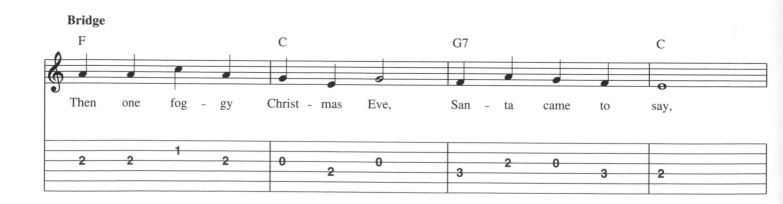

Then one fog - gy Christ - mas Eve, San - ta came to say,

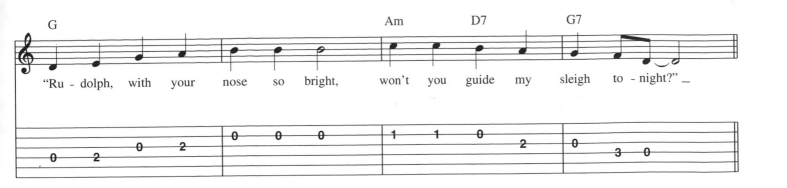

Verse

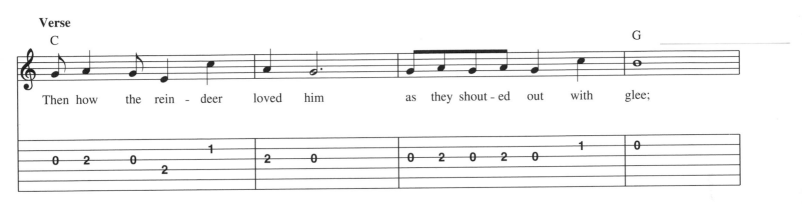

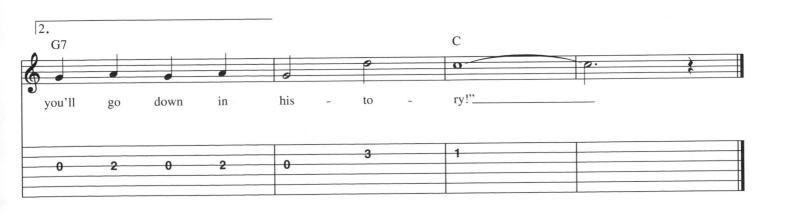

Rise Up, Shepherd, And Follow

African-American Spiritual

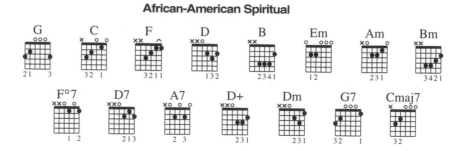

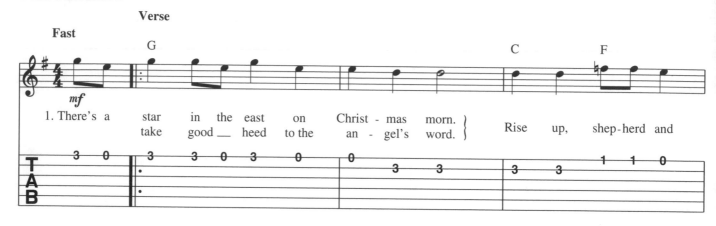

Strum Pattern: 3
Pick Pattern: 3

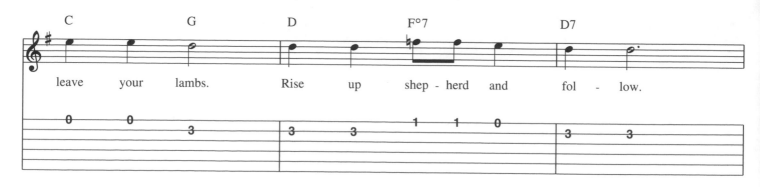

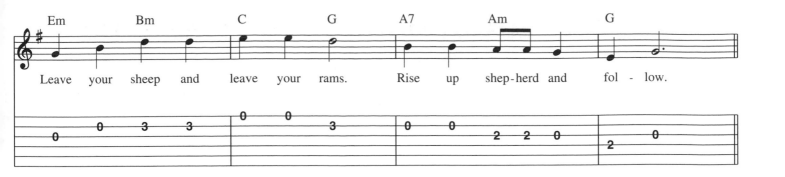

Leave your sheep and leave your rams. Rise up shep-herd and fol - low.

Chorus

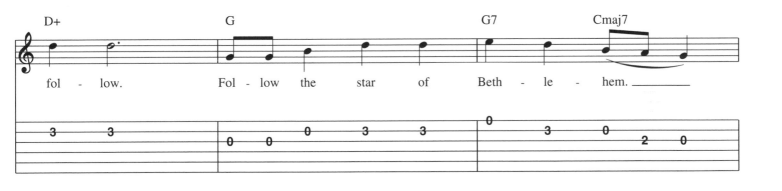

Fol - low, fol - low. Rise up shep - herd and

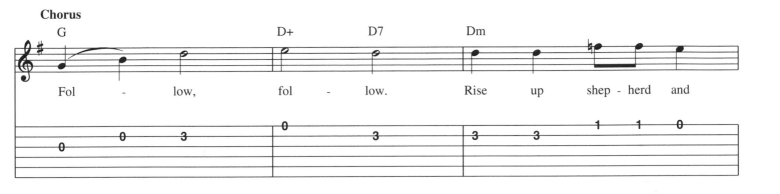

fol - low. Fol - low the star of Beth - le - hem.____

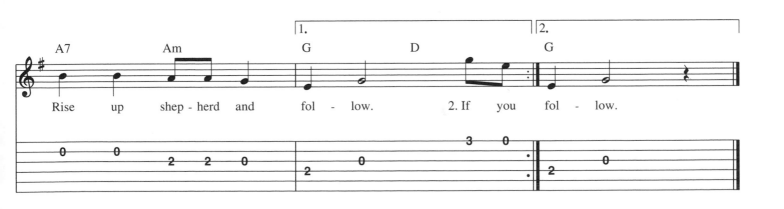

Rise up shep - herd and fol - low. 2. If you fol - low.

Rockin' Around the Christmas Tree

Music and Lyrics by Johnny Marks

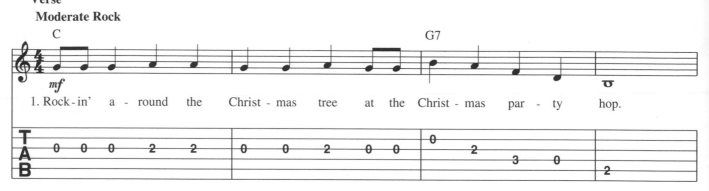

Strum Pattern: 2, 6
Pick Pattern: 4, 6

Verse
Moderate Rock

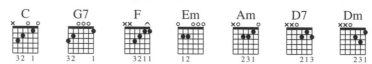

1. Rock-in' a - round the Christ-mas tree at the Christ-mas par-ty hop.

Mis-tle-toe hung where you can see ev-'ry cou-ple tries to stop.

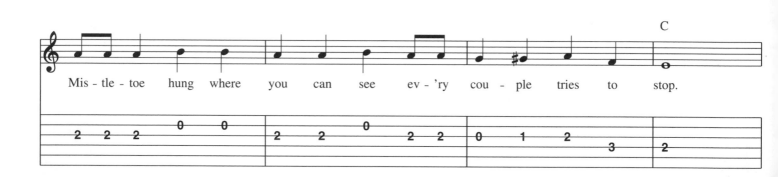

Rock-in' a - round the Christ-mas tree, let the Christ-mas spir-it ring.

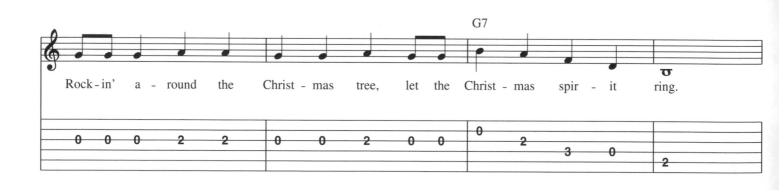

La-ter we'll have some pump-kin pie and we'll do some car-ol - ing.

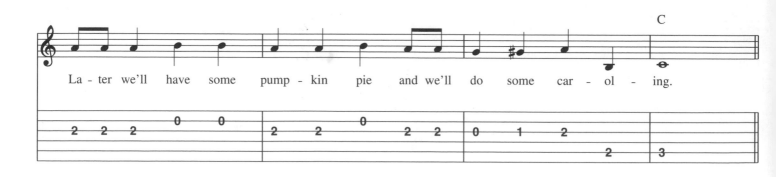

Bridge

You will get a sen - ti - men - tal feel - ing when you hear

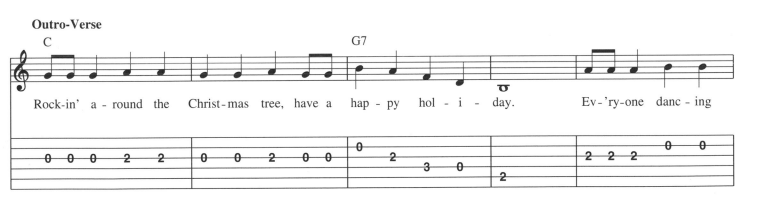

voic - es sing - ing, "Let's be jol - ly. Deck the halls with boughs of hol - ly."

Outro-Verse

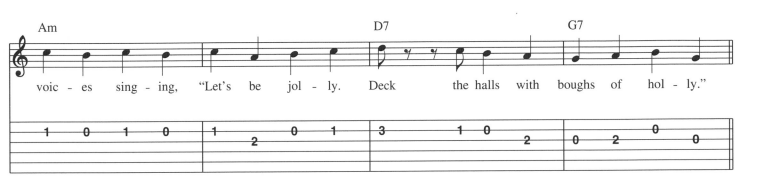

Rock-in' a - round the Christ-mas tree, have a hap - py hol - i - day. Ev-'ry-one danc - ing

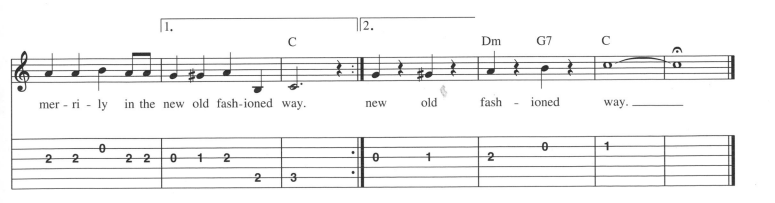

mer - ri - ly in the new old fash-ioned way. new old fash - ioned way. _____

Santa Baby

By Joan Javits, Phil Springer and Tony Springer

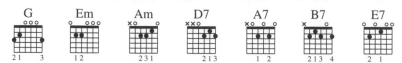

Strum Pattern: 1, 3
Pick Pattern: 2, 3

Intro
Moderately Slow

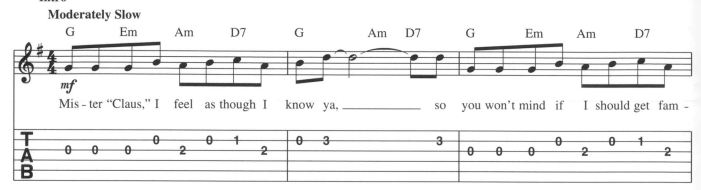

Mis-ter "Claus," I feel as though I know ya, _____ so you won't mind if I should get fam-

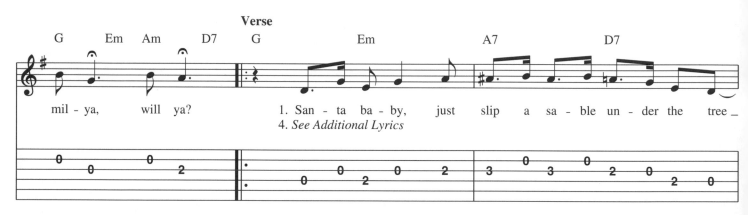

mil - ya, will ya?

1. San - ta ba - by, just slip a sa - ble un - der the tree _
4. *See Additional Lyrics*

_ for me; ___ been an aw - ful good girl. ___ San - ta ba - by, so

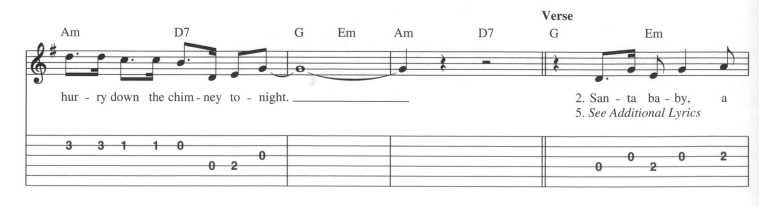

hur - ry down the chim - ney to - night. _____

2. San - ta ba - by, a
5. *See Additional Lyrics*

fif - ty four con - vert - i - ble, too, ____ light blue. __ I'll wait up for you dear. _

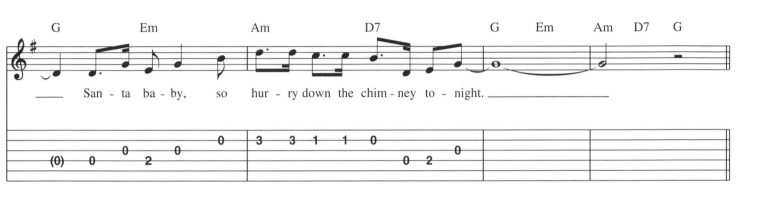

____ San - ta ba - by, so hur - ry down the chim - ney to - night. ____

Bridge

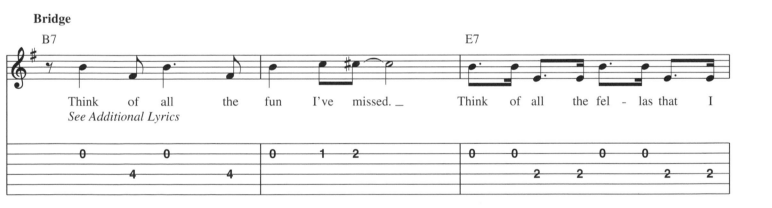

Think of all the fun I've missed. _ Think of all the fel - las that I
See Additional Lyrics

have - n't kissed. _ Next year I could be just as good _ if you check off my

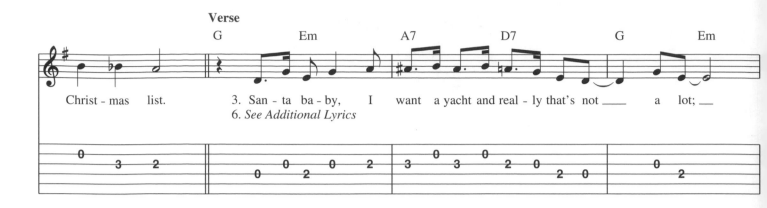

Verse

Christ - mas list.   3. San - ta ba - by, I want a yacht and real - ly that's not _____ a lot; _____
                      6. *See Additional Lyrics*

been an an - gel all year. _____ San - ta ba - by, so hur - ry down the chim - ney to - night. _

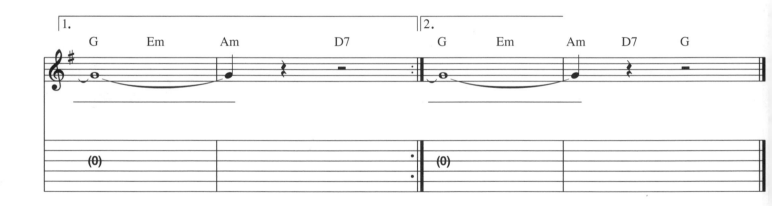

Additional Lyrics

4. Santa baby, one little thing I really do need;
   The deed to a platinum mine.
   Santa honey, so hurry down the chimney tonight.

5. Santa cutie and fill my stocking with a duplex and cheques.
   Sign your X on the line.
   Santa cutie, and hurry down the chimney tonight.

Bridge Come and trim my Christmas tree
   With some decorations at Tiffany.
   I really do believe in you.
   Let's see if you believe in me.

6. Santa baby, forgot to mention one little thing, a ring!
   I don't mean on the phone.
   Santa baby, so hurry down the chimney tonight.

Silent Night

Words by Joseph Mohr
Translated by John F. Young
Music by Franz X. Gruber

Strum Pattern: 7
Pick Pattern: 9

Verse
Quietly

1. Si - lent night, ho - ly night! All is calm,
2., 3. *See Additional Lyrics*

all is bright. Round yon Vir - gin Moth - er and Child.

Ho - ly In - fant so ten - der and mild, sleep in heav - en - ly

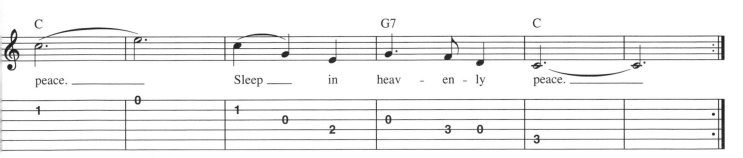

peace. _____ Sleep _____ in heav - en - ly peace. _____

Additional Lyrics

2. Silent night, holy night!
   Shepherds quake at the sight.
   Glories stream from heaven afar.
   Heavenly hosts sing Alleluia.
   Christ the Savior is born!
   Christ the Savior is born!

3. Silent night, holy night!
   Son of God, love's pure light.
   Radiant beams from thy holy face
   With the dawn of redeeming grace,
   Jesus Lord at Thy birth.
   Jesus Lord at Thy birth.

Santa, Bring My Baby Back (To Me)

Words and Music by Claude DeMetruis and Aaron Schroeder

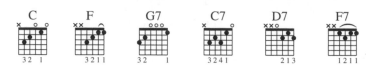

Strum Pattern: 4
Pick Pattern: 3

Verse
Moderate Rock

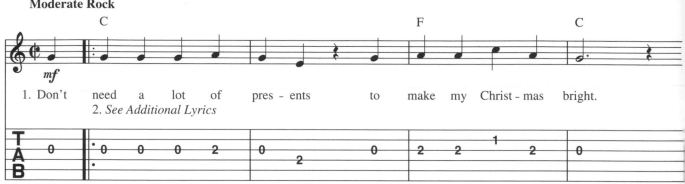

1. Don't need a lot of pres-ents to make my Christ-mas bright.
2. *See Additional Lyrics*

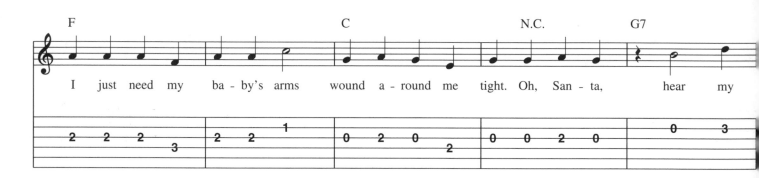

I just need my ba-by's arms wound a-round me tight. Oh, San-ta, hear my

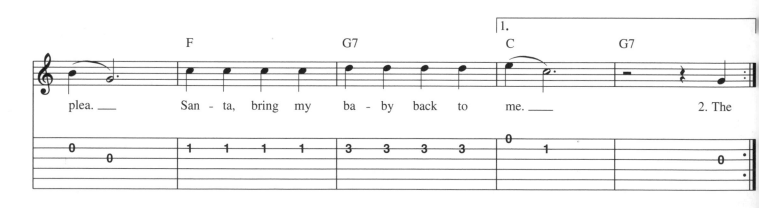

plea. __ San-ta, bring my ba-by back to me. __ 2. The

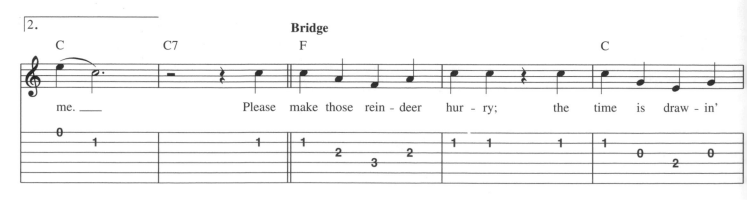

me. __ Please make those rein-deer hur-ry; the time is draw-in'

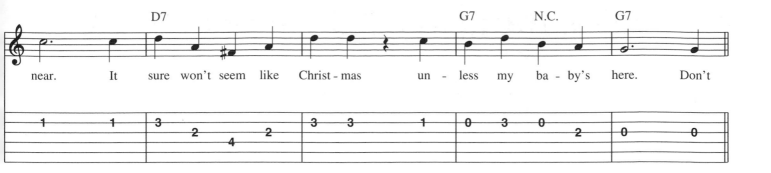

near.   It   sure   won't   seem   like   Christ-mas   un-less   my   ba-by's   here.   Don't

Outro

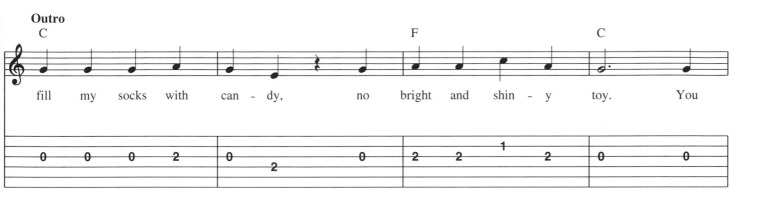

fill   my   socks   with   can-dy,   no   bright   and   shin-y   toy.   You

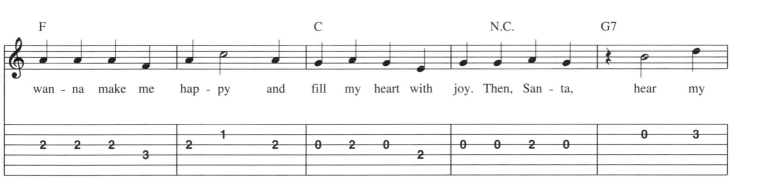

wan-na   make   me   hap-py   and   fill   my   heart   with   joy.   Then,   San-ta,   hear   my

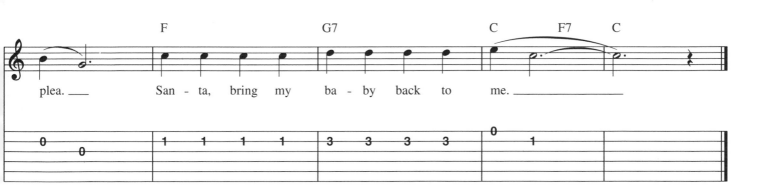

plea. ___   San-ta,   bring   my   ba-by   back   to   me. _____

Additional Lyrics

2. The Christmas tree is ready.
   The candles all aglow.
   But with my baby far away
   What good is mistletoe?
   Oh, Santa, hear my plea.
   Santa, bring my baby back to me.

Shout the Glad Tidings

Traditional

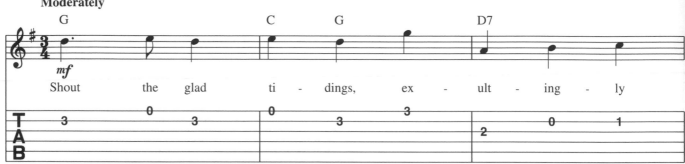

Strum Pattern: 7
Pick Pattern: 7

Chorus
Moderately

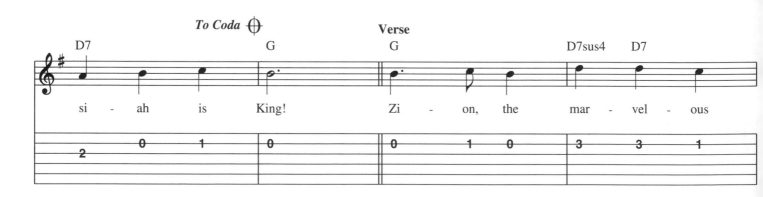

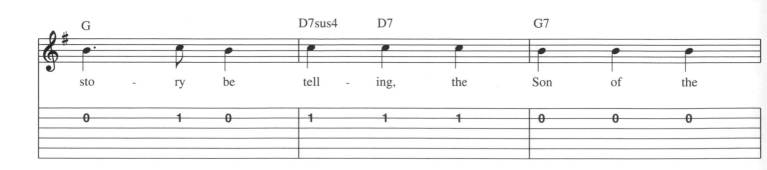

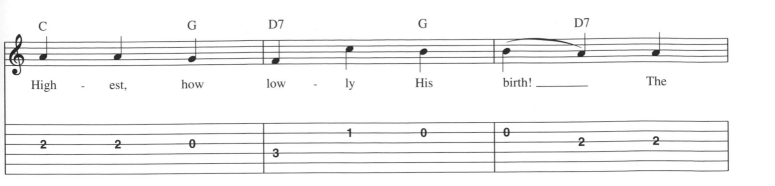

High - est, how low - ly His birth! _____ The

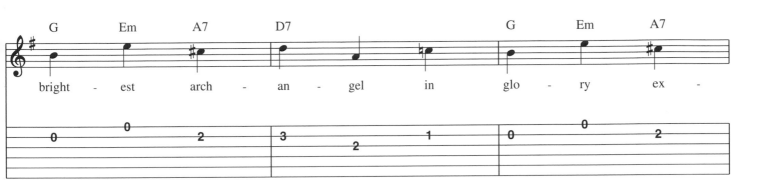

bright - est arch - an - gel in glo - ry ex -

cel - ling, He stoops to re - deem thee, He

D.C. al Coda   ⊕ *Coda*

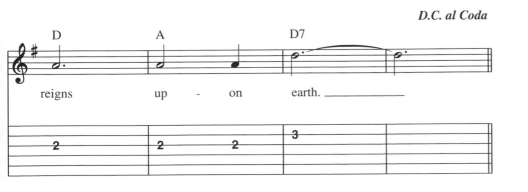

reigns up - on earth. _____

King!

Silver and Gold

Music and Lyrics by Johnny Marks

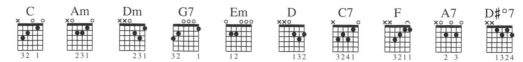

Strum Pattern: 8
Pick Pattern: 8

Verse
Slowly And Expressively

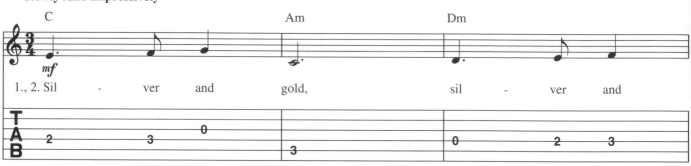

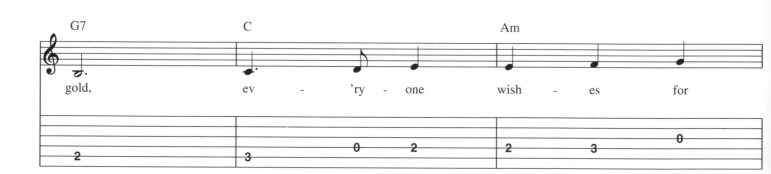

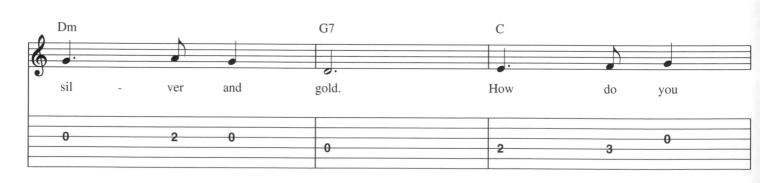

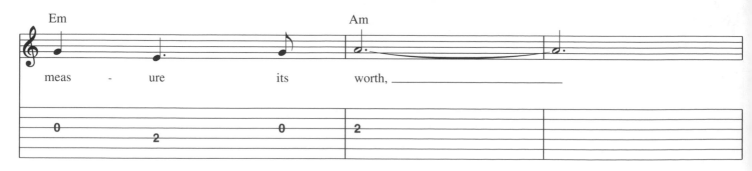

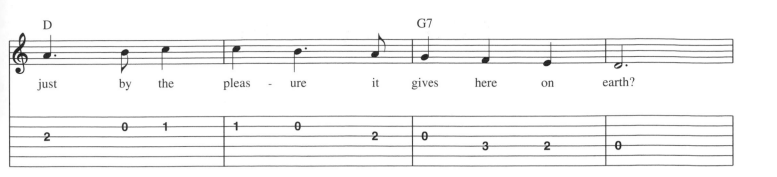

just by the pleas - ure it gives here on earth?

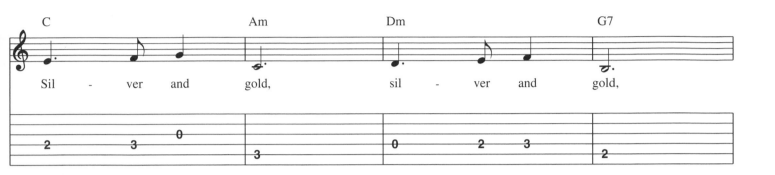

Sil - ver and gold, sil - ver and gold,

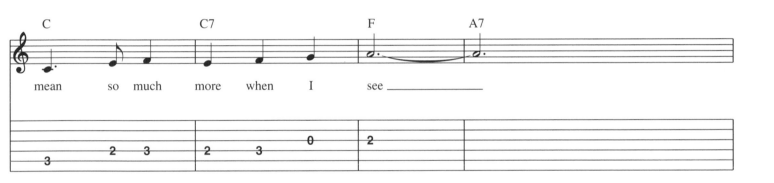

mean so much more when I see _____

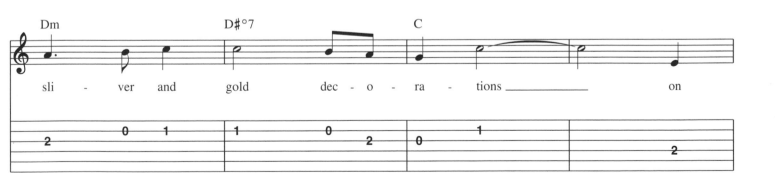

sli - ver and gold dec - o - ra - tions _____ on

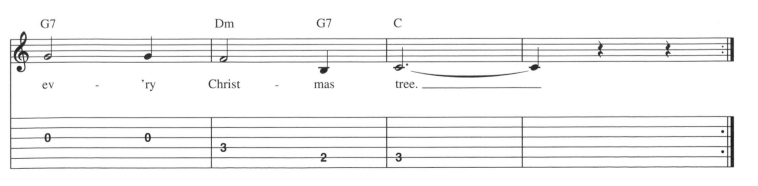

ev - 'ry Christ - mas tree. _____

Silver Bells

from the Paramount Picture THE LEMON DROP KID

Words and Music by Jay Livingston and Ray Evans

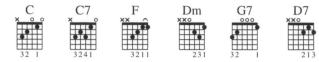

Strum Pattern: 9
Pick Pattern: 8

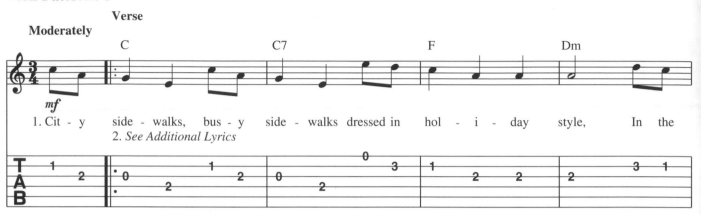

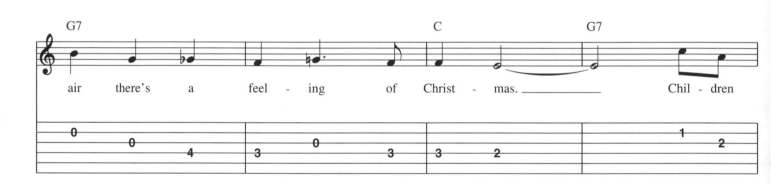

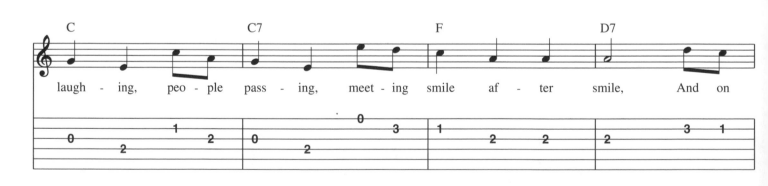

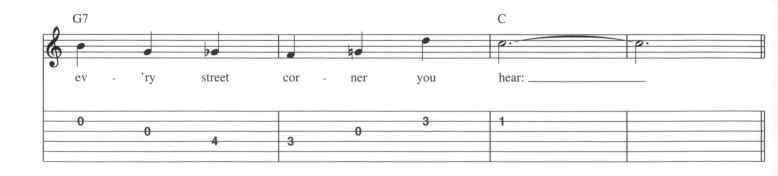

Chorus

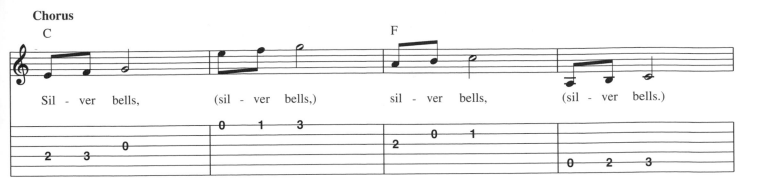

Sil - ver bells, (sil - ver bells,) sil - ver bells, (sil - ver bells.)

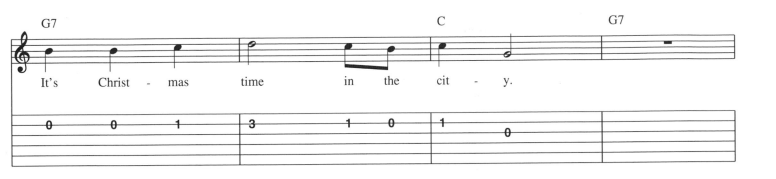

It's Christ - mas time in the cit - y.

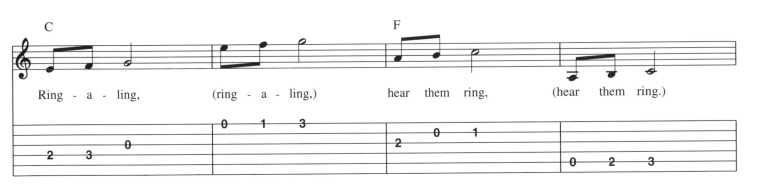

Ring - a - ling, (ring - a - ling,) hear them ring, (hear them ring.)

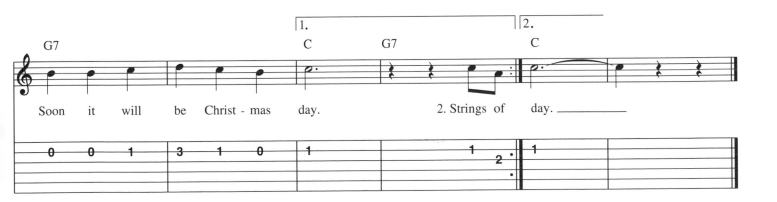

Soon it will be Christ - mas day. 2. Strings of day.

Additional Lyrics

2. Strings of street lights, even stop lights
   Blink a bright red and green,
   As the shoppers rush home with their treasures.
   Hear the snow crunch, see the kids bunch,
   This is Santa's big scene,
   And above all the bustle you hear:

Sing We Now of Christmas

Traditional

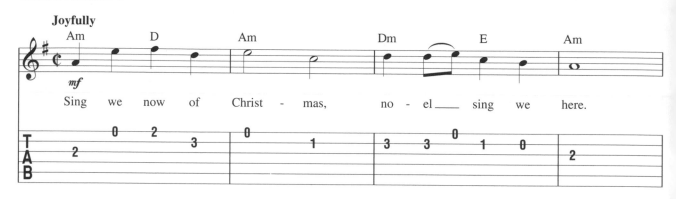

Strum Pattern: 4
Pick Pattern: 4

Joyfully

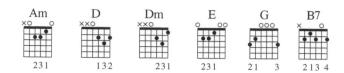

Sing we now of Christ - mas, no - el ___ sing we here.

Sing our grate - ful prais - es, to the ___ maid so dear.

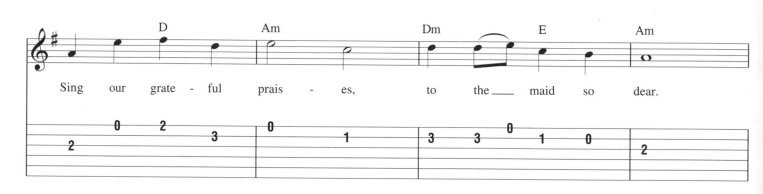

Sing we No - el! The King is born, No - el!

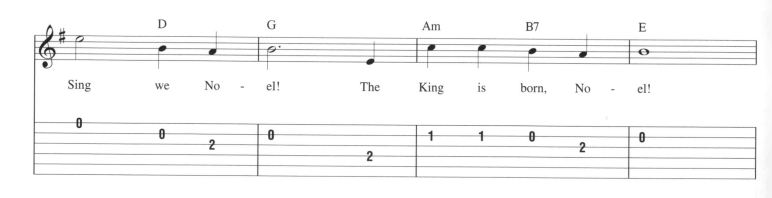

Sing we now of Christ - mas, sing we ___ here No - el.

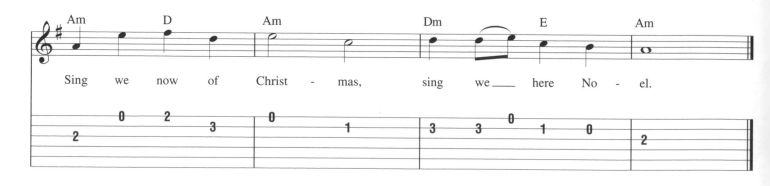

Sleep, Holy Babe

Words by Edward Caswell
Music by J.B. Dykes

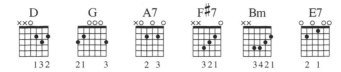

Strum Pattern: 1, 4
Pick Pattern: 1, 4

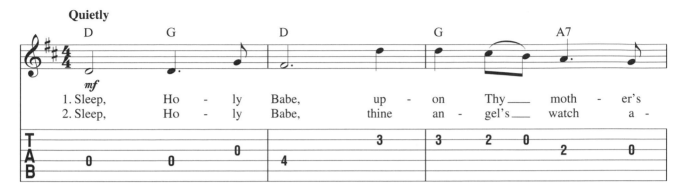

1. Sleep, Ho — ly Babe, up — on Thy____ moth — er's
2. Sleep, Ho — ly Babe, thine an — gel's____ watch a —

breast. Great Lord of earth and sea and sky, how
round, all bend — ing low with fold — ed wings; how be —

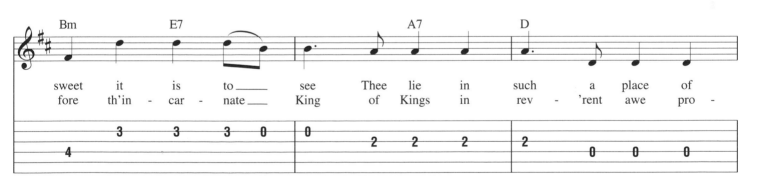

sweet it is to____ see Thee lie in such a place of
fore th'in — car — nate____ King of Kings in rev — 'rent awe pro —

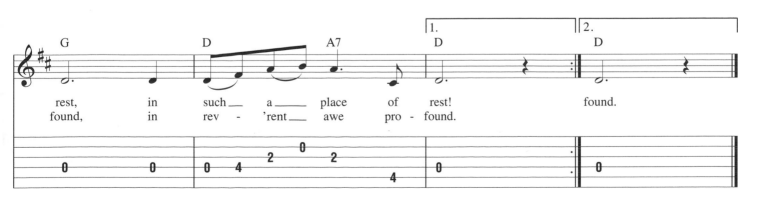

rest, in such___ a ___ place of rest!   found.
found, in rev — 'rent ___ awe pro — found.

The Snow Lay on the Ground

Traditional Irish Carol

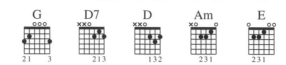

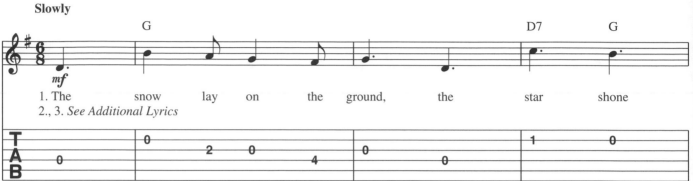

Strum Pattern: 7
Pick Pattern: 9

Verse
Slowly

1. The snow lay on the ground, the star shone
2., 3. *See Additional Lyrics*

bright when Christ our Lord was born on

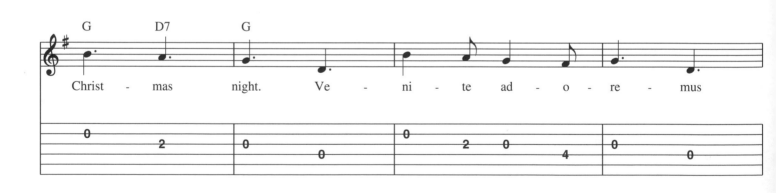

Christ - mas night. Ve - ni - te ad - o - re - mus

Do - mi - num; Ve - ni - te ad - o - re - mus

Chorus

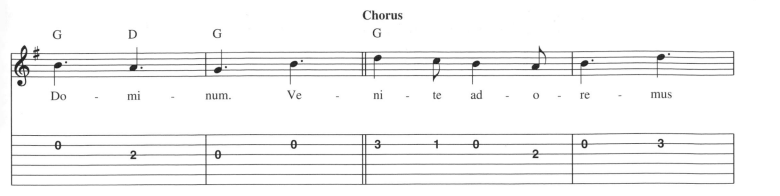

Do - mi - num. Ve - ni - te ad - o - re - mus

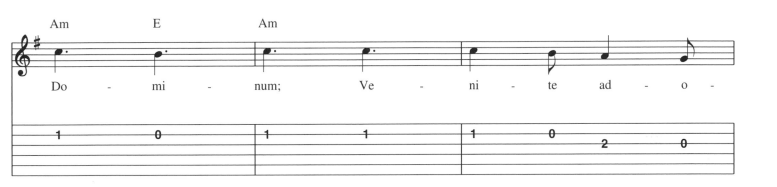

Do - mi - num; Ve - ni - te ad - o -

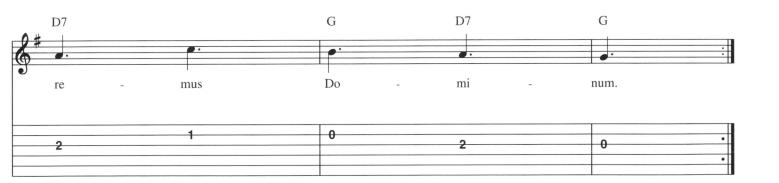

re - mus Do - mi - num.

Additional Lyrics

2. 'Twas Mary, virgin pure of Holy Anne
   That brought into this world the God made man.
   She laid him in a stall at Bethlehem.
   The ass and oxen share the roof with them.

3. Saint Joseph too, was by to tend the Child,
   To guard him and protect his mother mild.
   The angels hovered 'round and sang this song;
   Venite adoremus Dominum.

The Star Carol

Lyric by Wihla Hutson
Music by Alfred Burt

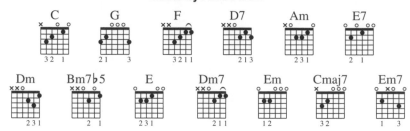

Strum Pattern: 8
Pick Pattern: 8

Verse
Tenderly

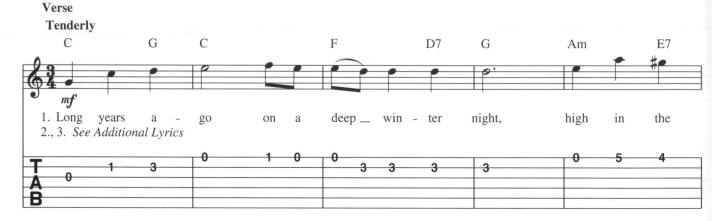

1. Long years a - go on a deep __ win - ter night, high in the
2., 3. *See Additional Lyrics*

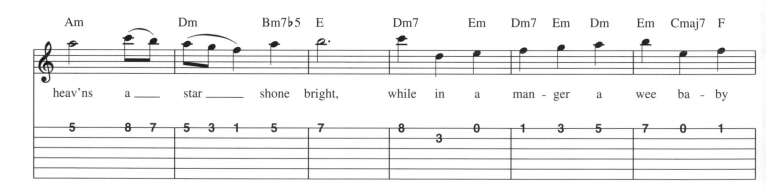

heav'ns a __ star __ shone bright, while in a man - ger a wee ba - by

lay. Sweet - ly a - sleep on a bed of hay. Thee.

Additional Lyrics

2. Jesus, the Lord was that Baby so small,
Laid down to sleep in a humble stall;
Then came the star and it stood overhead,
Shedding its light 'round His little bed.

3. Dear Baby Jesus, how tiny Thou art,
I'll make a place for Thee in my heart,
And when the stars in the heavens I see,
Ever and always I'll think of Thee.

Still, Still, Still

Salzburg Melody, c.1819
Traditional Austrian Text

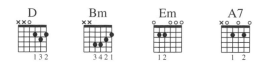

Strum Pattern: 4
Pick Pattern: 3

Verse
Moderately Slow

1. Still, _____ still, _____ still, to _____ sleep is _____ now His _____ will. On
2. *See Additional Lyrics*

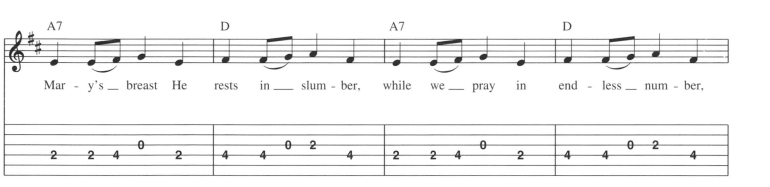

Mar - y's _____ breast He rests in _____ slum - ber, while we _____ pray in end - less _____ num - ber,

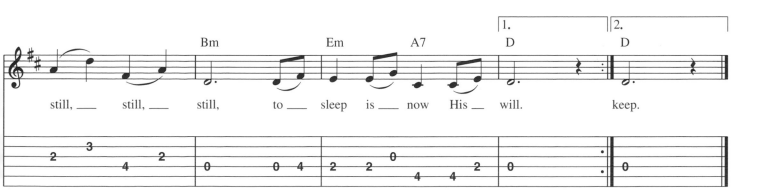

still, _____ still, _____ still, to _____ sleep is _____ now His _____ will. keep.

Additional Lyrics

2. Sleep, sleep, sleep, while we Thy vigil keep.
   And angels come from Heaven singing,
   Songs of jubilation bringing,
   Sleep, sleep, sleep, while we Thy vigil keep.

The Star Carol
(Canzone d'i Zampognari)

English Lyric and Music Adaptation by Peter Seeger

(Based on a Traditional Neapolitan Carol)

Strum Pattern: 8
Pick Pattern: 8

𝄋 Verse

Brightly

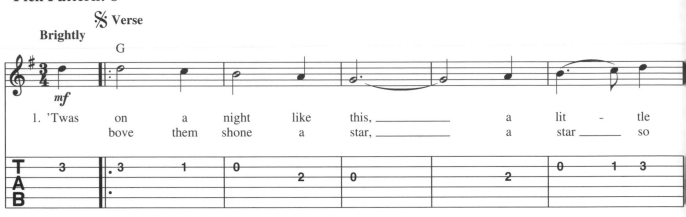

1. 'Twas on a night like this, _____ a lit - tle
'bove them shone like a star, _____ a star _____ so

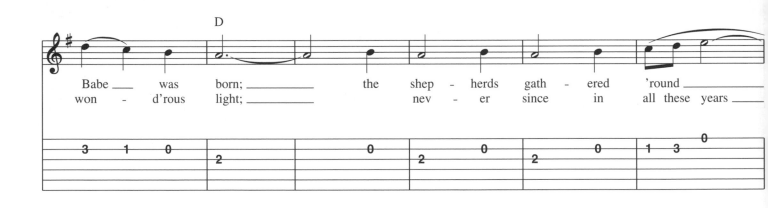

Babe ___ was born; _____ the shep - herds gath - ered 'round _____
won - d'rous light; _____ nev - er since in all these years _____

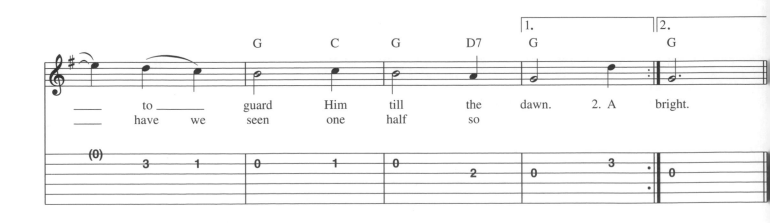

___ to guard Him till the dawn. 2. A bright.
___ have we seen one half so

Chorus

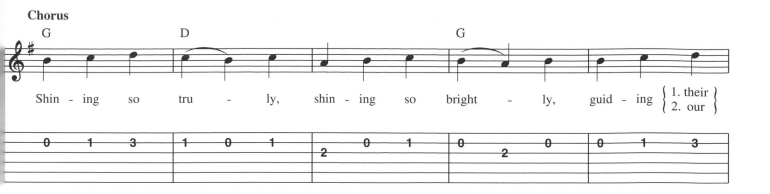

Shin - ing so tru - ly, shin - ing so bright - ly, guid - ing {1. their / 2. our}

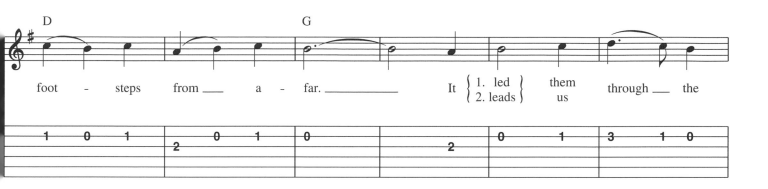

foot - steps from ___ a - far. _____ It {1. led / 2. leads} them us through ___ the

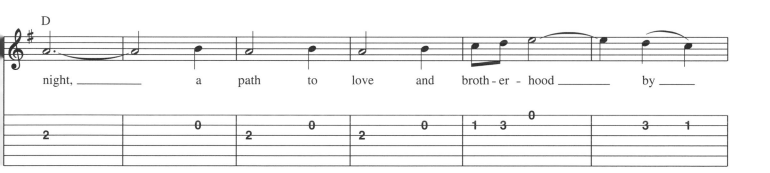

night, _____ a path to love and broth-er-hood _____ by _____

To Coda ⊕   *D.S. al Coda*
                               (take repeat)   ⊕ *Coda*

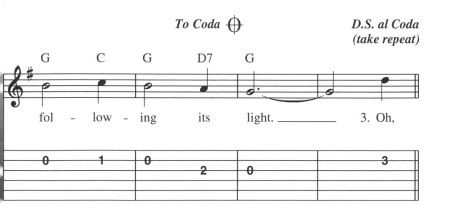

fol - low - ing its light. _____ 3. Oh,

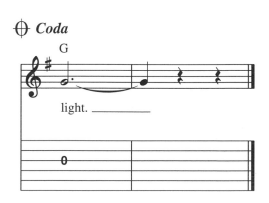

light. _____

Additional Lyrics

3. Oh, come with us tonight,
   And join us on our way;
   For we have found that star once more
   To greet a better day.

4. For though through out our land
   Men search the skies in vain,
   Yet turn their glance within their hearts
   They would find this star again.

Star of the East

Words by George Cooper
Music by Amanda Kennedy

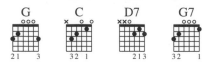

Strum Pattern: 9
Pick Pattern: 9

Verse
Joyfully

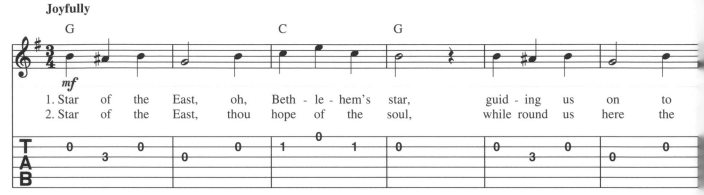

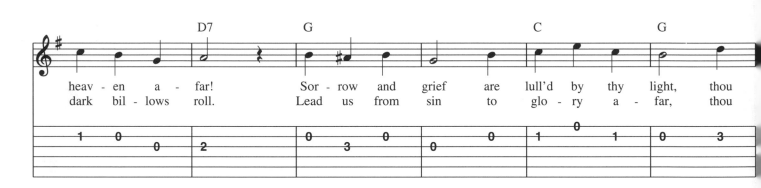

1. Star of the East, oh, Beth - le - hem's star, guid - ing us on to
2. Star of the East, thou hope of the soul, while round us here the

heav - en a - far! Sor - row and grief are lull'd by thy light, thou
dark bil - lows roll. Lead us from sin to glo - ry a - far, thou

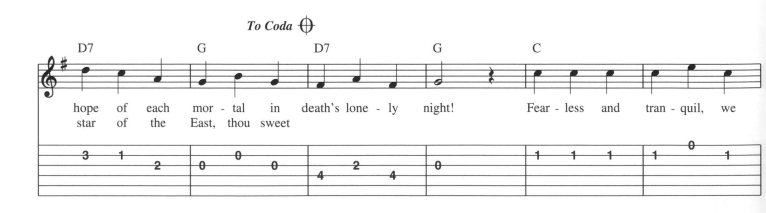

To Coda ⊕

hope of each mor - tal in death's lone - ly night! Fear - less and tran - quil, we
star of the East, thou sweet

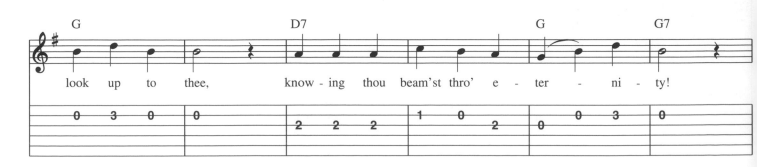

look up to thee, know - ing thou beam'st thro' e - ter - ni - ty!

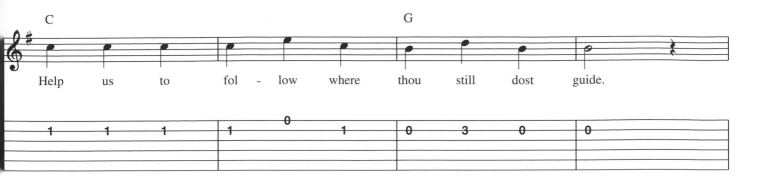

Help us to fol - low where thou still dost guide.

D.C. al Coda

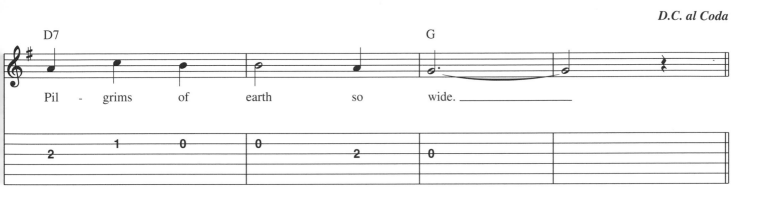

Pil - grims of earth so wide. _____

⊕ *Coda*

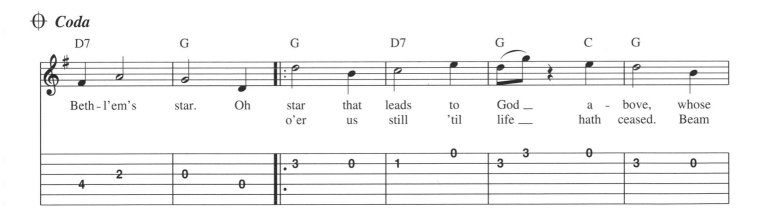

Beth - l'em's star. Oh star that leads to God __ a - bove, whose
o'er us still 'til life __ hath ceased. Beam

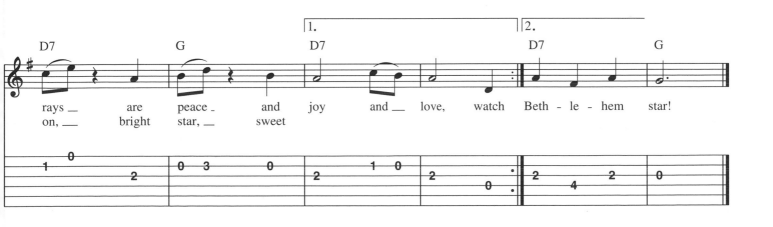

rays __ are peace __ and joy and __ love, watch Beth - le - hem star!
on, __ bright star, __ and sweet

Suzy Snowflake

Words and Music by Sid Tepper and Roy Bennett

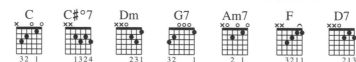

Strum Pattern: 3
Pick Pattern: 3

Verse
Moderately

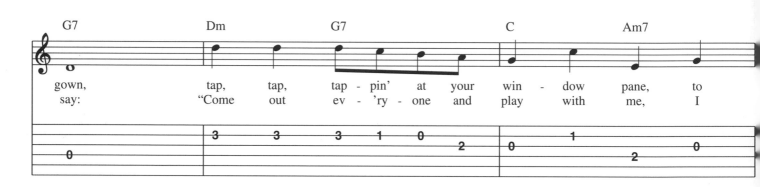

1. Here comes Su - zy Snow - flake, dressed in a snow white
2. Here comes Su - zy Snow - flake, soon you will hear her

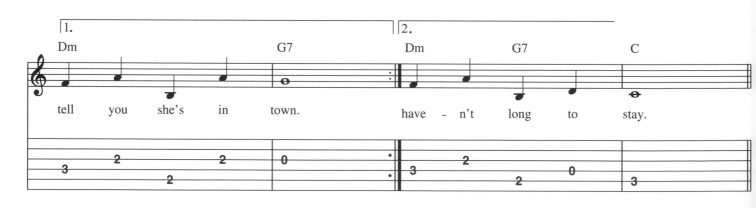

gown, tap, tap, tap - pin' at your win - dow pane, to
say: "Come out ev - 'ry - one and play with me, I

1.

tell you she's in town.

2.

have - n't long to stay.

𝄋 **Bridge**

If you wan - na make a snow - man, I'll help you make one,

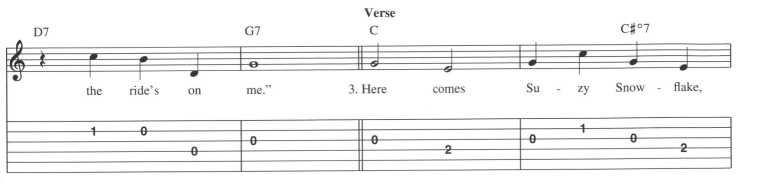

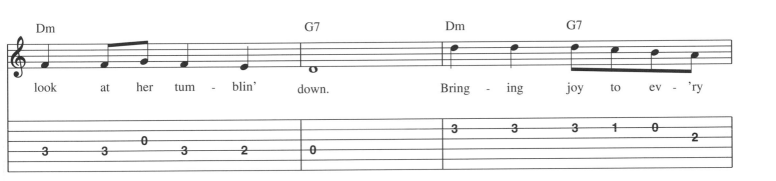

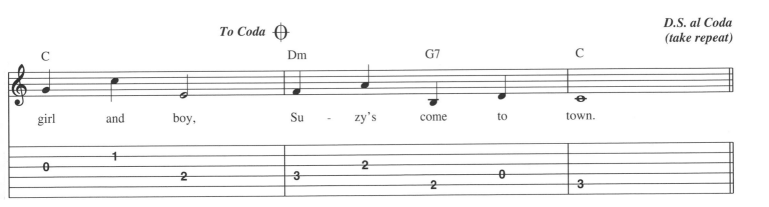

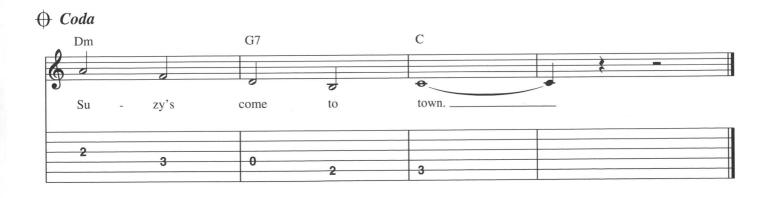

Tennessee Christmas

Words and Music by Amy Grant and Gary Chapman

Strum Pattern: 6
Pick Pattern: 3

Verse
Moderately

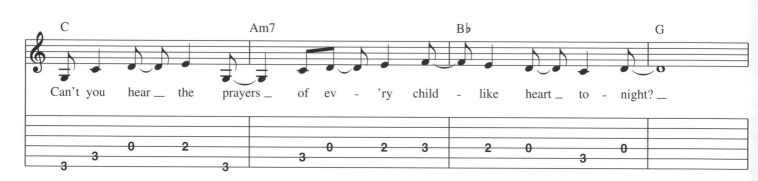

1. Come on weath - er - man __ give us __ a fore - cast snow - y white. __
2. *See Additional Lyrics*

Can't you hear __ the prayers __ of ev - 'ry child - like heart __ to - night? __

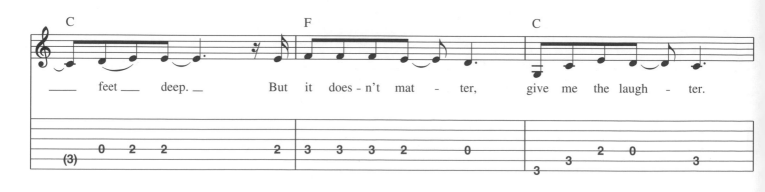

Rock - ies are call - in', Den - ver snow fall - in'. Some - bod - y said __ it's four __

___ feet __ deep. __ But it does - n't mat - ter, give me the laugh - ter.

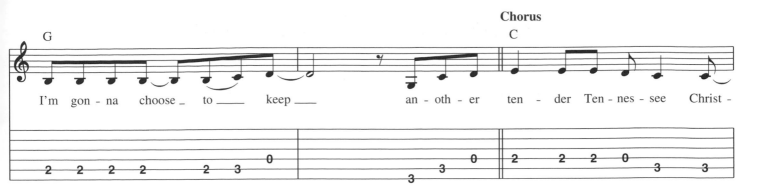

Chorus

I'm gon-na choose_ to_ keep_ an-oth-er ten-der Ten-nes-see Christ-

-mas, the on-ly Christ-mas for me. Where the

love cir-cles a-round_ us like the gifts_ a-round_ our tree._

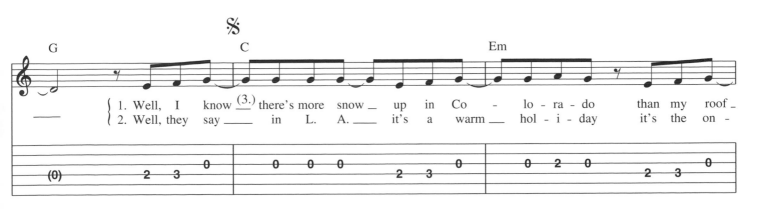

1. Well, I know_ (3.) there's more snow_ up in Co-lo-ra-do than my roof_
2. Well, they say_ in L. A._ it's a warm_ hol-i-day it's the on-

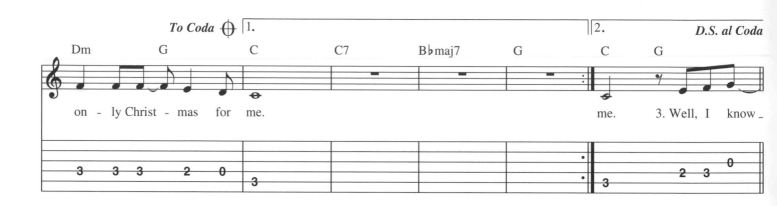

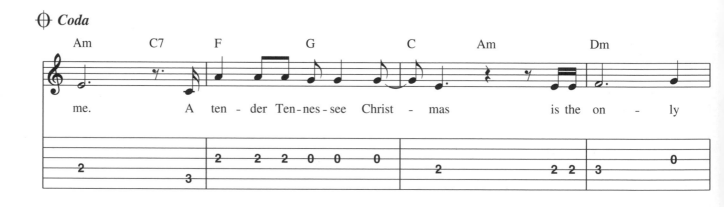

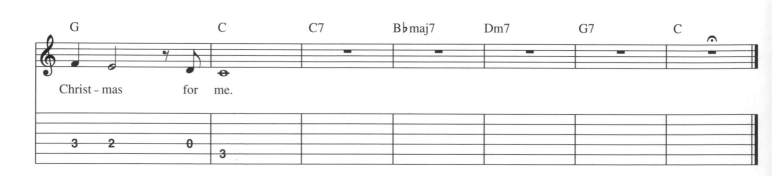

Additional Lyrics

2. Ev'ry now and then I get a wanderin' urge to see,
   Maybe California, maybe tinsel town's for me.
   There's a parade there, we'd have it made there.
   Bring home a tan for New Year's Eve.
   Sure sounds exciting, awfully inviting.
   Still I think I'm gonna keep...

There's a Song in the Air

Words and Music by Josiah G. Holland and Karl P. Harrington

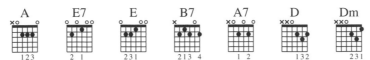

Strum Pattern: 7
Pick Pattern: 9

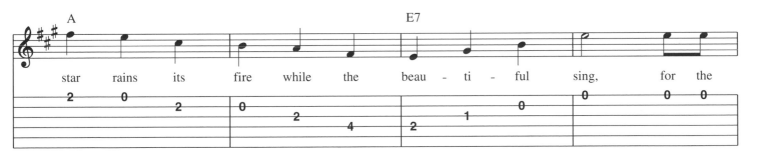

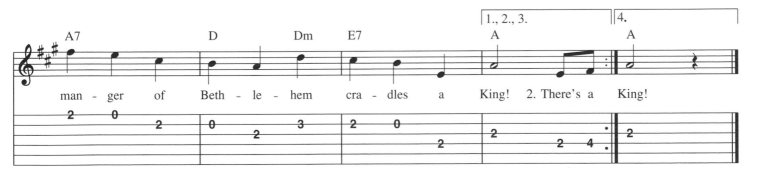

Additional Lyrics

2. There's a tumult of joy o'er the wonderful birth,
   For the Virgin's sweet boy is the lord of the earth.
   Ay! The star rains its fire while the beautiful sing,
   For the manger of Bethlehem cradles a King!

3. In the light of that star lie the ages impearled,
   And that song from afar was swept over the world.
   Ev'ry hearth is a flame and the beautiful sing
   In the homes of the nations that Jesus is King!

4. We rejoice in the light and we echo the song
   That comes down thro' the night from the heavenly throng.
   Ay! We should to the lovely Evangel they bring,
   And we greet in his cradle, our Savior and King!

That Christmas Feeling

Words and Music by Bennie Benjamin and George Weiss

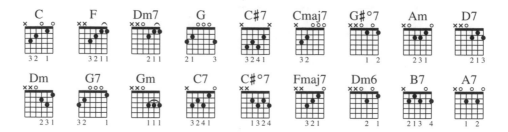

Strum Pattern: 3
Pick Pattern: 3

1., 2. How I love that Christ-mas feel - ing. _____

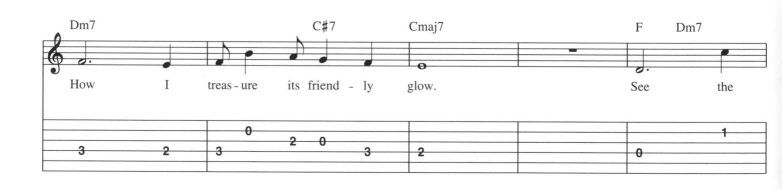

How I treas - ure its friend - ly glow. See the

way a strang - er greets you, _____ just as though you'd met him Christ-mas - es a-

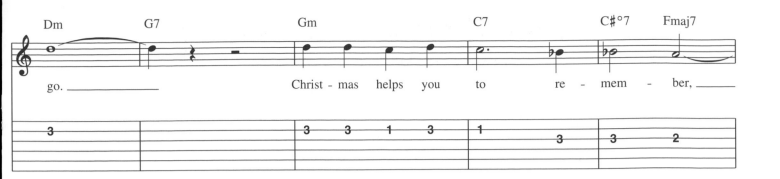

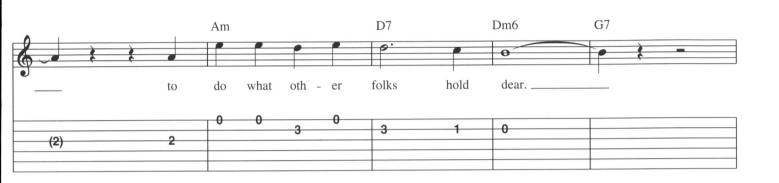

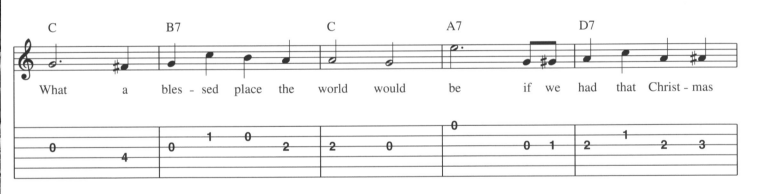

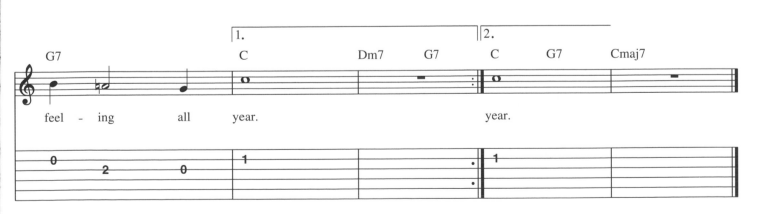

This Is Christmas
(Bright, Bright the Holly Berries)

Lyric by Wihla Hutson
Music by Alfred Burt

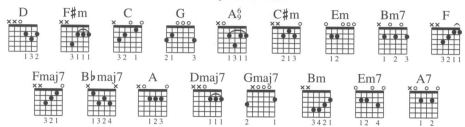

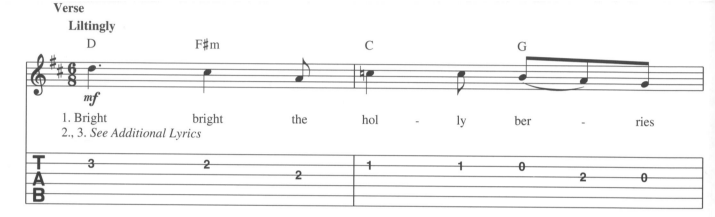

Strum Pattern: 7, 9
Pick Pattern: 7, 8

Verse

Liltingly

1. Bright   bright   the   hol - ly   ber - ries
2., 3. *See Additional Lyrics*

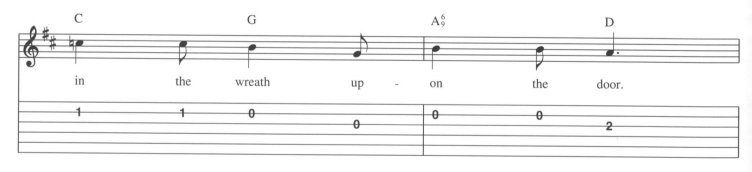

in   the   wreath   up - on   the   door.

Bright,   bright   the   hap - py   fac - es

with   the   thoughts   of   joys   in   store.

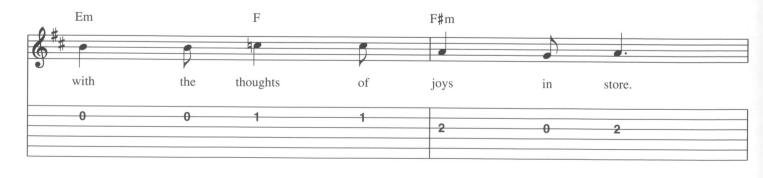

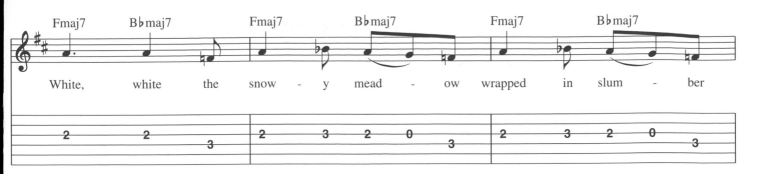

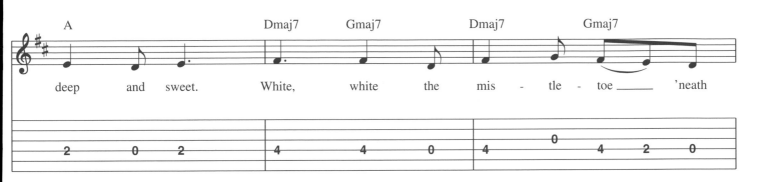

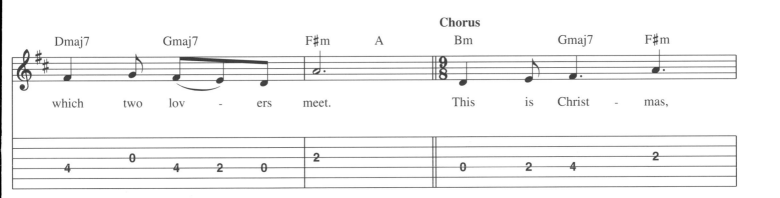

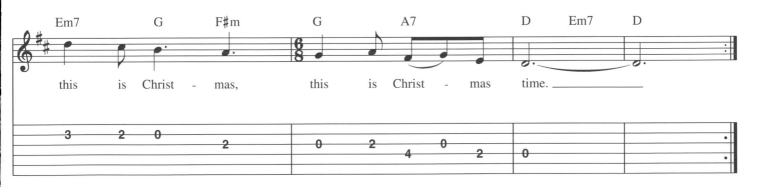

Additional Lyrics

2. Gay, gay the children's voices filled with laughter, filled with glee.
   Gay, gay the tinsled things upon the dark and spicy tree.
   Day, day when all mankind may hear the angel's song again.
   Day, day when Christ was born to bless the sons of men.

3. Sing, sing ye heav'nly host to tell the blessed Saviour's birth.
   Sing, sing in holy joy, ye dwellers all upon the earth.
   King, King yet tiny Babe, come down to us from God above.
   King, King of ev'ry heart which opens wide to love.

Toyland

from BABES IN TOYLAND

Words by Glen MacDonough

Music by Victor Herbert

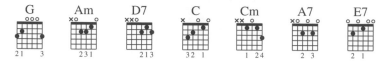

Strum Pattern: 9

Pick Pattern: 9

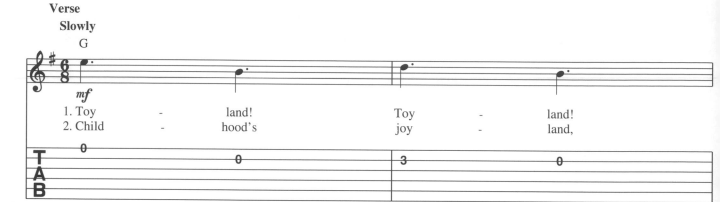

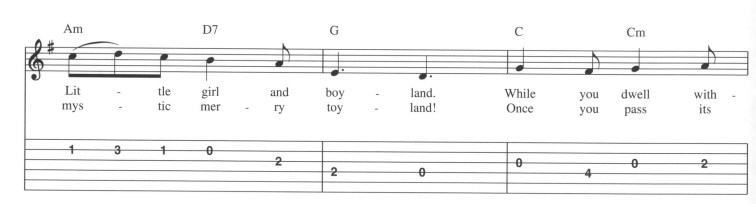

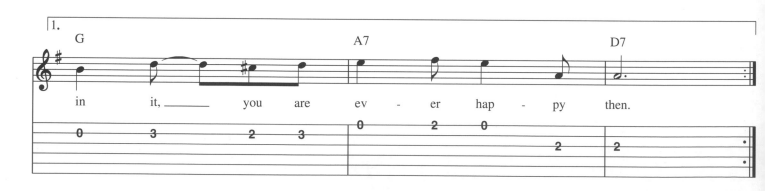

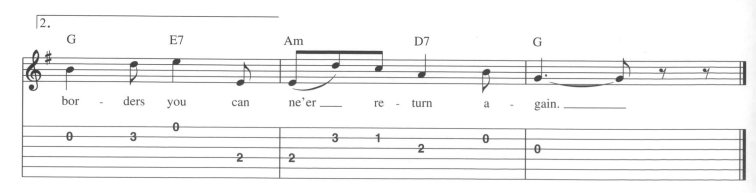

232

Up on the Housetop

Words and Music by B.R. Handy

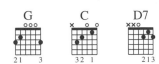

Strum Pattern: 4, 3
Pick Pattern: 5, 3

Additional Lyrics

2. First comes the stocking of Little Nell,
   Oh, dear Santa, fill it well.
   Give her a dollie that laughs and cries,
   One that will open and shut her eyes.

'Twas the Night Before Christmas

Words by Clement Clark Moore
Music by F. Henri Klickman

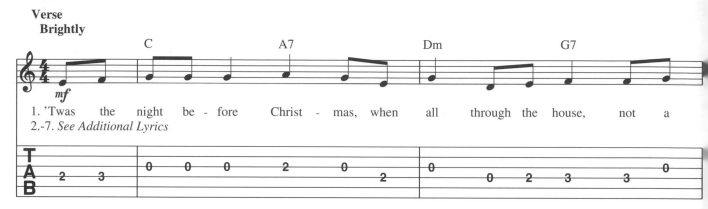

Strum Pattern: 4
Pick Pattern: 5

Verse
Brightly

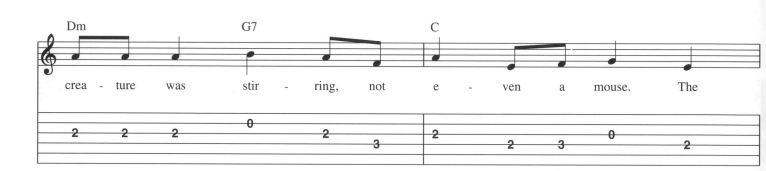

1. 'Twas the night be - fore Christ - mas, when all through the house, not a
2.-7. *See Additional Lyrics*

crea - ture was stir - ring, not e - ven a mouse. The

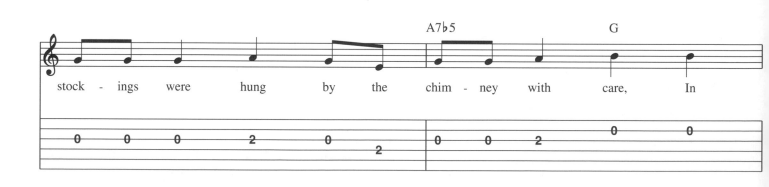

stock - ings were hung by the chim - ney with care, In

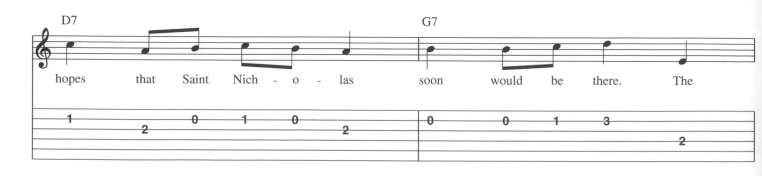

hopes that Saint Nich - o - las soon would be there. The

Additional Lyrics

2. When out on the lawn there arouse such a clatter;
   I sprang from my bed to see what was the matter.
   Away to the window I flew like a flash,
   Tore open the shutters and threw up the sash.
   The moon, on the breast of the new-fallen snow,
   Gave a lustre of midday to objects below.
   When what to my wondering eyes should appear.
   But a miniature sleigh and eight tiny reindeer.

3. With a little old driver; so lively and quick,
   I knew in a moment it must be Saint Nick.
   More rapid than eagles, his coursers they came
   And he whistled, and shouted, and called them by name;
   "Now, Dasher, Now, Dancer! Now, Prancer! Now, Vixen!
   On Comet! On, Cupid! On Donder and Blitzen!
   To the top of the porch, to the top of the wall!
   Now dash away, dash away, dash away all!"

4. As dry leaves that before the wild hurricane fly,
   When they meet with an obstacle, mount to the sky.
   So up to the house-top the coursers they flew,
   With the sleigh full of toys, and Saint Nicholas, too.
   And then in a twinkling I heard on the roof
   The prancing and pawing of each little hoof.
   As I drew in my head, and was turning around,
   Down the chimney Saint Nicholas came with a bound.

5. He was dressed all in fir from his head to his foot
   And his clothes were all tarnished with ashes and soot.
   And he looked like a peddler just opening his pack.
   His eyes how they twinkled! His dimples how merry!
   His cheeks were like roses, his nose like a cherry,
   His droll little mouth was drawn up like a bow
   And the beard of his chin was as white as the snow.

6. The stump of a pipe he held tight in his teeth
   And the smoke, it encircled his head like a wreath.
   He had a broad face, and a round little belly
   That shook, when he laughed, like a bowl full of jelly.
   He was chubby and plump, a right jolly old elf,
   And I laughed when I saw him, in spite of myself.
   A wink of his eye and a twist of his head,
   Soon gave me to know I had nothing to dread.

7. He spake not a word but went straight to his work,
   And filled all the stockings, then turned with a jerk,
   And laying his finger aside of his nose,
   And giving a nod, up the chimney he rose.
   He sprang to his sleigh, to his team gave a whistle,
   And away they all flew like the down of a thistle,
   But I heard him exclaim, ere he drove out of sight:
   "Happy Christmas to all, and all a Good-night!"

The Twelve Days of Christmas

Traditional English Carol

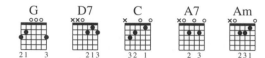

Strum Pattern: 3
Pick Pattern: 3

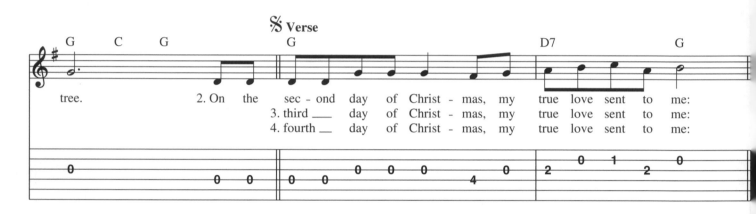

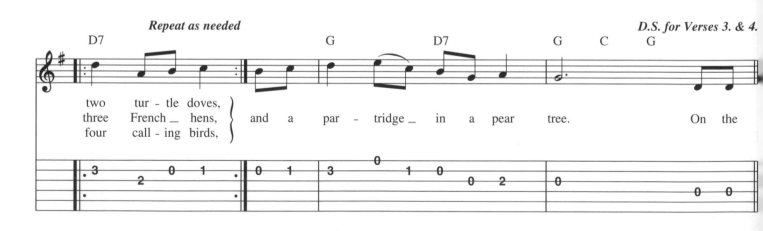

Copyright © 2002 by HAL LEONARD CORPORATION

237

A Virgin Unspotted

Traditional English Carol

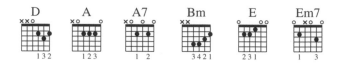

Strum Pattern: 8
Pick Pattern: 8

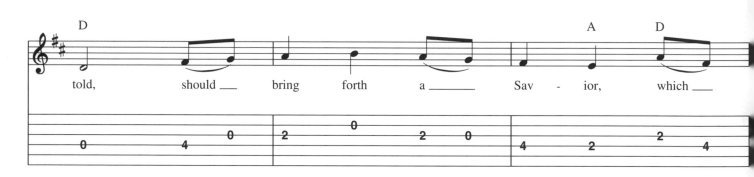

1. A ___ vir - gin un - spot - ted, the ___ proph - et fore -
2., 3., 4. See Additional Lyrics

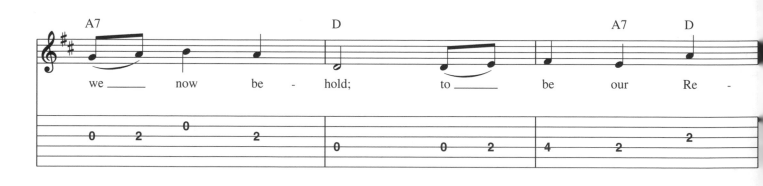

told, should ___ bring forth a ___ Sav - ior, which ___

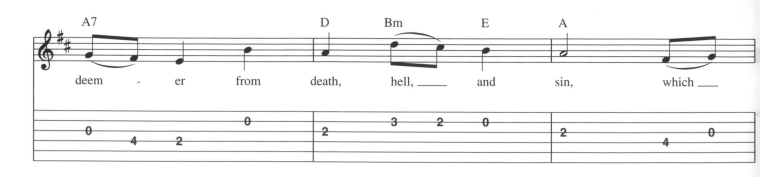

we ___ now be - hold; to ___ be our Re -

deem - er from death, hell, ___ and sin, which ___

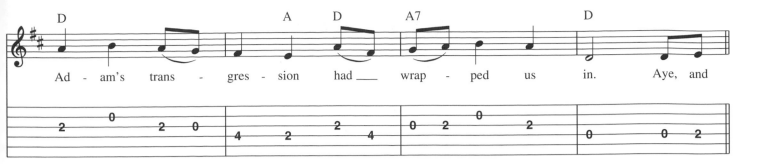

Ad - am's trans - gres - sion had __ wrap - ped us in. Aye, and

Chorus

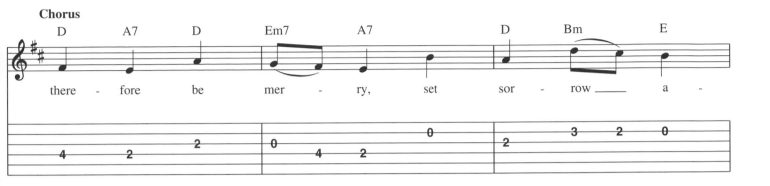

there - fore be mer - ry, set sor - row __ a -

side, Christ __ Je - sus, our __ Sav - ior, was

1., 2., 3. | 4.

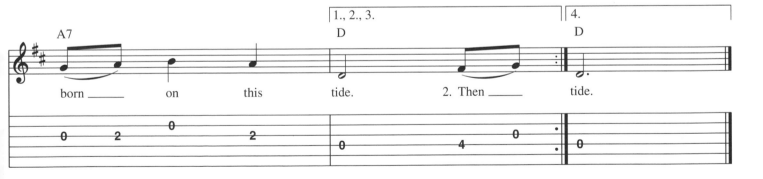

born __ on this tide. 2. Then __ tide.

Additional Lyrics

2. Then God sent an angel from Heaven so high,
   To certain poor shepherds in fields where they lie,
   And bade them no longer in sorrow to stay,
   Because that our Savior was born on this day.

3. Then presently after, the shepherds did spy
   Vast numbers of angels to stand in the sky;
   They joyfully talked and sweetly did sing:
   "To God be all glory, our heavenly King."

4. To teach us humility all this was done,
   And learn we form thence haughty pride for to shun;
   A manger His cradle who came from above,
   The great God of mercy, of peace and of love.

We Are Santa's Elves

Music and Lyrics by Johnny Marks

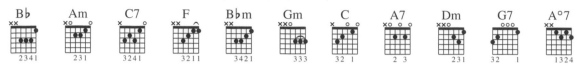

Strum Pattern: 3
Pick Pattern: 3

Intro

Happily

Ho, ho, ho! Ho, ho, ho! We are San-ta's elves.

Verse

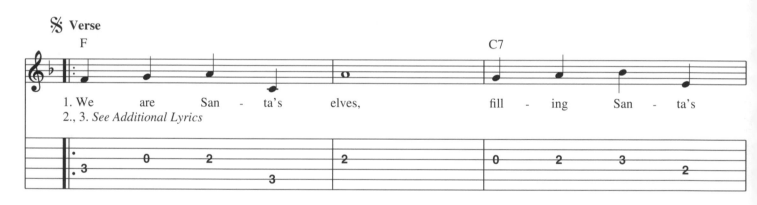

1. We are San-ta's elves, fill-ing San-ta's
2., 3. *See Additional Lyrics*

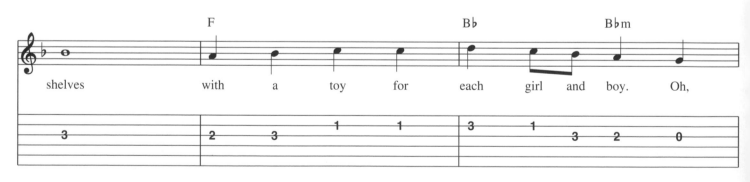

shelves with a toy for each girl and boy. Oh,

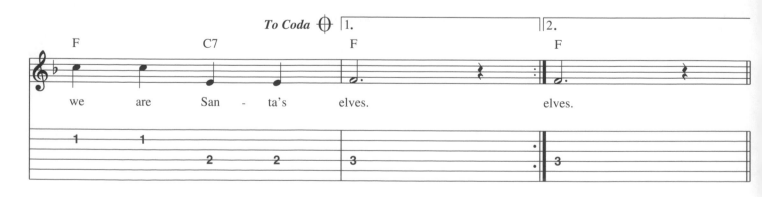

we are San-ta's elves. elves.

Bridge

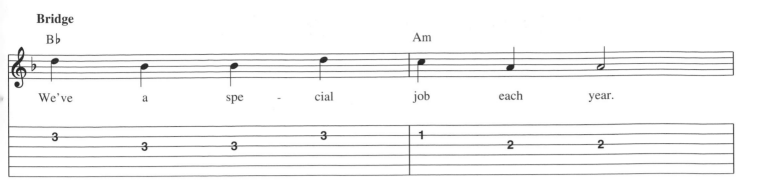

We've a spe - cial job each year.

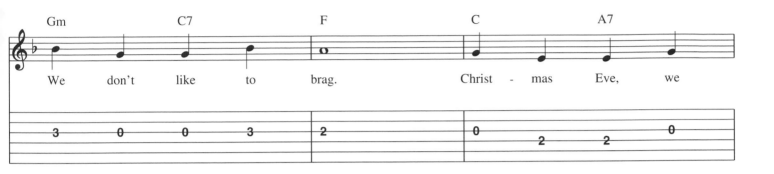

We don't like to brag. Christ - mas Eve, we

D.S. al Coda

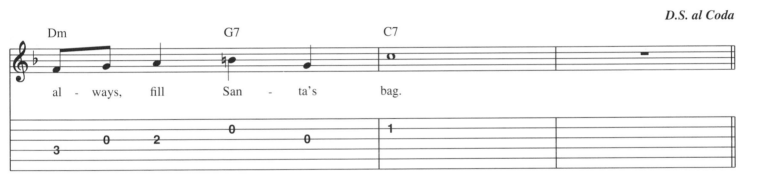

al - ways, fill San - ta's bag.

✛ *Coda*

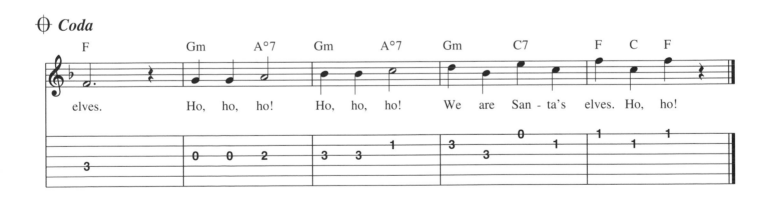

elves. Ho, ho, ho! Ho, ho, ho! We are San - ta's elves. Ho, ho!

Additional Lyrics

2. We work hard all day.
   But our work is play.
   Dolls we try out,
   See if they cry out
   We are Santa's elves.

3. Santa knows who's good.
   Do the things you should.
   And we bet you
   He won't forget you.
   We are Santa's elves.

241

We Three Kings of Orient Are

Words and Music by John H. Hopkins, Jr.

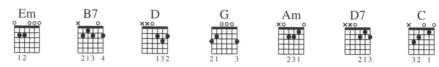

Strum Pattern: 8
Pick Pattern: 8

Verse

Moderately

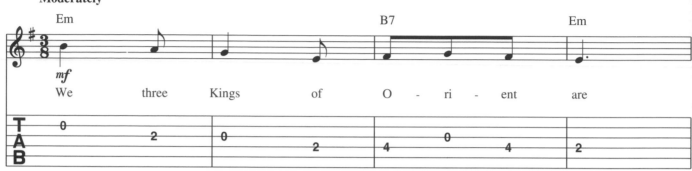

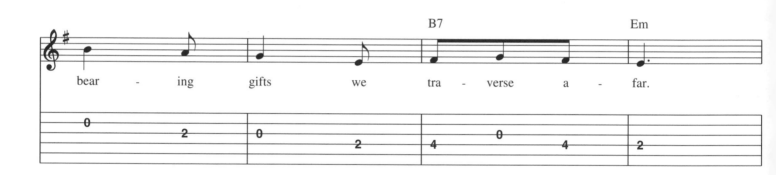

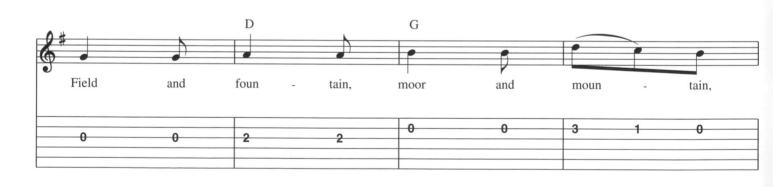

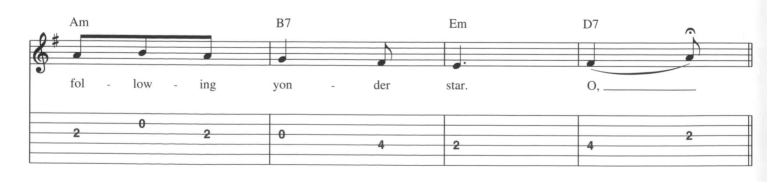

Chorus

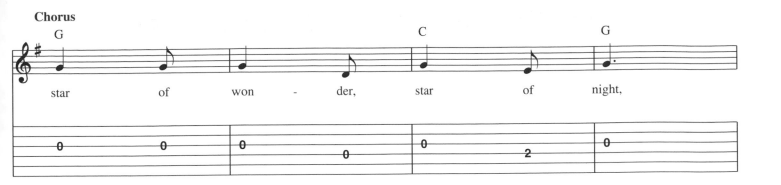

star of won - der, star of night,

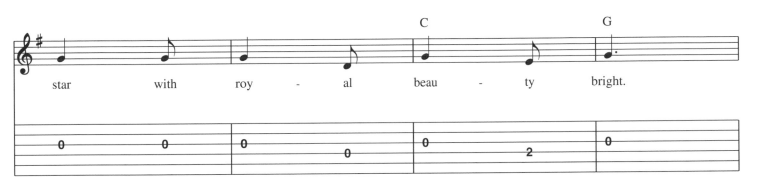

star with roy - al beau - ty bright.

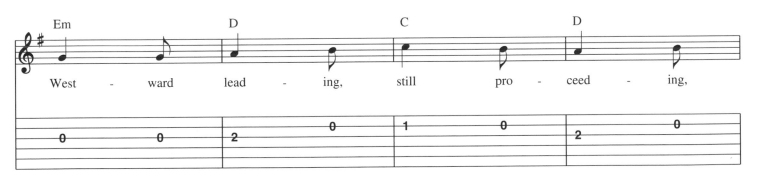

West - ward lead - ing, still pro - ceed - ing,

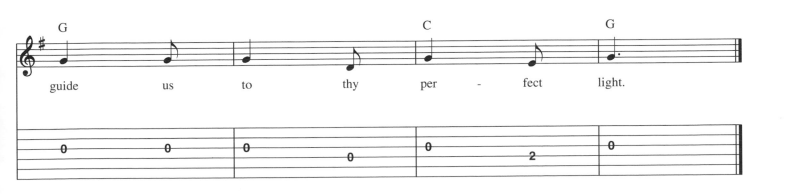

guide us to thy per - fect light.

We Wish You a Merry Christmas

Traditional English Folksong

Strum Pattern: 8, 9
Pick Pattern: 8, 9

Verse

Brightly

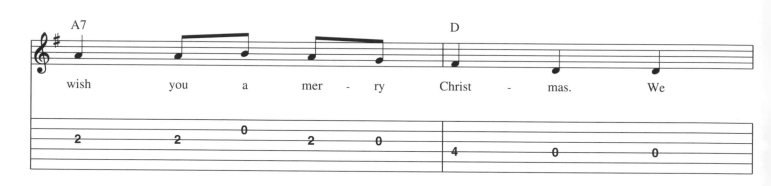

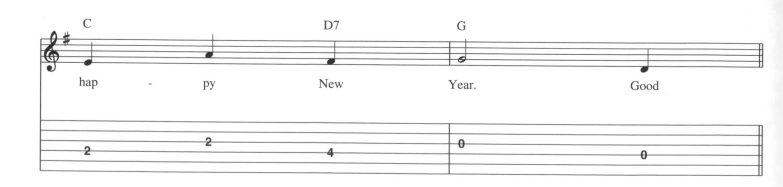

Bridge

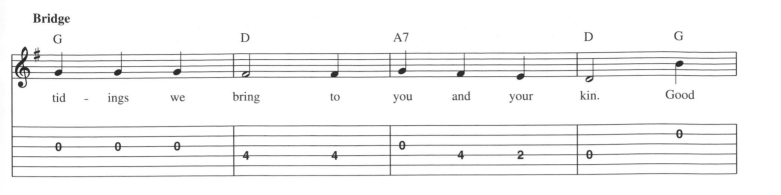

tid - ings we bring to you and your kin. Good

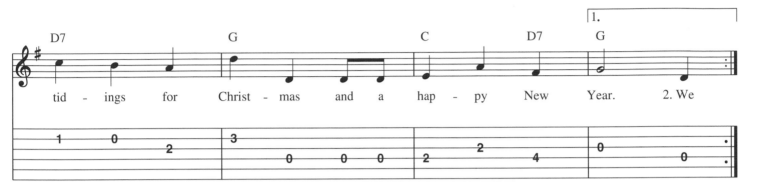

tid - ings for Christ - mas and a hap - py New Year. 2. We

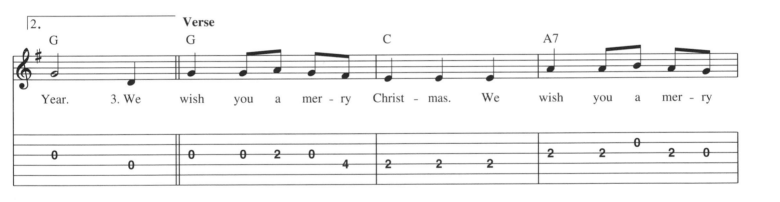

Year. 3. We wish you a mer - ry Christ - mas. We wish you a mer - ry

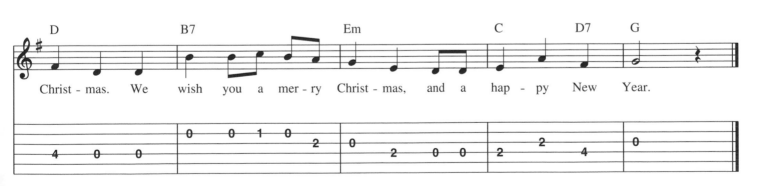

Christ - mas. We wish you a mer - ry Christ - mas, and a hap - py New Year.

Additional Lyrics

2. We all know that Santa's coming.
   We all know that Santa's coming.
   We all know that Santa's coming
   And soon will be here.

What Child Is This?

Words by William C. Dix

16th Century English Melody

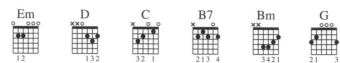

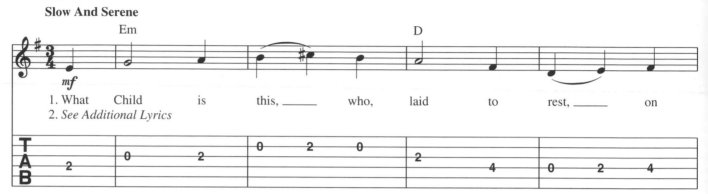

Strum Pattern: 8, 7
Pick Pattern: 8, 9

Verse

Slow And Serene

1. What Child is this, _____ who, laid to rest, _____ on
2. *See Additional Lyrics*

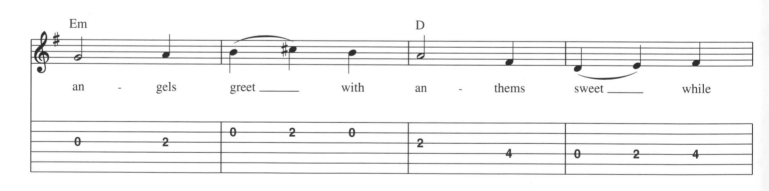

Ma - ry's lap _____ is sleep - ing? Whom

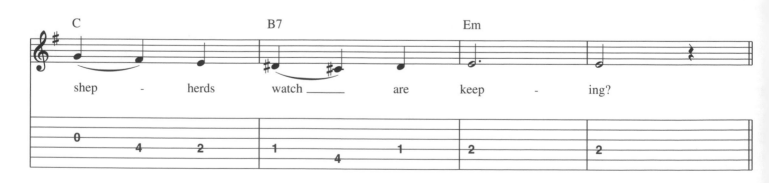

an - gels greet _____ with an - thems sweet _____ while

shep - herds watch _____ are keep - ing?

Chorus

This, this _____ is Christ the King, _____ whom

See Additional Lyrics

shep - herds guard _____ and an - gels sing:

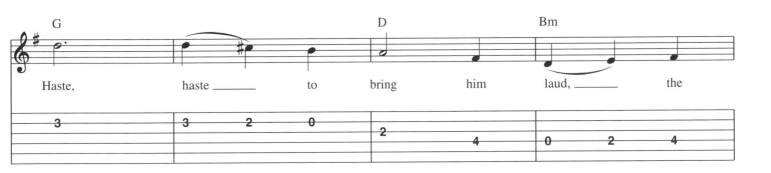

Haste, haste _____ to bring him laud, _____ the

Babe, _____ the Son _____ of Ma - ry.

Additional Lyrics

2. So bring Him incense, gold and myrrh,
   Come peasant king to own Him;
   The King of kings salvation brings.
   Let loving hearts enthrone Him,

Chorus Raise, raise the song on high,
   The Virgin sings her lullaby;
   Joy, joy for Christ is born,
   The Babe, the Son of Mary.

When Christ Was Born of Mary Free

Traditional English Carol

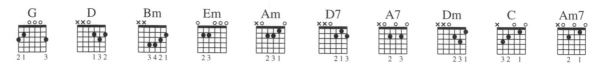

Strum Pattern: 3, 4
Pick Pattern: 3, 4

1. When Christ was born of __ Ma - ry __ free, in Beth - le - hem that fair ci - ty,
2., 3. *See Additional Lyrics*

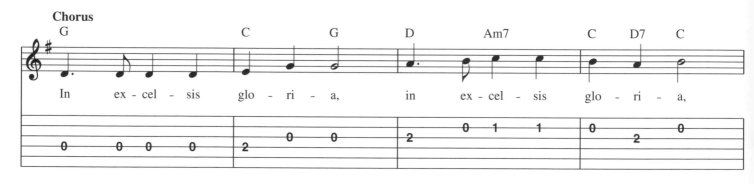

an - gels sang there with mirth and glee: "In ex - cel - sis __ glo - ri - a."

Chorus

In ex - cel - sis glo - ri - a, in ex - cel - sis glo - ri - a,

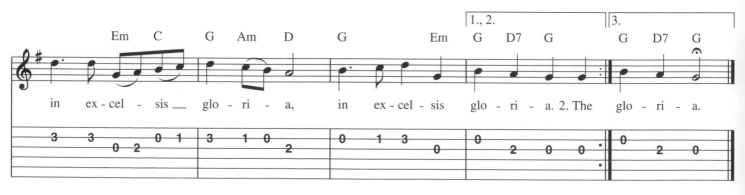

in ex - cel - sis __ glo - ri - a, in ex - cel - sis glo - ri - a. 2. The glo - ri - a.

Additional Lyrics

2. The King is come to save mankind,
As in the scripture truths we find.
Therefore this song we have in mind,
"In excelsis gloria."

3. Then, dearest Lord, for Thy great grace,
Grant us in bliss to see Thy face,
Thee we may sing to Thy solace,
"In excelsis gloria."

While Shepherds Watched Their Flocks

Words by Nahum Tate
Music by George Frideric Handel

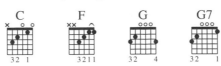

Strum Pattern: 3
Pick Pattern: 3

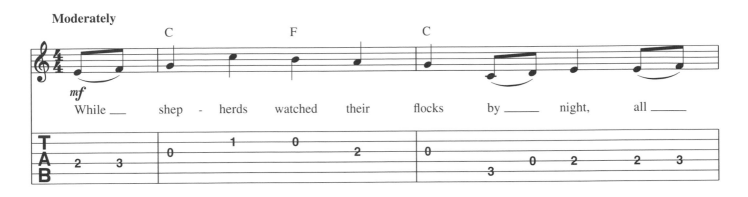

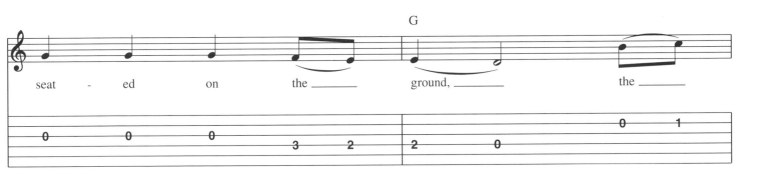

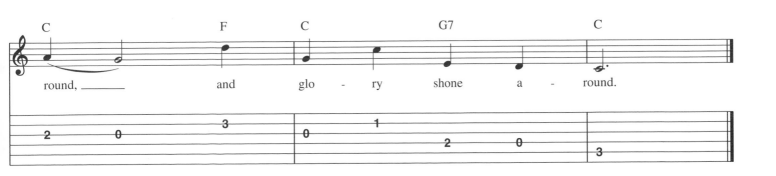

Winds Through the Olive Trees

19th Century American Carol

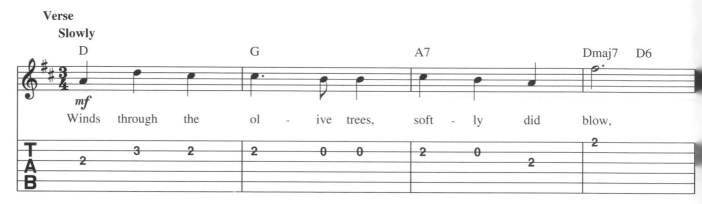

Strum Pattern: 7
Pick Pattern: 7

Verse
Slowly

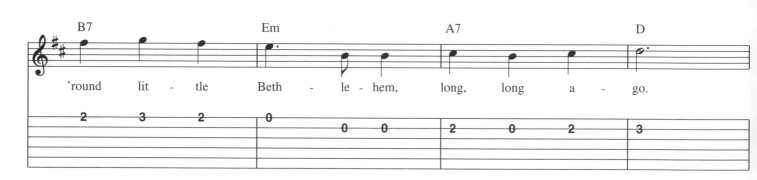

Winds through the ol - ive trees, soft - ly did blow,

'round lit - tle Beth - le - hem, long, long a - go.

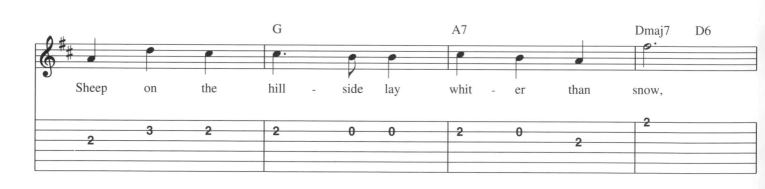

Sheep on the hill - side lay whit - er than snow,

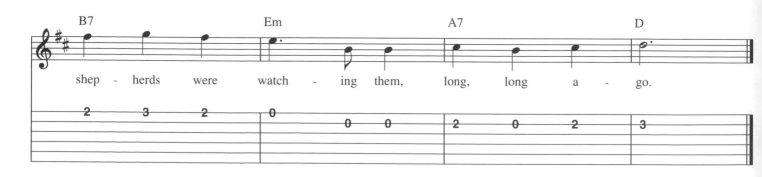

shep - herds were watch - ing them, long, long a - go.

Wonderful Christmastime

Words and Music by McCartney

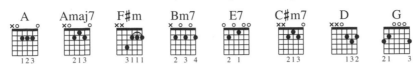

Strum Pattern: 2
Pick Pattern: 4

Verse
Brightly

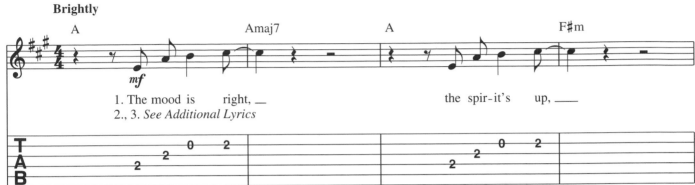

1. The mood is right, the spir-it's up,
2., 3. *See Additional Lyrics*

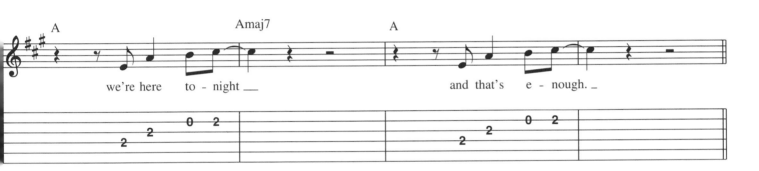

we're here to - night and that's e - nough.

Chorus

Sim - ply hav - ing a won - der - ful Christ - mas - time.

Sim - ply hav - ing a won - der - ful Christ - mas - time. time.

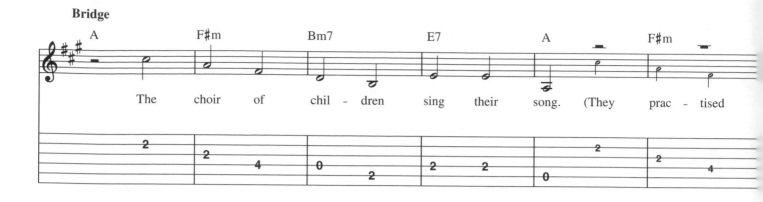

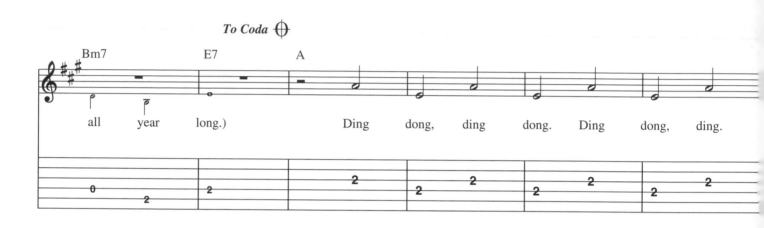

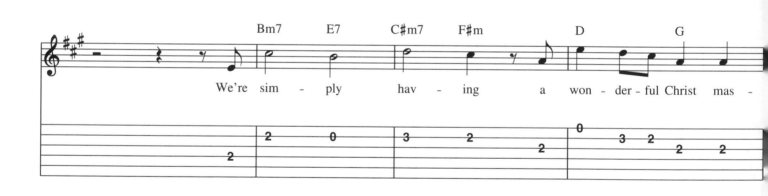

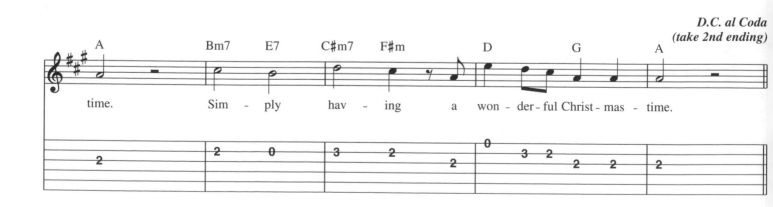

⊕ *Coda*

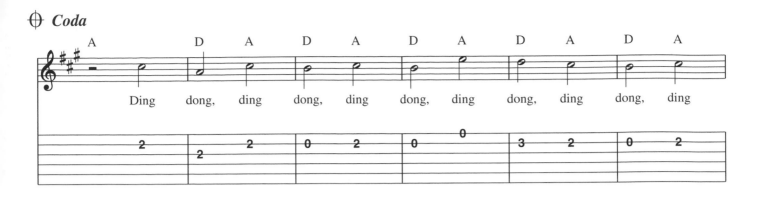

Ding dong, ding dong, ding dong, ding dong, ding dong, ding

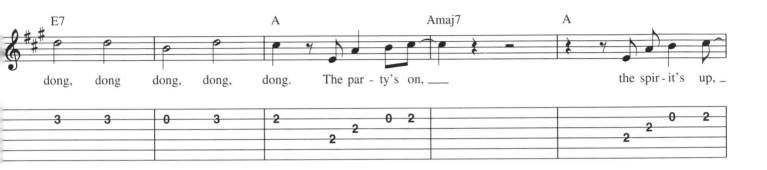

dong, dong dong, dong, dong. The par - ty's on, ___ the spir - it's up, _

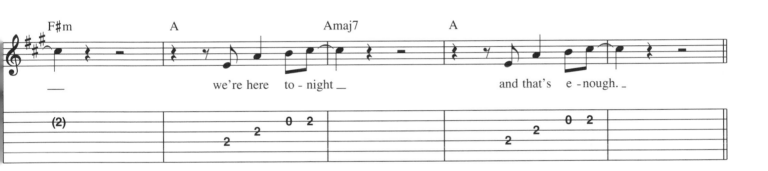

_ we're here to - night _ and that's e - nough. _

Repeat & Fade

Sim - ply hav - ing a won - der - ful Christ - mas - time. We're

Additional Lyrics

2. The party's on,
   The feeling's here
   That only comes
   This time of year.

3. The word is out
   About the town,
   To lift a glass.
   Oh, don't look down.

The Wonderful World of Christmas

Words by Charles Tobias
Music by Al Frisch

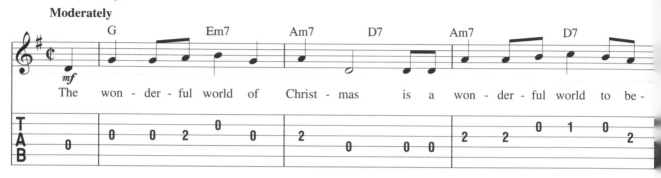

Strum Pattern: 3, 4
Pick Pattern: 3, 4

Moderately

The won-der-ful world of Christ-mas is a won-der-ful world to be-

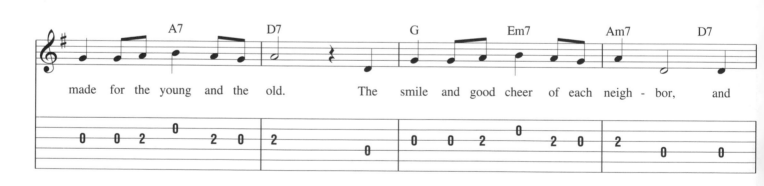

hold. The won-der-ful world of Christ-mas was

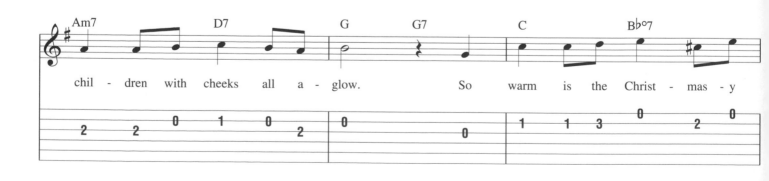

made for the young and the old. The smile and good cheer of each neigh-bor, and

chil-dren with cheeks all a-glow. So warm is the Christ-mas-y

feel - ing   with the tree - tops all wrapped up in snow.

Lis - ten to those won - drous bells   and you'll hear them say:

"O - pen up your hearts to all   on the hol - i - day."   The

won - der - ful world of Christ - mas   is a joy from the mo - ment it starts.   The

won - der - ful world of Christ - mas   should re - main ev - 'ry day in our hearts.

You Make It Feel Like Christmas

Words and Music by Neil Diamond

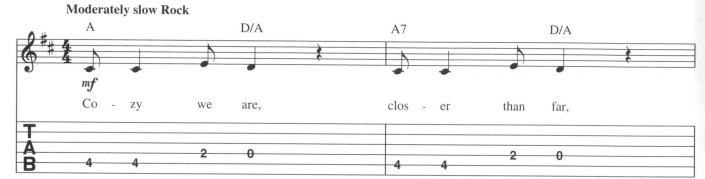

Strum Pattern: 4
Pick Pattern: 3

Intro

Moderately slow Rock

Co - zy we are, clos - er than far,

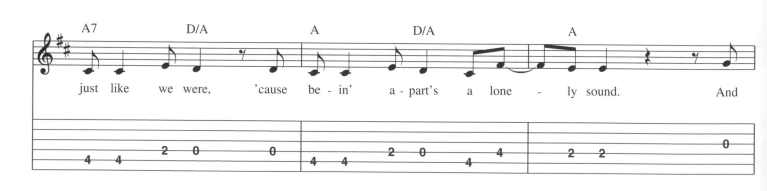

sounds of for - ev - er still ___ a - round.

Verse

1. Lov - ers in love,
2., 3. *See additional lyrics*

just like we were, 'cause be - in' a - part's a lone - ly sound. And

when peo - ple ask how ___ we stay to - geth - er, I say you nev - er let ___

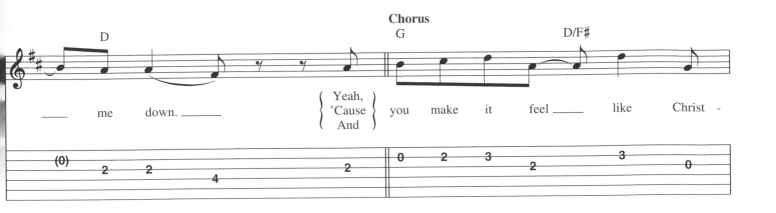

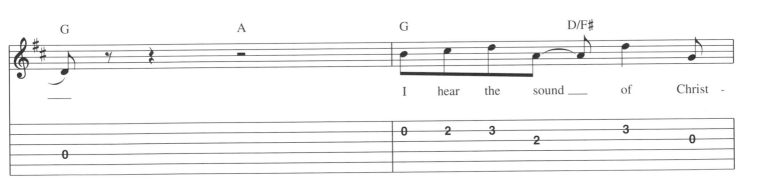

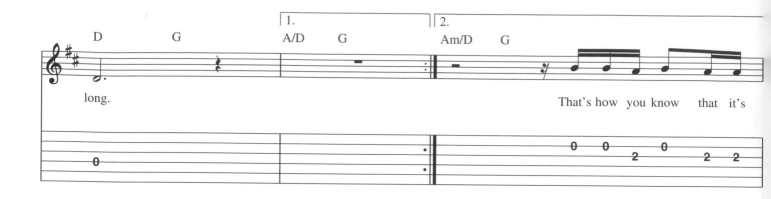

long.

That's how you know that it's

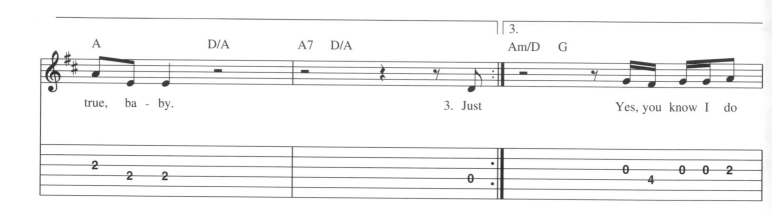

true, ba - by.

3. Just

Yes, you know I do

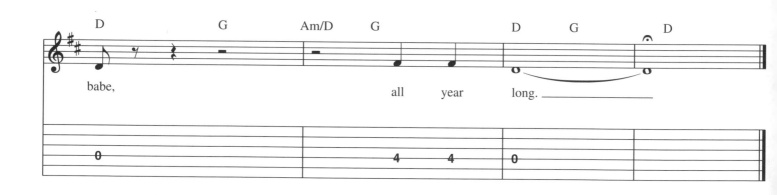

babe,

all year long. _____

Additional Lyrics

2. Look at the sun shining on me;
   Nowhere could be a better place.
   Lovers in love, yeah, that's what we'll be.
   When you're here with me, it's Christmas Day.

3. Just look at us now, part of it all.
   In spite of it all, we're still around.
   So wake up the kids, and put on some tea.
   Let's light up the tree; it's Christmas Day.

STRUM AND PICK PATTERNS

This chart contains the suggested strum and pick patterns that are referred to by number at the beginning of each song in this book. The symbols ⊓ and ∨ in the strum patterns refer to down and up strokes, respectively. The letters in the pick patterns indicate which right-hand fingers plays which strings.

p = thumb
i = index finger
m = middle finger
a = ring finger

For example; Pick Pattern 2
is played: thumb - index - middle - ring

Strum Patterns   ## Pick Patterns

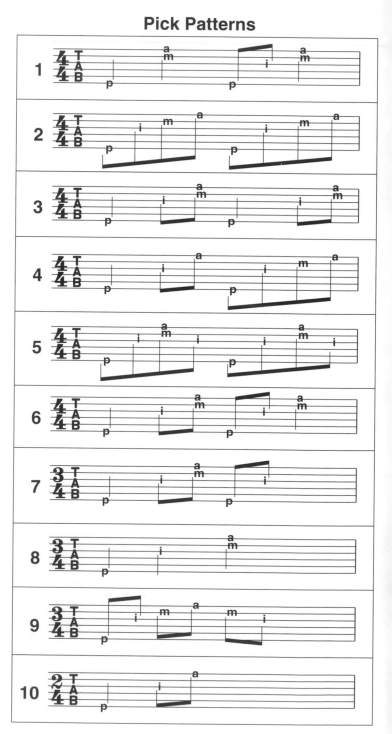

You can use the 3/4 Strum or Pick Patterns in songs written in compound meter (6/8, 9/8, 12/8, etc.). For example, you can accompany a song in 6/8 by playing the 3/4 pattern twice in each measure. The 4/4 Strum and Pick Patterns can be used for songs written in cut time (¢) by doubling the note time values in the patterns. Each pattern would therefore last two measures in cut time.

FAKE BOOKS FOR GUITAR

These giant songbooks feature the lyrics, melodies and chords to hundreds of your favorite songs.

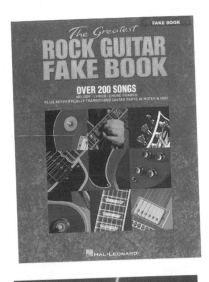

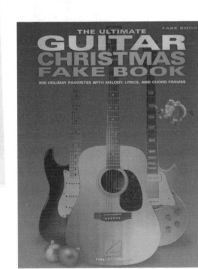

Prices, contents and availability subject to change without notice.

For More Information, See Your Local Music Dealer, Or Write To:

HAL•LEONARD®
CORPORATION

7777 W. Bluemound Rd. P.O. Box 13819 Milwaukee, WI 53213

www.halleonard.com

THE GREATEST ROCK GUITAR FAKE BOOK
INCLUDES TAB

The ultimate rock guitar collection featuring 200 classics and contemporary hits with melody, lyrics and chord frames plus authentically transcribed guitar parts in notes and tab! Songs include: All Day and All of the Night • American Woman • Another One Bites the Dust • Bang a Gong (Get It On) • Black Hole Sun • Carry On Wayward Son • Change the World • Come Out and Play • Don't Fear the Reaper • Dust in the Wind • Every Breath You Take • Give Me One Reason • Heartache Tonight • The House Is Rockin' • Iris • Layla • Little Sister • Money • My Generation • Nights in White Satin • Owner of a Lonely Heart • Paranoid • Pride and Joy • Rhiannon • Roxanne • Semi-Charmed Life • Smoke on the Water • Suffragette City • Sultans of Swing • Twist and Shout • Two Princes • Welcome to the Jungle • Woman from Tokyo • and more.
00240148...$29.95

THE ULTIMATE ROCK GUITAR FAKE BOOK
 INCLUDES TAB

A collection of 200 rock guitar classics. Includes lyrics, chords with music notation and tablature, all in appropriate guitar keys. Includes special guitar and solos made famous by Hendrix, Eric Clapton, Randy Rhoads, Jeff Beck, Ratt, Bon Jovi, U2 and many others.

An incredible selection of songs, including:
Blue Suede Shoes • Born to Be Wild • Day Tripper • Doctor, My Eyes • Every Breath You Take • Foxy Lady • Free Bird • Gloria • Good Lovin' • I Can See for Miles • Layla • Lola • Louie, Louie • Maggie May • Magic Carpet Ride • Maniac • Money • My Generation • Pipeline • Purple Haze • Reelin' in the Years • Spinning Wheel • Steal Away (The Night) • Summertime Blues • Sunshine of Your Love • That'll Be the Day • Tuesday Afternoon • Walk on the Wild Side • Walk This Way • White Room • With or Without You • You Give Love a Bad Name • You Really Got Me.
00240070...$29.95

THE MASTERS OF ROCK GUITAR FAKE BOOK
INCLUDES TAB

137 of the hottest rock guitar tunes ever compiled into one incredible book. Each song includes lyrics, chords, and melody line in standard notation and tablature. Also features special guitar locks and solos. Songs include: After Midnight • Bad Case of Loving You • Bad Medicine • Barracuda • Black Magic Woman • Brown Eyed Girl • Dude (Looks Like a Lady) • Dust in the Wind • Every Rose Has Its Thorn • Gimme Three Steps • Hey Joe • Hysteria • I Love Rock 'N' Roll • Jailhouse Rock • Long Cool Woman (In a Black Dress) • On Broadway • Once Bitten Twice Shy • Pour Some Sugar on Me • Red, Red Wine • Rikki, Don't Lose That Number • Rock and Roll Hoochie Koo • Running on Empty • School's Out • Sweet Emotion • Turn, Turn, Turn • Where the Streets Have No Name • Wind Cries Mary.
00290173...$24.95

THE BEST CHRISTMAS GUITAR FAKE BOOK EVER
 INCLUDES TAB

Over 150 Christmas classics for guitar. Songs include:
Blue Christmas • The Chipmunk Song • The Christmas Song (Chestnuts Roasting on an Open Fire) • Frosty the Snow Man • Happy Holiday • A Holly Jolly Christmas • I Saw Mommy Kissing Santa Claus • I Wonder As I Wander • Jingle-Bell Rock • My Favorite Things • Rudolph, The Red-Nosed Reindeer • Santa Bring My Baby Back (To Me) • Suzy Snowflake • Tennessee Christmas • You Make It Feel Like Christmas • and more. Includes notes and tab as well as a chord diagram chart and strum and picking patterns.
00240053...$19.95

THE ULTIMATE GUITAR CHRISTMAS FAKE BOOK
200 Holiday Favorites with Melody, Lyrics and Chord Frames
No guitarist should be without this stellar collection of Christmas classics! It includes fake book arrangements of 200 terrific tinsel-time tunes, all in one convenient collection. Please note: this collection does not include tablature.
00240158...$19.95

GUITAR SONGBOOKS FOR THE HOLIDAYS

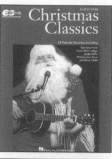
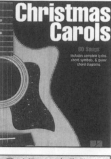

THE BIG CHRISTMAS COLLECTION FOR EASY GUITAR

Includes over 70 Christmas favorites, such as: Ave Maria • Blue Christmas • Deck the Hall • Feliz Navidad • Frosty the Snow Man • Happy Holiday • A Holly Jolly Christmas • Joy to the World • O Holy Night • Silver and Gold • Suzy Snowflake • You're All I Want for Christmas • and more.
00698978   Easy Guitar with Notes and Tab $16.95
INCLUDES TAB

CHRISTMAS CHEER FOR EASY GUITAR

26 songs, including: Blue Christmas • The Christmas Song (Chestnuts Roasting) • Frosty, the Snow Man • Happy Xmas • It's Beginning to Look Like Christmas • Rudolph the Red-Nosed Reindeer • Wonderful Christmastime • and more.
00702048   Easy Guitar with Notes and Tab $10.95
INCLUDES TAB

CHRISTMAS CLASSICS

Over 25 easy guitar arrangements of Christmas favorites: Auld Lang Syne • Away in a Manger • Deck the Hall • The First Noel • I Saw Three Ships • Jingle Bells • O Christmas Tree • Once in a Royal David's City • Silent Night • Up on the Housetop • What Child Is This? • and more. Easy guitar arrangements in standard notation and tablature.
00702028   Easy Guitar with Notes and Tab $7.95
INCLUDES TAB

CHRISTMAS FAVORITES - 2ND EDITION

A collection of 33 seasonal songs in standard notation and tab. Includes: Angels We Have Heard on High • The First Noel • I Saw Three Ships • Joy to the World • O Come All Ye Faithful • O Holy Night • What Child Is This • and more.
00698978   Easy Guitar with Notes and Tab $16.95
INCLUDES TAB

CHRISTMAS TIDINGS

23 easy arrangements of Christmas favorites, including: Blue Christmas • The Chipmunk Song • Feliz Navidad • Grandma Got Run Over by a Reindeer • Happy Holiday • I'll Be Home for Christmas • Rudolph the Red-Nosed Reindeer • Silver Bells • and more.
00698978   Easy Guitar with Notes and Tab $16.95
INCLUDES TAB

CONTEMPORARY CHRISTIAN CHRISTMAS

19 contemporary favorites recorded by top artists: Breath of Heaven (Mary's song) • Celebrate the Child • Child of Bethlehem • Emmanuel • Good News • Jesus is Born • One Small Child • Precious Promise • A Strange Way to Save the World • This Gift • This Little Child • and more.
00698978   Easy Guitar with Notes and Tab $16.95
INCLUDES TAB

CHRISTMAS CAROLS — GUITAR CHORD SONGBOOK

Includes complete lyrics, chord symbols, and guitar chord diagrams. A convenient reference of 80 Christmas carols for the player who just needs the lyrics and chords. Songs include: Angels We Have Heard on High • Away in a Manger • Deck the Hall • Good King Wenceslas • The Holly and the Ivy • I Heard the Bells on Christmas Day • Jingle Bells • Joy to the World • O Holy Night • Silent Night • Up on the Housetop • We Wish You a Merry Christmas • Welsh Carol • What Child Is This? • and more.
00699536   Guitar Chords/Lyrics $12.95

CHRISTMAS SONGS FOR GUITAR

The Strum It! series lets guitar players strum the chords (and sing along) with their favorite songs. The songs in each book have been selected because they can be played with regular open chords, barre chords, or other moveable chord types. All songs are shown in their original keys complete with chords, strum patterns, melody and lyrics. This book features over 45 Christmas favorites, including: The Christmas Song (Chestnuts Roasting on an Open Fire) • Feliz Navidad • Frosty the Snow Man • Grandma Got Run over by a Reindeer • The Greatest Gift of All • (There's No Place Like) Home for the Holidays • I'll Be Home for Christmas • It's Beginning to Look like Christmas • The Most Wonderful Time of the Year • Rockin' Around the Christmas Tree • Rudolph the Red-Nosed Reindeer • Silver Bells • and more.
00699247   Strum It Guitar $9.95

A FINGERSTYLE GUITAR CHRISTMAS

Over 20 songs for fingerstyle guitar: Auld Lang Syne • Ave Maria • Away in a Manger • The Coventry Carol • Deck the Hall • The First Noel • Good King Wenceslas • I Saw Three Ships • Joy to the World • Silent Night • Up on the Housetop • What Child Is This? • and more.
00699038   Easy Guitar with Notes and Tab $7.95
INCL TAB

THE GUITAR STRUMMER'S CHRISTMAS SONGBOOK

A great collection of 80 favorite Christmas tunes that can be played with open chords, barre chords or other moveable chord types - all in their original keys, complete with chords, strum patterns, melody and lyrics. Includes: The Christmas Song (Chestnuts Roasting on an Open Fire) • Christmas Time Is Here • Do They Know It's Christmas? • Feliz Navidad • Frosty the Snow Man • Grandma Got Run over by a Reindeer • A Holly Jolly Christmas • I Heard the Bells on Christmas Day • I've Got My Love to Keep Me Warm • It's Christmas in New York • Let It Snow! Let It Snow! Let It Snow! • My Favorite Things • O Holy Night • Rudolph the Red-Nosed Reindeer • Silver Bells • We Wish You a Merry Christmas • You Make It Feel like Christmas • and more.
00699527   Melody/Lyrics/Chords $14.95

HAPPY HOLIDAY

20 holiday favorites arranged for fingerstyle guitar, including: Happy Holiday • I'll Be Home for Christmas • My Favorite Things • Rockin' Around the Christmas Tree • Silver Bells • and more.
00699209   Fingerstyle Guitar $10.95
INCL TAB

LET IT SNOW!

22 songs for fingerstyle guitar, including: Blue Christmas • The Christmas Song (Chestnuts Roasting on an Open Fire) • Feliz Navidad • Frosty the Snow Man • Jingle-Bell Rock • We Need a Little Christmas • and more.
00699206   Fingerstyle Guitar $10.95
INCL TAB

STRUM IT GUITAR

• AUTHENTIC CHORDS • ORIGINAL KEYS • COMPLETE SONGS •

The *Strum It* series lets players strum the chords and sing along with their favorite hits. Each song has been selected because it can be played with regular open chords, barre chords, or other moveable chord types. Guitarists can simply play the rhythm, or play and sing along through the entire song. All songs are shown in their original keys complete with chords, strum patterns, melody and lyrics. Wherever possible, the chord voicings from the recorded versions are notated.

Acoustic Classics
Play along with the recordings of 21 acoustic classics. Songs include: And I Love Her • Angie • Barely Breathing • Free Fallin' • Maggie May • Melissa • Mr. Jones • Only Wanna Be with You • Patience • Signs • Teach Your Children • Wonderful Tonight • Wonderwall • Yesterday • and more.
00699238 $10.95

The Beatles Favorites
Features 23 classic Beatles hits, including: Can't Buy Me Love • Eight Days a Week • Hey Jude • I Saw Her Standing There • Let It Be • Nowhere Man • She Loves You • Something • Yesterday • You've Got to Hide Your Love Away • and more.
00699249 $14.95

Celtic Guitar Songbook
Features 35 complete songs in their original keys, with authentic chords, strum patterns, melody and lyrics. Includes: Black Velvet Band • Cockles and Mussels (Molly Malone) • Danny Boy (Londonderry Air) • Finnegan's Wake • Galway Bay • I'm a Rover and Seldom Sober • The Irish Washerwoman • Kerry Dance • Killarney • McNamara's Band • My Wild Irish Rose • The Rose of Tralee • Sailor's Hornpipe • Whiskey in the Jar • Wild Rover • and more. 00699265 $9.95

Christmas Songs for Guitar
Over 40 Christmas favorites, including: The Christmas Song (Chestnuts Roasting on an Open Fire) • Feliz Navidad • Frosty the Snow Man • Grandma Got Run Over by a Reindeer • The Greatest Gift of All • I'll Be Home for Christmas • It's Beginning to Look Like Christmas • Rockin' Around the Christmas Tree • Silver Bells • and more. 00699247 $9.95

Christmas Songs with Three Chords
30 all-time favorites: Angels We Have Heard on High • Away in a Manger • Deck the Hall • Go, Tell It on the Mountain • Here We Come A-Wassailing • I Heard the Bells on Christmas Day • Jolly Old St. Nicholas • Silent Night • Up on the Housetop • and more.
00699487 $8.95

Country Strummin'
Features 24 songs: Achy Breaky Heart • Adalida • Ain't That Lonely Yet • Blue • The Beaches of Cheyenne • A Broken Wing • Gone Country • I Fall to Pieces • My Next Broken Heart • She and I • Unchained Melody • What a Crying Shame • and more.
00699119 $8.95

Jim Croce - Classic Hits
Authentic chords to 22 great songs from Jim Croce, including: Bad, Bad Leroy Brown • I'll Have to Say I Love You in a Song • Operator (That's Not the Way It Feels) • Time in a Bottle • and more.
00699269 $10.95

Disney Favorites
A great collection of 34 easy-to-play Disney favorites. Includes: Can You Feel the Love Tonight • Circle of Life • Cruella De Vil • Friend Like Me • It's a Small World • Some Day My Prince Will Come • Under the Sea • Whistle While You Work • Winnie the Pooh • Zero to Hero • and more. 00699171 $10.95

Disney Greats
Easy arrangements with guitar chord frames and strum patterns for 39 wonderful Disney classics including: Arabian Nights • The Aristocats • Beauty and the Beast • Colors of the Wind • Go the Distance • Hakuna Matata • Heigh-Ho • Kiss the Girl • A Pirate's Life • When You Wish Upon a Star • Zip-A-Dee-Doo-Dah • Theme from Zorro • and more. 00699172 $10.95

Best of The Doors
Strum along with more than 25 of your favorite hits from The Doors. Includes: Been Down So Long • Hello I Love You Won't You Tell Me Your Name? • Light My Fire • Riders on the Storm • Touch Me • and more. 00699177 $10.95

Favorite Songs with 3 Chords
27 popular songs that are easy to play, including: All Shook Up • Blue Suede Shoes • Boot Scootin' Boogie • Evil Ways • Great Balls of Fire • Lay Down Sally • Semi-Charmed Life • Surfin' U.S.A. • Twist and Shout • Wooly Bully • and more.
00699112 $8.95

Favorite Songs with 4 Chords
22 tunes in this great collection, including: Beast of Burden • Don't Be Cruel • Get Back • Gloria • I Fought the Law • La Bamba • Last Kiss • Let Her Cry • Love Stinks • Peggy Sue • 3 AM • Wild Thing • and more. 00699270 $8.95

Irving Berlin's God Bless America
25 patriotic anthems: Amazing Grace • America, the Beautiful • Battle Hymn of the Republic • From a Distance • God Bless America • Imagine • The Lord's Prayer • The Star Spangled Banner • Stars and Stripes Forever • This Land Is Your Land • United We Stand • You're a Grand Old Flag • and more.
00699508 $9.95

Great '50s Rock
28 of early rock's biggest hits, including: At the Hop • Blueberry Hill • Bye Bye Love • Hound Dog • Rock Around the Clock • That'll Be the Day • and more. 00699187 $8.95

Great '60s Rock
Features the chords, strum patterns, melody and lyrics for 27 classic rock songs, all in their original keys. Includes: And I Love Her • Crying • Gloria • Good Lovin' • I Fought the Law • Mellow Yellow • Return to Sender • Runaway • Surfin' U.S.A. • The Twist • Twist and Shout • Under the Boardwalk • Wild Thing • and more. 00699188 $8.95

Great '70s Rock
Strum the chords to 21 classic '70s hits! Includes: Band on the Run • Burning Love • If • It's a Heartache • Lay Down Sally • Let It Be • Love Hurts • Maggie May • New Kid in Town • Ramblin' Man • Time for Me to Fly • Two Out of Three Ain't Bad • Wild World • and more. 00699262 $8.95

Great '80s Rock
23 arrangements that let you play along with your favorite recordings from the 1980s, such as: Back on the Chain Gang • Centerfold • Crazy Little Thing Called Love • Free Fallin' • Got My Mind Set on You • Kokomo • Should I Stay or Should I Go • Uptown Girl • Waiting for a Girl Like You • What I Like About You • and more. 00699263 $8.95

Best of Woody Guthrie
20 of the Guthrie's most popular songs, including: Do Re Mi • The Grand Coulee Dam • I Ain't Got No Home • Ramblin' Round • Roll On, Columbia • So Long It's Been Good to Know Yuh (Dusty Old Dust) • Talking Dust Bowl • This Land Is Your Land • Tom Joad • and more. 00699496 $12.95

The John Hiatt Collection
This collection includes 17 classics: Angel Eyes • Feels Like Rain • Have a Little Faith in Me • Memphis in the Meantime • Perfectly Good Guitar • A Real Fine Love • Riding with the King • Thing Called Love (Are You Ready for This Thing Called Love) • The Way We Make a Broken Heart • and more.
00699398 $12.95

Hymn Favorites
Includes: Amazing Grace • Battle Hymn of the Republic • Down by the Riverside • Holy, Holy, Holy • Just as I Am • Rock of Ages • This Is My Father's World • What a Friend We Have in Jesus • and more. 00699271 $9.95

Best of Sarah McLachlan
20 of Sarah's most popular hits for guitar, including: Adia • Angel • Building a Mystery • I Will Remember You • Ice Cream • Sweet Surrender • and more. 00699231 $10.95

A Merry Christmas Songbook
Easy arrangements for 51 holiday hits: Away in a Manger • Deck the Hall • Fum, Fum, Fum • The Holly and the Ivy • Jolly Old St. Nicholas • O Christmas Tree • Star of the East • The Twelve Days of Christmas • and more! 00699211 $8.95

Pop-Rock Guitar Favorites
31 songs, including: Angie • Brown Eyed Girl • Crazy Little Thing Called Love • Eight Days a Week • Fire and Rain • Free Bird • Gloria • Hey Jude • Let It Be • Maggie May • New Kid in Town • Surfin' U.S.A. • Wild Thing • Wonderful Tonight • and more. 00699088 $8.95

Best of George Strait
Strum the chords to 20 great Strait hits! Includes: Adalida • All My Ex's Live in Texas • The Best Day • Blue Clear Sky • Carried Away • The Chair • Does Fort Worth Ever Cross Your Mind • Lovebug • Right or Wrong • Write This Down • and more.
00699235 $10.95

Best of Hank Williams Jr.
24 of Hank's signature standards. Includes: Ain't Misbehavin' • All My Rowdy Friends Are Coming Over Tonight • Attitude Adjustment • Family Tradition • Honky Tonkin' • Texas Women • There's a Tear in My Beer • Whiskey Bent and Hell Bound • and more. 00699224 $10.95

Women of Rock
22 hits from today's top female artists. Includes: Bitch • Don't Speak • Galileo • Give Me One Reason • I Don't Want to Wait • Insensitive • Lovefool • Mother Mother • Stay • Torn • You Oughta Know • You Were Meant for Me • Zombie • and more.
00699183 $9.95

FOR MORE INFORMATION, SEE YOUR LOCAL MUSIC DEALER, OR WRITE TO:

HAL•LEONARD® CORPORATION
7777 W. BLUEMOUND RD. P.O. BOX 13819 MILWAUKEE, WI 53213

www.halleonard.com

Prices, contents & availability subject to change without notice. Disney characters & artwork ©Disney Enterprises, Inc.

0102

EASY GUITAR
WITH NOTES & TAB

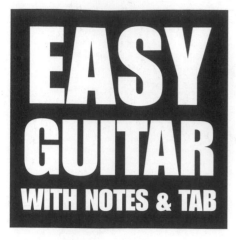

This series features simplified arrangement with notes, TAB, chord charts, and strum an pick patterns.

00702002	Acoustic Rock Hits	$12.95
00702001	Best of Aerosmith	$12.95
00702040	Best of Allman Brothers	$9.95
00702166	All-Time Best Guitar Collection	$16.95
00702169	Best of The Beach Boys	$10.95
00702143	Best Chart Hits	$8.95
00702066	Best Contemporary Hits	$9.95
00702140	Best of Brooks and Dunn	$10.95
00702095	Best of Mariah Carey	$10.95
00702043	Best of Johnny Cash	$12.95
00702033	Best of Steven Curtis Chapman	$12.95
00702073	Steven Curtis Chapman – Favorites	$10.95
00702115	Blues Classics	$10.95
00385020	Broadway Songs for Kids	$9.95
00702149	Christian Children's Songbook	$7.95
00702090	Eric Clapton's Best	$10.95
00702086	Eric Clapton from "Unplugged"	$10.95
00702016	Classic Blues	$12.95
00702141	Classic Rock	$8.95
00702053	Best of Patsy Cline	$10.95
00702170	Contemporary Christian Christmas	$9.95
00702006	Contemporary Christian Favorites	$9.95
00702091	Contemporary Country Ballads	$9.95
00702089	Contemporary Country Pickin'	$9.95
00702065	Contemporary Women of Country	$9.95
00702121	Country from the Heart	$9.95
00702145	Best of Jim Croce	$10.95
00702085	Disney Movie Hits	$9.95
00702122	The Doors	$10.95
00702041	Favorite Hymns	$9.95
00702068	Forty Songs for a Better World	$10.95
00702159	Best of Genesis	$10.95
00702174	God Bless America and Other Songs for a Better Nation	$8.95
00702057	Golden Age of Rock	$8.95
00699374	Gospel Favorites	$14.95
00702099	Best of Amy Grant	$9.95
00702113	Grease Is Still the Word	$9.95
00702160	Great American Country Songbook	$12.95
00702050	Great Classical Themes	$6.95
00702131	Great Country Hits of the '90s	$8.95
00702116	Greatest Hymns for Guitar	$7.95
00702130	The Groovy Years	$9.95
00702136	Best of Merle Haggard	$10.95
00702037	Hits of the '50s	$10.95
00702035	Hits of the '60s	$10.95
00702046	Hits of the '70s	$8.95
00702047	Hits of the '80s	$8.95
00702054	Best of Hootie and the Blowfish	$9.95
00702059	Hunchback of Notre Dame & Hercules	$9.95
00702032	International Songs	$12.95
00702045	Jailhouse Rock, Kansas City and Other Hits by Leiber & Stoller	$10.95
00702021	Jazz Standards	$14.95
00702051	Jock Rock	$9.95
00702087	New Best of Billy Joel	$10.95
00702088	New Best of Elton John	$9.95
00702162	Jumbo Easy Guitar Songbook	$19.95
00702011	Best of Carole King	$12.95
00702112	Latin Favorites	$9.95
00702097	John Lennon – Imagine	$9.95
00699003	Lion King & Pocahontas	$9.95
00702005	Best of Andrew Lloyd Webber	$12.95
00702061	Love Songs of the '50s & '60s	$9.95
00702062	Love Songs of the '70s & '80s	$9.95
00702063	Love Songs of the '90s	$9.95
00702129	Songs of Sarah McLachlan	$12.95
00702138	Mellow Rock Hits	$10.95
00702147	Motown's Greatest Hits	$9.95
00702112	Movie Love Songs	$9.95
00702039	Movie Themes	$10.95
00702117	My Heart Will Go On & Other Top Hits	$9.95
00702096	Best of Nirvana	$14.95
00702026	'90s Rock	$12.95
00702067	The Nutcracker Suite	$5.95
00699261	Oasis	$14.95
00702030	Best of Roy Orbison	$12.95
00702158	Songs from Passion	$9.95
00702125	Praise and Worship for Guitar	$9.95
00702139	Elvis Country Favorites	$9.95
00702038	Elvis Presley – Songs of Inspiration	$10.95
00702004	Rockin' Elvis	$9.95
00699415	Best of Queen	$12.95
00702155	Rock Hits for Guitar	$9.95
00702128	Rockin' Down the Highway	$8.95
00702135	Rock'n'Roll Romance	$9.95
00702092	Best of the Rolling Stones	$10.95
00702093	Rolling Stones Collection	$17.95
00702101	17 Chart Hits	$9.95
00702137	Solid Gold Rock	$9.95
00702110	The Sound of Music	$8.95
00702010	Best of Rod Stewart	$12.95
00702049	Best of George Strait	$10.95
00702042	Today's Christian Favorites	$8.95
00702124	Today's Christian Rock	$8.95
00702171	Top Chart Hits for Guitar	$8.95
00702029	Top Hits of '95-'96	$12.95
00702034	Top Hits of '96-'97	$12.95
00702007	TV Tunes for Guitar	$12.95
00702108	Best of Stevie Ray Vaughan	$10.95
00702123	Best of Hank Williams	$9.95
00702111	Stevie Wonder – Guitar Collection	$9.95

0102